Advances in
Relationship
Marketing

Titles in the Cranfield Management Series include:

The Challenge of Strategic Management
Corporate Strategy and Financial Decisions
Strategic Marketing Planning
Strategy Planning in Logistics and Transportation
Making Sense of Competition Policy
European Developments in Human Resource Management
Executive Redundancy and Outplacement
The Challenge of International Business
The Future of Services Management
Advances in Consumer Marketing
Examining Business Process Re-engineering
Advances in Relationship Marketing

These books are available from all good bookshops or directly from
Kogan Page Ltd, 120 Pentonville Road, London N1 9JN.
Tel: 0171 278 0433 Fax 0171 837 6348

Advances in
Relationship
Marketing

Edited by

Adrian Payne

KOGAN
PAGE

First published in 1995

Kogan Page Limited
120 Pentonville Road
London N1 9JN

© Adrian Payne, 1995

British Library Cataloguing in Publication Data

A CIP record for this book is available from the British Library.

ISBN 0 7494 1636 X

Typeset by Books Unlimited (Nottm), Mansfield NG19 7QZ

Printed in England by Clays Ltd, St Ives plc

CONTENTS

PART TWO — Internal Marketing

PART THREE — Managing Relationships Before, During and After the Sale

---

PART FOUR — Service Quality Themes in Relationship Marketing

Contents

LIST OF FIGURES

LIST OF TABLES

THE CRANFIELD MANAGEMENT SERIES

The Cranfield Management Series represents an exciting joint initiative between the Cranfield School of Management and Kogan Page.

As one of Europe's leading post-graduate business schools, Cranfield is renowned for its applied research activities, which cover a wide range of issues relating to the practice of management.

Each title in the Series is based on current research and authored by Cranfield faculty or their associates. Many of the research projects have been undertaken with the sponsorship and active assistance of organizations from the industrial, commercial or public sectors. The aim of the Series is to make the findings of direct relevance to managers through texts which are academically sound, accessible and practical.

For managers and academics alike, the Cranfield Management Series will provide access to up-to-date management thinking from some of the world's leading academics and practitioners. The series represents both Cranfield's and Kogan Page's commitment to furthering the improvement of management practice in all types of organizations.

THE SERIES EDITORS

Frank Fishwick
Reader in Managerial Economics
Director of Admissions at Cranfield School of Management

Dr Fishwick joined Cranfield from Aston University in 1966, having previously worked in textiles, electronics and local government (town and country planning). Recent research and consultancy interests have been focused on business concentration, competition policy and the book publishing industry. He has been directing a series of research studies for the Commission of the European Communities, working in collaboration with business economists in France and Germany. He is permanent economic adviser to the Publishers Association in the UK and is a regular consultant to other public and private sector organisations in the UK, continental Europe and the US.

Gerry Johnson

Professor of Strategic Management
Director of the Centre for Strategic Management and Organisational Change
Director of Research at Cranfield School of Management

After graduating from University College London, Professor Johnson worked for several years in management positions in Unilever and Reed International before becoming a management consultant. Since 1976, he has taught at Aston University Management Centre, Manchester Business School, and from 1988 at Cranfield School of Management. His research work is primarily concerned with processes of strategic decision making and strategic change in organisations. He also works as a consultant on issues of strategy formulation and strategic change at a senior level with a number of UK and international firms.

Shaun Tyson

Professor of Human Resource Management
Director of the Human Resource Research Centre
Dean of the Faculty of Management and Administration at Cranfield School of Management

Professor Tyson studied at London University and spent eleven years in senior positions in industry within engineering and electronic companies.

For four years he was lecturer in personnel management at the Civil Service College, and joined Cranfield in 1979. He has acted as a consultant and researched widely into human resource strategies, policies and the evaluation of the function. He has published 14 books.

THE CONTRIBUTORS

Colin Armistead is the Royal Mail Chair of Business Performance Improvement Group at Bournemouth University. Colin was previously head of the Operations Management Group at Cranfield School of Management, where he was also Research Director for the Centre for Services Management. Colin's research interests are in the formulation of operations strategy, the design of service delivery systems and the re-engineering of service business processes, and the management of capacity, quality and resource productivity in service organisations.

David Ballantyne is Linfox Fellow of Logistics Management at the Syme Department of Marketing, Monash University, Melbourne, Australia. He was a director of the Total Quality Management Institute in Australia and more recently was a Senior Associate at the Centre for Services Management at Cranfield School of Management, UK. He has worked in many senior quality and marketing roles in a large bank. More recently he has been directly involved at executive level in organisational change strategies which focus on service quality improvement.

Martin Christopher is Head of the Marketing and Logistics Group and teaches those subjects at Cranfield School of Management. He has lectured widely in Europe, North America and Australasia and has had appointments as Visiting Professor at the University of British Columbia, University of South Florida and the University of New South Wales. Professor Christopher is currently a Deputy Director of the School and Chairman of Continuing Studies in the School of Management.

Graham Clark was trained as a mechanical engineer with J Lucas Limited. A period as a development engineer was followed by a Master's Degree in Management Science and 12 years in manufacturing management. He joined Cranfield School of Management in 1986, where he has carried out research in after-sales service, quality management, and service operations strategy. He is co-director of the Service Operations Research and Development Club and is co-author (with Colin Armistead) of *Customer Service and Support* (Financial Times/Pitman Publishing).

Moira Clark is a Teaching Fellow in services marketing in the Cranfield School of Management. Prior to joining Cranfield, Moira was an international marketing consultant based in Munich where she was involved with a wide range of industries including construction and related fields, engineering, local radio, consumer and industrial goods manufacturers and service industries.

Brett Collins is a management consultant and visiting academic at a number of universities. He was previously Chairman of the Marketing Group at the Royal Melbourne Institute of Technology and has also held positions at Deakin University and the University of Melbourne in Australia. He has extensive management experience with a number of Australian companies.

Christian Grönroos is a former visiting professor at Arizona State University and a research fellow of its First Interstate Center for Services Marketing. He currently holds a position as Professor of Marketing and Chairman of the Department of Marketing and Corporate Geography at the Swedish School of Economics and Business Administration in Helsinki. He is also a member of the board of directors of the School.

Deborah Helman is currently undertaking Doctoral studies at the Open University. She has worked as a research assistant at both the Cranfield School of Management at Cranfield University and at Templeton College at Oxford University. She completed her M.Phil degree at Templeton College.

Uta Jüttner is a research fellow in marketing at the Cranfield School of Management and a regular guest lecturer at the University of Zurich, Switzerland. Her main research interests are in relationship marketing and strategic marketing and management. She holds a Masters degree in public administration and a Doctorate in business administration.

Simon Knox is a reader in marketing at the Cranfield School of Management, Cranfield University. Since joining Cranfield, he has published over 40 papers on branding and consumer purchasing styles. Simon is the Co-Director of the Institute for Advanced Research in Marketing in the School and is a brand consultant to a number of multinationals including Rank, Hovis, McDougall and Shell.

Tony Millman is Professor of Business at the University of Buckingham School of Business. His research and consultancy interests include: strategic marketing in industrial companies, international technology transfer, and key account management. Prior to joining Buckingham he was with the Marketing Group at Cranfield School of Management.

Adrian Payne is Professor of Services Marketing and Director of the Centre for Services Management at the Cranfield School of Management. His current research interests are in strategic marketing and management in service industries, customer service, corporate acquisitions, global competition and developing marketing oriented organisations. He has published five books and over thirty papers in the areas of strategy, marketing and financial markets.

Helen Peck is a researcher with the Marketing and Logistics Group at Cranfield. She is involved in the development of teaching material for graduate programmes and research and consultancy for corporate clients. Previously Helen worked with the School's management advisory service in the development of in-company programmes and in the library where she specialised in the retrieval and analysis of business information.

Paula Stanley is Senior Research Officer for the Centre for Services Management at Cranfield School of Management, and a member of the Operations Management group. Paula's research interests in the area of services management include: service quality in public services, service recovery and service pledges and charters. Paula is a member of the Operations Management Association, the British Academy of Management and the British Society of Criminology.

Kaj Storbacka is the Founder and President of CRM—Customer Relationship Management Limited, a management consulting firm specialising in developing customer relationship strategies for financial services companies. He also holds a position as Research Director in CERS—Centre for Relationship Marketing and Service Management at the Swedish School of Economics and Business Administration in Helsinki.

Tore Strandvik is Director of the recently founded CERS—Centre for Relationship Marketing and Services Management at the Swedish School of Economics and Business Administration in Helsinki. He is currently Associate Professor (acting) at the Department of Marketing and Corporate Geography. His research interests are service quality management, customer satisfaction measurement, service management and relationship marketing.

Hans Peter Wehrli is Professor of Marketing at the University of Zurich, Switzerland and a visiting professor at the University of St Gallen in business administration, economics, law and social sciences. He has published numerous books and articles on strategic marketing, relationship marketing and time-based competition.

INTRODUCTION

Adrian Payne

In the 1990s relationship marketing has become a topic of great interest to many organisations. Relationship marketing has its origins in industrial and business-to-business markets. However, much of the more recent interest and research activity in relationship marketing has been in services markets. Currently consumer goods companies are now seeking to develop stronger relationships with their final consumers, in addition to the traditional business-to-business relationships with their immediate customers. Thus all sectors – industrial, services and consumer – are increasingly examining ways to develop greater competitive advantage through relationship-based strategies.

The traditional approach to marketing has been increasingly questioned in recent years. This approach emphasised management of the key marketing mix elements such as product, price, promotion and place within a functional context. The new relationship approach, whilst recognising these key elements still need to be addressed, reflects the need to create an integrated cross-functional focus of marketing – one which emphasises keeping as well as winning customers. Thus the focus is shifting from customer acquisition to customer retention, and ensuring the appropriate amounts of time, money and managerial resources are directed at both of these key tasks.

The new relationship marketing paradigm reflects a change from traditional marketing to what a number of authors are now describing as customer-focused management, or market-oriented management. Hence, the term relationship marketing embraces an organisation-wide perspective of marketing rather than a narrow functional focus. Although the term relationship marketing has now become widely adopted, perhaps a better term to describe the emphasis on cross-functional activities might have been relationship management.

TYPES OF RELATIONSHIP MARKETING

Relationship marketing is a broad topic and many researchers have approached its study from different perspectives. There are at least four broad groups of researchers working on relationship marketing within institutions or groups around the world. This book focuses on work initiated at the Cranfield School of Management since 1988. It includes work by a number of researchers whose work is now described as the 'Anglo-Australian' school of relationship marketing. This work has several key elements that are explored within the book and which are described shortly. However, it is appropriate at this point to acknowledge other groups of researchers working within institutions or groups elsewhere.

Within Europe, the work of Scandinavian professors, including Christian Gronroos, Evert Gummesson and their colleagues working at the Swedish School of Economics and Business Administration in Finland and at Stockholm University, is well known. Their research in relationship marketing represents development of their work in services marketing and service quality.

Another group is the International (or Industrial) Marketing and Purchasing (IMP) Group. The IMP Group have been highly influential in the study of industrial markets and their work has received wide coverage, especially within Europe. Originally starting with twelve European researchers from France, Sweden, Germany, Italy and the United Kingdom, the group has now expanded to include academics from many countries including the USA and Australasia.

Within North America, the development of relationship marketing can be traced to the work of Theodore Levitt and Barbara Bund Jackson at the Harvard Business School in industrial markets, and Len Berry and his colleagues at the Texas A&M University in service markets. More recently Jagdish Sheth and his colleagues at Emory University in Atlanta have formed a Center for Relationship Marketing. Emory hosted a major research conference, especially devoted to relationship marketing, in 1994, at which over 50 papers from a world-wide group of researchers were presented. In the view of those attending this conference, this event marked the coming of age of relationship marketing as a separate discipline in its own right.

RELATIONSHIP MARKETING AT CRANFIELD

Many researchers have concerns about the relevance of much of traditional marketing theory, with its inherent short-term transactional emphasis, emphasised by many, but not all of its proponents. This approach has been found to be lacking, especially in industrial and service business-to-business marketing where establishing and maintaining long-term relationships with customers is critical to organisational success. These concerns were the motivation for an ongoing research programme, started at Cranfield University in 1988, on relationship marketing and customer retention.

The Cranfield approach builds on the concept of relationship marketing as first introduced by Berry, but discussed by many others when describing a longer-term approach to marketing. This approach to relationship marketing has extended from the work of Christopher, Payne and Ballantyne, who have developed a theory of relationship marketing based on broader considerations than the North American perspective. The key elements of this theory include:

- emphasising a relationship rather than a transaction approach to marketing;
- understanding the economics of customer retention and thus ensuring the right amount of money and other resources are appropriately allocated between the two tasks of retaining and attracting customers;
- highlighting the critical role of internal marketing in achieving external marketing success;
- showing how the principles of relationship marketing can be applied to a range of diverse market domains – not just customer markets;
- recognising that quality, customer service and marketing need to be integrated in a much closer manner than has previously been the case in many organisations;
- illustrating how the traditional marketing mix concept of the four Ps does not adequately capture all the key elements which must be addressed in building and sustaining relationships with markets;
- ensuring that marketing is considered in a broad cross-functional context.

The research papers in this book emphasise many of the issues outlined above.

STRUCTURE AND CONTENT OF THE BOOK

This book is divided into five parts which reflect our broad perspective of relationship marketing. They are:

- Part One – Relationship Marketing and Customer Retention;
- Part Two – Internal Marketing;
- Part Three – Managing Relationships Before, During and After the Sale;
- Part Four – Service Quality Themes in Relationship Marketing;
- Part Five – Value Creation Through Relationship Marketing.

In Part One two interrelated topics, relationship marketing and customer retention, are examined. In the first chapter Adrian Payne outlines the broadened perspective of relationship marketing and explains how the six markets framework is used for relationship development. In the second and third chapters by Moira Clark and Adrian Payne the theme of customer retention is explored in more detail. The second chapter examines the evolution of customer retention, strategies for improving customer retention and linkages between customer retention and employee satisfaction. It then raises a number of key areas for research, many of which are the subject of our current research programmes at Cranfield. The third chapter provides a brief overview of a strategic approach to achieving long-term customer loyalty. It consists of a three-stage framework of customer retention measurement, identification of causes of defection and key service issues, and corrective action to improve retention. It also provides a brief overview of research aimed at measuring the profit impact of customer retention strategies.

In Part Two the topic of internal marketing is explained. It is now becoming increasingly evident that in most organisations – and especially in services, retailing and business-to-business marketing – that a strong internal marketing programme needs to be in place before excellent external service quality can be provided to customers. The first chapter in this part, by Deborah Helman and Adrian Payne, provides a summary of an initial research study on internal marketing. It sets the scene by defining several forms of internal marketing and outlines the results of a pilot study aimed at identifying the scope, formal objectives and organisation of internal marketing activities. The second chapter by Helen Peck provides a detailed literature review of internal marketing and examines linkage with customer service, service delivery systems and improving the customer interface. The third chapter by Brett Collins and Adrian Payne examines the internal marketing of a specific function within an organisation, the human resource department. It compares external marketing with the internal market of an HRM department. It illustrates how the traditional concepts used in external marketing such as mission statements, market segmentation, marketing mix determination and new product development are equally applicable to the marketing of internal services.

In Part Three the management of relationships before, during and after the sale is addressed. The first chapter in this part is by Tony Millman who examines the critical role of key account management in building relationships in business-to-business markets. His study draws on empirical research in the area of industrial sales management, key account management and observations from working with many key account managers in a management development context. The second chapter by Kaj Storbacka, Tore Strandvik and Christian Gronroos explores customer relationship economics issues. They develop a conceptual framework for exploring issues of service quality and customer profitability. Their chapter provides a dynamic perspective of service quality and ties service management to perceived service quality, two key constructs within services marketing, to relationship marketing. The third chapter by Colin Armistead, Graham Clark and Paula Stanley explores managing service recovery. The chapter presents the findings of a survey of UK service managers from a range of services sectors and interprets the findings with reference to a model of empowerment for front-line service staff.

Part Four focuses on service quality themes in relationship marketing and draws upon the work of David Ballantyne, Martin Christopher and Adrian Payne. The first chapter in this part examines the service quality literature. The chapter then develops a framework for monitoring service quality involving the integration of the six market monitors. The second chapter looks at what goes wrong when company-wide quality initiatives are introduced. It describes seven prescriptions for failure and outlines a framework for the diagnostic review of work processes and a strategy for continuous improvement.

The final section, Part Five, explores value creation through relationship marketing. The first chapter by Uta Juttner and Hans Peter Wehrli examines relationship marketing from a value system perspective. This article extends our thinking and understanding of transactions and relationships within the context of exchange theory. It emphasises the role of marketing management in coordinating all the interactive value-generating activities to improve performance. The second chapter by Simon Knox focuses on building value through re-engineering brand management practices. The chapter reflects the pivotal role that branding can have in creating a process-oriented organisation which delivers improved value. The final chapter by Moira Clark, Helen Peck, Adrian Payne and Martin Christopher provides a framework for managing relationship marketing. It develops the concept of the relationship chain as a means of integrating a range of cross-functional elements in the value delivery process and emphasises the need to manage external and internal markets in a structured way.

IMPORTANT NOTE TO READERS

The emerging array of research approaches in relationship marketing and the focus of different groups of academics working in this area has resulted in a broad range of topics being addressed here. The breadth of the issues addressed means that all readers may not wish to read this book from cover to cover. One of the difficult tasks in putting this book together was to seek to satisfy both those who wish to read only those areas of specific interest to them, and those who wish to read it in its entirety. These two different groups of readers present a particular problem when there is some overlap between the literature reviews covered in different chapters. For those reading all the book, inclusion of some of the literature reviews will, at times, seem repetitive. On the other hand those who are only interested in specific articles will wish to read these articles fully. After considering this problem a decision was made to reduce the literature review sections of these chapters only slightly so as to not impair the context of the authors' work. Thus each chapter may be read separately without the need to read through earlier chapters. Those who read the book in its entirety may wish to skip some of the discussion of the research literature when it is not of relevance to them or where it has been covered earlier.

SCOPE AND PRACTICAL RELEVANCE

There are likely to be three audiences for this book: practising managers, academics and students. In particular the chapters in this book have been selected and structured in a way to give practising managers a view of some of the important developments which apply within the relationship marketing arena and especially the work that is being conducted at Cranfield.

The scope of the work presented in this book is not intended to cover all interpretations of relationship marketing, but rather to represent a selection of key issues which will enable readers to have a better understanding of the topic of relationship marketing from a managerial perspective.

Our view of relationship marketing reflects an emerging paradigm of marketing that is cross-functional, relationship-driven and focuses upon processes as well as functions in achieving long-term customer satisfaction. This is an area of research that has significant practical relevance for managers.

The implementation of relationship marketing strategies will require managers to go beyond their traditional roles. They will need to take a broader perspective and develop stronger cross-functional capabilities leading to much closer relationships between suppliers, internal staff, customers and other relevant markets. This represents a significant challenge to senior managers to reorient their thinking and actions towards building a more relationship-oriented and customer-focused organisation.

All the research in this book has been undertaken by academics who are associated with the Cranfield School of Management and who are currently engaged in the theoretical and practical development of relationship marketing. This includes present and former members of academic and research staff at Cranfield and a small number of colleagues who collaborate with researchers at Cranfield.

Most of the chapters included in this book have been subject to peer scrutiny through publication in academic journals and academic conferences. Presentation of papers from the Cranfield Relationship Marketing Group have been made at over a dozen conferences including the Academy of Management in the USA, the British Academy of Management and the Marketing Education Group of the UK annual conferences.

Our thanks go to both the contributors and the publishers who have permitted us to include their work in this book.

PART ONE

RELATIONSHIP MARKETING AND CUSTOMER RETENTION

1

RELATIONSHIP MARKETING: A BROADENED VIEW OF MARKETING*

Adrian Payne

INTRODUCTION

The emergence of relationship marketing in the 1980s has been not so much a discovery, but a rediscovery, of an approach which has long formed the cornerstone of many successful businesses. This approach emphasises the development and enhancement of relationships over the customer life cycle rather than new customer acquisition. Despite the increasing recognition of the importance of retention of existing customers, relatively little effort has been directed at developing frameworks and analytical tools to help achieve this. However, recent research activity has focused on the critical activities and issues that need to be managed in order for organisations to achieve increased performance and success in the market-place through relationship marketing.

Concerns about the validity of the traditional marketing approach and recognition of the increasing importance of relationships in the mature and complex markets of today led to a research initiative being undertaken at Cranfield University in 1988. The Cranfield research programme in relationship marketing reflects concerns regarding the relevance of traditional marketing especially when applied to services and industrial markets. These concerns, discussed in greater detail elsewhere in this book, led to a number of research projects on relationship marketing and customer retention. This chapter commences by discussing some of the key elements of the Cranfield approach to relationship marketing and then outlines a model – the six markets framework – for understanding the broadened context of relationship marketing.

---

* This chapter is based on Payne, A (1991) 'Relationship Marketing: The Six Markets Framework', Working Paper, Cranfield School of Management. © Cranfield School of Management. Reprinted with permission.

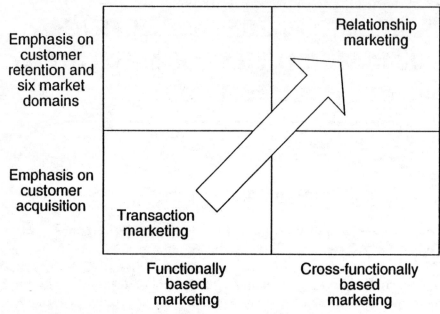

Figure 1.1 The transition to relationship marketing

Our approach to relationship marketing is summarised in Figure 1.1 which illustrates three key elements in the transition from transaction marketing to relationship marketing. As Figure 1.1 shows, these three elements include:

- A move from functionally-based marketing to cross-functionally based marketing
- A shift from marketing activities which have an emphasis on customer acquisition to marketing activities which emphasise customer retention
- An approach which addresses a total of six key markets, not just the traditional customer market.

It is this first element that is addressed in this chapter. It argues for a broadening in approach to marketing which recognises that the principles of marketing can, and should, be applied to a range of 'markets' or 'market domains'. The last two elements are addressed in greater detail elsewhere in this book, so are only discussed briefly here.

The move to cross-functional marketing reflects the difficulties encountered by traditional hierarchically- structured and functionally-oriented organisations which adopt a departmental or functional approach to marketing. Relationship marketing emphasises the organisation of marketing activities around cross-functional processes as opposed to organisational functions. This cross-functional approach is discussed in much greater detail in Chapter 14, and elsewhere, within this book.

The relationship marketing philosophy also stresses the need to shift from marketing strategies which are based mainly on customer acquisition to ones which focus on customer retention. Customer retention is at the heart of relationship marketing and this topic is developed in Chapters 2 and 3.

To achieve success in the complex and fast moving market-place of today it is increasingly being recognised that there are a number of key market areas, six in total, which need to be considered if the customer is to be served satisfactorily. Central to these considerations is the need for strong internal marketing, as well as marketing activities aimed at other key markets.

Figure 1.2 The relationship marketing six markets model

THE SIX MARKETS FRAMEWORK

The six markets framework, shown in Figure 1.2, illustrates an expanded view of where marketing can be applied. It identifies six key market domains where organisations should direct marketing activity and where the development of detailed marketing strategies may be needed. Apart from existing and potential customers, those markets are: referral markets; supplier markets; employee recruitment markets; influence markets; and internal markets. Below, each market is considered in turn.

Customer Markets

Customer markets are at the centre of the six markets framework. Customers must, of course, remain the prime focus area for marketing activity. However, marketing activities need to be less directed at transactional marketing – an emphasis on the acquiring of a new customer – and more on building long-term customer relationships.

Transaction marketing has a number of specific characteristics including:

- Focus on a single sale
- Orientation on product features
- Short time-scale
- Little emphasis on customer service
- Limited customer commitment
- Moderate customer contact
- Quality is primarily a concern of production.

Relationship marketing, by contrast, has a:

- Focus on customer retention
- Orientation to customer values
- Long time-scale
- High customer service emphasis
- High customer contact
- Quality is the concern of all.

It is clear that while a relationship focus has been fully adopted by some businesses it is noticeably absent in others. Many companies take the transactional route. The investment made in winning a new customer, once successful, is immediately transferred to the next prospect. Little effort goes into keeping that customer.

However, organisations are now starting to recognise that existing customers are easier to sell to and are frequently more profitable. While managers intellectually concur with this view, often much greater emphasis and resources are placed on attracting new customers and existing customers are taken for granted. It is only when some breakdown in service quality occurs, and the customer leaves or is on the point of defection, that the spotlight focuses more on the existing customer.

An actual example from a large city firm of solicitors provides a good illustration of how marketing effort may be misdirected. In this firm two events occurred within a short period of each other. The first involved the gaining of a contentious piece of litigation work from a new client. This work, worth around £200,000, was likely to be a one-off piece of business as the client's existing law firm did not wish to handle it. The law firm's partners were delighted with the litigation partner's brilliant coup in bringing in this new client. Six weeks later another partner persuaded a large corporate client, who dealt with several law firms, to give his firm all the company's conveyancing work. Prior to this the firm had worked only in one area of the law for this client. This represented additional work of about £300,000 in the first year and this would be a continuing and growing source of fees. There was little reaction to this news in the partnership. This conveyancing assignment represented an on-going source of work for this firm. As such it represented, in net present value terms perhaps five times as much profit, yet it received little attention in the firm.

This illustration is not meant to suggest that new customers are not important, indeed they are vital to most service businesses' futures. Rather, a balance is needed between the effort directed toward existing and new customers. Often it is the existing customer who does not receive sufficient attention.

The marketing ladder of customer loyalty in Figure 1.3 emphasises this point. It is apparent that many organisations put their main emphasis on the lower rungs of identifying prospects and attempting to turn them into customers than on the higher 'relationship' – and ultimately more rewarding – rungs of turning them into regular clients and subsequently into strong supporters and eventually active advocates for the company and its products. However, moving customers up the loyalty ladder is not simple. Organisations need to know explicitly and in depth exactly what each customer is buying – and every customer is different – and how it can continue to offer additional satisfactions that will differentiate its offering. Essentially, the only way to move someone from customer to advocate is to replace customer satisfaction with customer delight – by offering service quality that exceeds expectations.

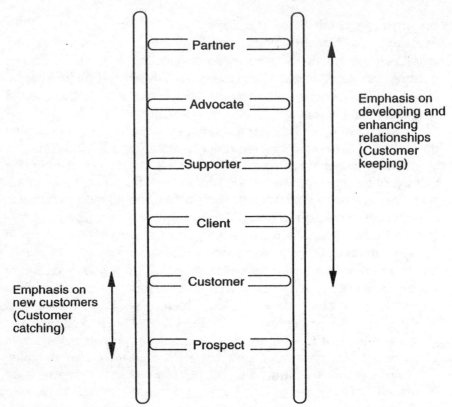

Figure 1.3 The relationship marketing ladder of customer loyalty

Referral Markets

What is the best form of marketing? Our view is that the best marketing is that done for you by your own customers, which is why the customer loyalty ladder and the creation of advocates is so important. But existing customers are not the only sources of referral – there are also other groups who can refer business to organisations. Referral markets go under many names – intermediaries, connectors, multipliers, agencies, and so on.

We will consider an example from a bank to illustrate this point. Referral sources for the bank included insurance companies, real estate brokers, accountancy and law firms as well as existing customers and internal referrals. For this bank, an internal study was undertaken of the amount of business, (both historic and projected), which arose through referral sources. This showed how important these sources were – though the bank had traditionally done little to promote this area.

Shortly after undertaking this study the bank held a strategy retreat. This included discussions on referral sources and presentations from several important intermediaries. The bank was surprised at the criticism it received from them during these presentations. Aware through its research of the importance of this business, the bank then established a task force to develop better relations with referral sources and establish a marketing plan to deal with the referral markets. As a result, noticeable and continued improvements in business generated by referral sources followed.

Most organisations need to consider both existing customers and often intermediaries as a source of future business. The current and potential importance of referral sources should be established and a plan developed for allocating marketing resources to them. Efforts should also be made to monitor results and cost benefits. However, it is worth emphasising that the benefits of increased marketing activity in this area may take some time to come to fruition.

Supplier Markets

Organisations' relationships with their suppliers are undergoing some fundamental changes. The old adversarial relationship – where a company tried to squeeze its suppliers to its own advantage – is giving way to one based much more on partnership and collaboration. There is good commercial sense in this. Manufacturers in the US typically spend over 60 per cent of total revenue on goods and services from outside suppliers.

The new relationship with supplier markets is being described under a number of different names. At AT&T it is 'vendorship partnership'; at electronics group Philips in Europe it is called 'co-makership'. In the US it is being referred to as 'reverse marketing'. Whatever the term, it aims at close co-operation between customer and supplier from a very early stage, mutual concentration on quality, commitment to flexibility, lowest costs and long-term relationships.

From the marketing point of view, the concern is to 'sell' the new attitudes implicit in such a collaborative arrangement both to suppliers and, equally important, inside the company as well, since in the past reward systems may have been geared to a traditional antagonistic relationship.

Recruitment Markets

Perhaps the scarcest resource for most organisations is no longer capital or raw materials – it is skilled people, a vital, perhaps the most vital, element in customer service delivery. And the situation is not getting any easier, even if unemployment levels climb to historic levels. The reason is demographic trends.

In the US the percentage of people in the age range 16-24 is expected to fall from around 200 per cent in 1985 to 16 per cent in 2000 and in the 25-34 age group from 23 per cent to 19 per cent over the same period. The same broad pattern exists in most western countries.

Obviously these age groups represent the key markets for new skilled workers entering the labour market. If attracting the best quality recruits is important then this market will become a vital success factor. A brief case example shows the kind of effort that may have to be made.

A large and well known accountancy practice was suffering problems attracting newly qualified recruits. The reasons were not hard to discover. Its recruitment literature was old fashioned and lacked visual impact. On visits to university campuses – a traditional recruitment source – the company was represented by an old and uninspiring partner and disinterested administrative staff. A marketing plan to try to improve the situation involved redesigning recruitment literature (with the help of recent graduates), sending the brightest partners on university visits accompanied by managers with interesting experiences to recount, and sponsoring awards and prizes at target universities. As a result of this recruitment marketing plan, the firm's offers to acceptances ratio increased dramatically.

Influence Markets

'Influence' markets cover a range of markets and tend to vary according to the type of industry or industry sector that an organisation is in. Companies involved in selling infrastructure items, such as communications or utilities, will place government departments and regulatory bodies high in importance on their lists on markets they must address. Companies listed on stock markets also face the financial community in its various forms – brokers, analysts, financial journalists and so on – and fall within the influencer market. Other examples include shareholders, standards bodies, consumer associations, environmental control authorities, etc.

A good example of the influence markets that needs to be addressed is provided by MCI Communications Corporation in the US. William G McGowan, who was Chairman and Chief Executive of MCI Communications, faced some key marketing tasks, with respect to influence markets in the early days of MCI. These influence markets included:

- **The venture capital business**: McGowan had a start up that was a capital starved communications company, and he had to raise sufficient finance from venture capitalists
- **The regulators**: who needed to be convinced that McGowan could construct and satisfactorily operate a long distance telecommunications network
- **Lobbyists**: communications is an industry highly subject to regulation by the Federal Communications Commission and one which was dominated by AT&T. MCI had to become skilled as a lobbyer. It was for this reason they established their headquarters in Washington DC.
- **Litigators:** in challenging AT&T's domination of long distance telephone lines by way of a private anti-trust case, MCI got involved in a complex litigation business. Relationships with law firms and lawyers became critical.

MCI had to focus on their important influence markets as well as their original core mission. This suggests that involvement in other activities may be essential to protect the core business. These key activities were the principal focus of McGowan's efforts in the early stages of MCI's development.

While this activity is often carried out under the heading of 'public relations' or 'public affairs', it is important that it is recognised as being an essential element in the overall marketing activity and that appropriate resources are devoted to it.

Internal Markets

Internal marketing encompasses many issues of management, but has two main aspects. The first is the idea that every employee and every department in an organisation is both an internal customer and an internal supplier. The aim is to ensure that the operation of the organisation is optimised by ensuring that every individual and department both provides and receives excellent service.

The second aspect is making sure that all staff work together in a way that is aligned with the organisation's stated mission, strategy and goals. The importance of this has become particularly transparent in service firms, where there is a close interface with the customer. In this context, internal marketing aims at ensuring that all staff provide the best representation of the organisation through successfully handling telephone, mail, electronic and personal contacts with customers (including customers from the other markets outlined above).

Internal marketing is recognised as an important activity in developing a customer-focused organisation. In practice, internal marketing is concerned with communications, with developing responsiveness, responsibility and unity of purpose. Fundamental aims of internal marketing are to develop internal and external customer awareness and remove functional barriers to organisational effectiveness.

While relatively little empirical work has been undertaken regarding internal marketing practice it is clear that a consideration of internal markets is essential. Where internal marketing is concerned with the development of a customer orientation, the alignment of internal and external marketing ensures coherent relationship marketing. Further, it plays an important role in employee motivation and retention. Internal marketing is examined in greater detail in Chapters 4, 5 and 6.

DETERMINING MARKET EMPHASIS IN RELATIONSHIP MARKETING

These six-markets – customer, referral, supplier, recruitment, influence, and internal – do not necessarily each need their own formal written marketing plan, though some organisations will find it useful to do that. But companies do need to develop some form of marketing strategy to address each of them. The adoption of the relationship philosophy as a key strategic issue is more important than a written plan. For example, a formal marketing plan for an internal market is of little value if customer contact staff are not motivated and empowered to deliver the level of service quality required. The needs of members of all these markets need to be addressed in exactly the same way as customer markets – and high levels of service quality are essential in establishing and maintaining relationships with them.

However, not all markets require equal levels of attention and resources. A decision on the appropriate level of attention can be arrived at through the following steps:

- Identify key participants in each of the markets
- Research to identify expectations and requirements of key participants
- Review current and proposed level of emphasis in each market
- Formulate desired relationship strategy and determine if a formal market plan is necessary.

To consider the present level of effort and desired level of emphasis on each market, the relationship marketing network diagram shown in Figure 1.4 can be used. The diagram has seven axes – two for customers

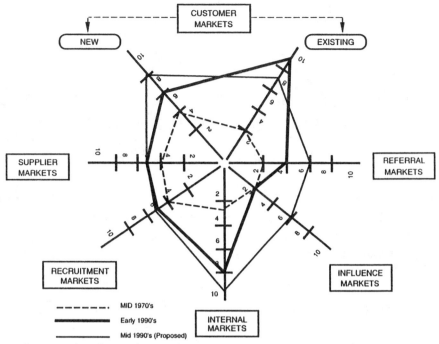

Figure 1.4 Relationship marketing network diagram for British Airways

(existing and new) and one each for the other five relationship markets. The division of customers into new and existing reflects the two tasks of customer attraction and customer retention.

As noted earlier many companies place too much emphasis on attention of customer and too little on retention. An objective approach to determining the level of emphasis is to examine in detail the resources, in terms of both money and executive time, expended on each of these two tasks. In a number of companies we have studied, where a quantitative assessment was undertaken, it was clear the majority of the marketing mix, marketing expenditure and managerial time was still being directed at attraction of new customers.

The approach to the six markets shown is illustrated by reference to British Airways (BA) in Figure 1.4. This is based on views of a number of people including two former senior executives in BA and represents an external view of developments in BA. In the 1970s BA was in poor shape. Its financial position was terrible and it lacked market focus. Following the appointment of Lord King and Colin Marshall in the 1980s a revolution took place in BA. Considerable emphasis was placed on the internal market and a series of customer care programmes including 'Putting the

Customer First' and 'A Day in the Life' were conducted for all staff. Towards the end of the 1980s, BA recognised the importance of customer retention and this led to a number of initiatives aimed at retention including the 'Airmiles' and 'Latitudes' programmes. Marketing greatly improved to existing and new customers, and travel agents and other referral markets. Saatchi and Saatchi developed a series of outstanding global television commercials aimed at many of the relationship markets.

In the early 1990s BA might consider a number of issues in the relationship markets, as shown in '1990's proposed' in Figure 1.4. These involve:

- Greater attention towards gaining new customers (BA has placed much emphasis on customer retention. Should more attention now be directed at new customers?)
- A reinforcement of customer care and service quality issues with internal staff
- Greater attention on 'influence markets' – especially government. (The granting of rights to several US carriers to Heathrow slots, the departure of Mrs Thatcher as Prime Minister, [with whom Lord King had a close relationship] and the failure to fully acquire a US carrier raised an important issue. Should stronger influence relationships have been forged – especially within government and the opposition?).

The six markets framework illustrates how organisations have a network of relationships with different markets. Each of these interactions needs to be managed, where appropriate, with a formal strategy and marketing plan. At this point the framework does not have empirically based quantification. Our next task is to develop a more rigorous means of quantifying the amount of effort, the 'quality' of that effort and the expectation on each market domain. Each market domain can then be further sub-divided into the relevant market segments within it.

The six markets framework has now been used in a diverse range of over 20 organisations to develop plans for each of the six markets and to illustrate the relationship marketing concept. This model has proved a robust means of considering the network of relationships that organisations need to address. In each the important areas were highlighted, that were not previously receiving attention, as a result of using the approach outlined above.

2

CUSTOMER RETENTION: DOES EMPLOYEE RETENTION HOLD A KEY TO SUCCESS?*

Moira Clark and Adrian Payne

INTRODUCTION

Over a decade ago Schneider (1980: 54) wrote 'What is surprising is that (1) researchers and businessmen have concentrated far more on how to attract consumers to products and services than on how to retain customers, (2) there is almost no published research on the retention of service consumers'. Despite the passing of more than twelve years there is still very little published research in the area of retention marketing. Certainly little rigorous work is evident in the area of the relationship between employee satisfaction and customer retention.

The specific objectives of this chapter are:

1. to review and provide a critique on the literature on customer retention and employee satisfaction;
2. to consider appropriate strategies for improving customer retention;
3. to examine the relationship between customer retention and employee satisfaction;
4. to identify major potential areas for future research.

LITERATURE REVIEW

The concepts of relationship marketing (Berry, 1983; Levitt, 1983; Rosenberg and Czepiel, 1984; Jackson, 1985; Gummesson, 1987a; Christopher, Payne and Ballantyne 1991; McKenna, 1992) and interactive marketing (Gronroos, 1982) are receiving increasing attention as

---

* A version of this chapter was presented to the Annual Conference of the Marketing Education Group, July 1993.

marketers focus more on how to maintain and enhance customer relationships with existing customers rather than attract new customers.

According to Gronroos (1990) 'the traditional view of marketing as a function for specialists planning and executing a marketing mix may not be altogether true where services are concerned.' The marketing mix approach is frequently too limited and does not cover all the activities that appear in customer relationships at various stages of the customer relationship lifecycle (Gronroos, 1989; Gronroos and Gummesson, 1986; Gummesson, 1987a,b).

Instead of this narrow transactional view of marketing, marketing is now increasingly seen as being concerned with relationships. Whilst some relationships do not involve any social relationship or interaction, other relationships may involve many interactions between customers and employees and evolve over long periods of time (Gronroos, 1990).

Berry (1983) introduced the concept of relationship marketing to describe a longer-term approach to marketing (see also Rosenberg and Czepiel, 1984; Jackson, 1985; Gummesson, 1987b). According to Gummesson (1987b) long-term relationships with customers are especially important in services, where relationships can be more expensive to establish. The emphasis on relationships is also important in industrial markets (Hakansson, 1982; Jackson, 1985). This does not mean that short-term sales are not desirable. In fact, they may be very profitable (Jackson, 1985). However, if close and long-term relationships can be achieved, this will lead to increased profitability for the company and reduced costs and make market entry or share gain difficult for competitors (Buchanan, 1990).

According to Berry (1983): 'Relationship marketing is applicable when there is an ongoing and periodic desire for the service and when the customer controls the selection of a service supplier and has alternatives from which to choose.'

Customer service is a key ingredient in relationship marketing and therefore also in customer retention. However, Lewis (1989) points out that emphasising service is one thing; delivering it is another. In fact, he considers that emphasising service is not the most appropriate approach to adopt. His basic idea is that emphasis should be placed on the customer and that focusing on the customer renders marketing and service inseparable. Thus management policies that enhance customer-based service often prove to be a firm's best marketing strategy. Christopher, Payne and Ballantyne (1991) go further than this to describe a new synthesis between quality, customer service and marketing. They argue that quality is also a key linkage in the exchange relationship between the organisation and its customer. They maintain that 'unless management can bring these activities together with new forms of collaboration and cross-functional coordination there can be no sustainable market-orientated performance improvement and therefore no sustainable competitive advantage.' Relationship marketing can therefore be seen as a focal point for integrating customer service and quality with a marketing orientation.

Much of the literature on retention marketing draws on the philosophy of relationship marketing and focuses primarily on the impact of retention marketing on company profitability and various strategies and plans to improve customer retention rates (Buchanan and Gillies, 1990; Buchanan, 1990; Reichheld and Kenny, 1990; Dawkins and Reichheld, 1990; Reichheld and Sasser, 1990; Carroll and Reichheld, 1991/92; DeSouza, 1992).

Buchanan and Gillies (1990), Dawkins and Reichheld (1990), Berry (1983), DeSouza (1992) and others, argue that service firms devote most of their resources to attracting new customers, but few take equal trouble to retain existing customers.

Bain & Co maintain that 'one of the key elements of business success and profitability is customer satisfaction, the more satisfied the customer, the more durable the relationship. And the longer this lasts, the more money the company stands to make' (Buchanan and Gillies, 1990: 523). The effect of longevity on profits can be explained by several factors:

- Acquiring a new customer costs more than retaining an existing one. The costs of acquiring a new customer are incurred only at the beginning of the relationship, thus the longer the relationship the lower the amortised cost of acquisition.
- Retaining customers means that account maintenance costs as a percentage of income tend to decline over the life of the relationship leading to increased revenues
- Long-time customers tend to be less price sensitive, permitting higher prices to be charged.
- Long-time, satisfied customers are likely to provide free, word-of-mouth advertising and referrals.
- Long-time customers are likely to purchase additional products/services.
- Retaining customers makes it difficult for competitors to enter a market or increase share.
- Regular customers tend to place frequent, consistent orders and, therefore, usually cost less to serve.

- Improved customer retention can also lead to an increased employee retention which feeds back into even greater customer longevity.

Bain & Co have developed approaches for measuring customer retention and linking it to company profitability. The customer retention rate is the rate at which customers are kept and is expressed as the percentage of customers at the beginning of the year that still remain at the end of the year. Therefore, the average life of a customer relationship doubles from five to ten years as a company's retention rate goes from 80 to 90 per cent (Dawkins and Reichheld 1990).

Bain & Co have also quantified the potential impact of improving customer retention for several banks and many other service businesses. They conclude that a five-point improvement in customer retention can lead to profit swings of 25 per cent to 80 per cent (Reichheld and Kenny, 1990; Buchanan and Gillies, 1990).

STRATEGIES FOR IMPROVING CUSTOMER RETENTION

There are a number of core ideas relating to customer retention strategies that can be identified:

1. Companies must measure customer retention rates over time and by line of business and in each of the areas that the company does business. This information and its importance must then be communicated to the employees (Dawkins and Reichheld, 1990; Reichheld and Kenny, 1990; Buchanan and Gillies, 1990; DeSouza, 1992).
2. It is then essential to analyse the root causes of customer defections, because it is only by understanding why customers are leaving the company that the company can begin to implement a customer retention programme to increase satisfaction and thereby improve customer retention and profitability (Dawkins and Reichheld, 1990; Buchanan, 1990; Reichheld and Kenny, 1990; DeSouza, 1992).
3. A further strategy involves focusing attention on internal marketing and particularly front-line employees to ensure that they are offering service quality that consistently meets the requirements of the target market. These employees can often make or break service organisations (Berry, 1983, 1986; Reichheld and Kenny, 1990).
4. Best demonstrated practice is also recommended as a technique for improving customer retention rates (Buchanan, 1990; Reichheld and Kenny, 1990).

Other suggested strategies include: senior management commitment; customer focussed culture and incentive schemes (Reichheld and Kenny,

1990); building value-managed relationships (Buchanan and Gillies, 1990); focusing attention on the most profitable customers and setting clear targets and measuring results (Buchanan, 1990) and identifying switching barriers (DeSouza, 1992).

The prevailing idea behind retaining customers has been maintaining quality. However, research undertaken in the financial services sector by Temple, Barker & Sloan, a US firm of management and economic consultants, indicates that quality programmes no longer have the power to keep customers satisfied (Intindola, 1991). Their work suggests that quality is not always the major determinant of customer turnover for which there are four primary causes – rate increases, competitive solicitation, service deficiency and poor reputation. According to Temple, Barker & Sloan, the initial step for implementing a sound customer retention plan is to determine price volatility and service intensity for particular products. The findings from their research are summarised in Figure 2.1. Essentially, the research found that quality is important but insufficient when it comes to high service, high volatility products such as car insurance, and that for low volatility and high service intensity

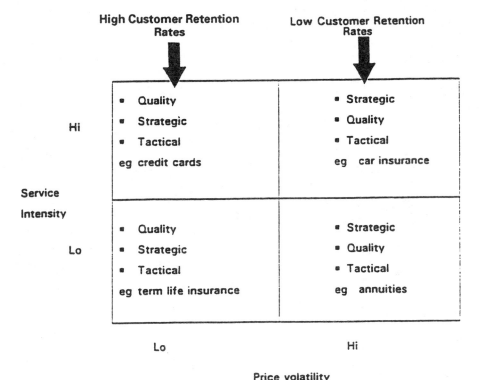

Figure 2.1 Summary of research by Temple, Barker and Sloan

products, quality is the key driver. The research suggests that financial service firms must effect a comprehensive retention strategy composed of quality, strategy and tactical programmes.

In the same way that Christopher, Payne and Ballantyne (1991) describe relationship marketing as a focal point for integrating quality and customer service with a marketing orientation, many of the strategies/plans for improving customer retention as described above, integrate concepts from marketing, quality management and customer service and apply them specifically to keeping customers.

CUSTOMER RETENTION AND EMPLOYEE SATISFACTION

Little evidence has emerged in the literature of research into the relationship between employee satisfaction and customer retention. However, the work undertaken by Bain & Co (Buchanan, 1990; Reichheld and Kenny, 1990) suggests a strong link between these two variables (Figure 2.2). They maintain that high customer retention will lead to higher employee satisfaction as employees find their job much easier dealing with satisfied customers rather than dissatisfied customers. As a result employees will tend to stay longer with the company. 'Higher retention of the right calibre of employees creates a stable and experienced labour force that delivers higher service quality at lower cost … this leads to higher customer retention' and of course increased profitability (Buchanan, 1990).

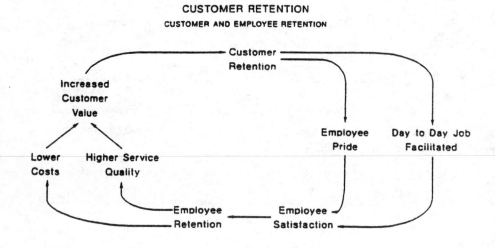

CUSTOMER RETENTION
CUSTOMER AND EMPLOYEE RETENTION

Source : Bain & Company

Figure 2.2 Link between employee satisfaction and customer retention

The advantages of long-term employees is that they are often able to form personal relationships with customers, understand their needs, and possibly are able to preempt dissatisfied customers leaving the company. Reichheld (1991/92: 24) maintains that there are:

> powerful insights available from probing into root causes of customer and employee defections. This is the most powerful pool of untapped insight in any business. It clarifies what is and what is not working in the business system and this is the first step toward a meaningful and measurable improvement program.

In labour-intensive organisations the quality of service is determined mostly by the skills and attitudes of the people producing the services. All employees are part of the process which connects with the customer at the point of sale. Employees remain the key to success at these service encounters or 'moments of truth' (Carlzon, 1987). The extent, therefore, to which these organisations can attract, keep and motivate quality personnel will influence their capability to offer quality services to their customers. Consistently offering services that match the requirements of the external customer will be an important factor in building strong long-lasting customer relationships.

The concept of internal marketing has emerged in the literature in the last 15 years as a way of enabling companies to get, motivate and retain customer-conscious employees (Gronroos, 1981, 1985; Berry, 1981; George *et al.*, 1986; George, 1990), and was then described more widely in the services management literature (Carlzon, 1987). The aims of internal marketing are to improve internal marketing relationships, quality and customer service in order to satisfy internal and external customer needs (Helman and Payne, 1991). Schneider and Bowen (1985) have found that when employees identify with the norms and values of an organisation, they are less inclined to leave and, furthermore, customers are likely to be more satisfied with the service. In addition to this '... when employee turnover is minimised, service values and norms are more transmitted to newcomers and successive generations of service employees' (Bowen and Schneider, 1988: 63). Employee satisfaction in internal markets is, therefore, a prerequisite to customer satisfaction in external markets. The basic philosophy is that if management wants its employees to do a great job with customers, then it must be prepared to do a great job with its employees (George, 1990). Unhappy employees will make for unhappy customers so unless employees can be success-fully taken care of, the success of the organisation in its ultimate, external markets will be jeopardised.

Internal marketing therefore involves creating, developing and maintaining an organisational service culture that will lead to the right service personnel performing the service in the right way. It tells employees how to respond to new, unforeseen and even awkward situations (Schneider, 1986). The service culture has a vital impact on how service-orientated employees act and thus how well they perform their tasks as 'part-time marketers' (Bowen and Schneider, 1988). 'When internal customers perform, the likelihood of external customers continuing to buy is increased' (Berry, 1981). Lewis (1989) argues that the success of the internal marketing concept ultimately lies with management. It is unreasonable to expect lower-level employees to be customer orientated if management is not customer orientated.

CONCLUSIONS

Because of the implications for profitability and growth, customer retention is potentially one of the most powerful weapons that companies can employ in their fight to gain a strategic advantage and survive in today's ever increasing competitive environment. It is vital that we understand the issues and the mechanisms behind customer and employee retention and the role that retention marketing can play in formulating strategies and plans. However, in order to do that, much more research needs to be undertaken to provide us with the relevant information on which to base management decisions.

There are three major areas for research in this field: an evaluation of current practice; an examination of factors affecting customer retention rates and a consideration of retention management strategies. The key research questions relating to each of these areas are listed below.

Current practice
- To what extent are service businesses measuring customer retention? Is it measured in aggregate or is it broken down to measure retention rates by market segment?
- To what extent have service companies implemented customer retention programmes?
- What have been the results of customer retention programmes?
- Do successful companies factor customer retention into performance measures, job evaluation and career advancement?

Factors affecting customer retention rates
- What are the factors that affect customer retention rates?
- Why do some companies have high retention rates and other companies have low retention rates?

- Why do some regions/branches with the same company have higher retention rates than others?
- Is there a strong link between employee satisfaction and customer retention? What are the key factors that determine this?
- To what extent do satisfied employees tend to be long-service employees?
- What is the impact of the company's culture on customer and employee retention rates?
- Are referred customers retained longer than customers who are not referred?

Retention marketing strategies
- What frameworks and structures can be formulated in order to explain the theory of retention marketing?
- How can organisations create, develop and maintain an effective service culture? What are the critical success factors and what are the barriers which must be broken down in order to achieve this goal?
- What retention marketing strategies can be adopted to build an organisational climate which will encourage quality customer conscious employees to stay with the company and at the same time ensure that the company maintains long-lasting relationships with its customers?
- What are the most effective organisational structures which will facilitate building a customer-orientated culture?

The second of these – factors affecting customer retention rates – represents an especially interesting area for research. It would be particularly appropriate to examine the different performance amongst branch activities in the same company within organisations such as banks and building societies, for example, since these provide an opportunity to explore best demonstrated practice on a comparative basis. It also provides the opportunity to examine linkages between employee retention and customer satisfaction.

Within this, the key to customer satisfaction, it can be argued, is based upon the extent to which an appropriate climate can be engendered whereby employees see as their major priority the retention of customers. Some preliminary evidence is provided by Schneider (1973), Schneider, Parkington and Buxton (1980) and Schlesinger and Heskett (1991) regarding possible linkages between the internal customer service climate and its impact upon employee retention and customer satisfaction. A critical research issue, therefore, lies in establishing the major determinants of employee satisfaction and hence the willingness of employees to work as part of a team that feels itself empowered to create an atmosphere in which customers willingly commit themselves to a continued relationship with the organisation.

Customer retention provides a fertile ground for a number of related research projects. The next phase of our work will focus on examining the relationship between customer satisfaction and employee retention.

References

Berry, L L (1981) 'The employee as customer', *Journal of Retail Banking*, Vol 3, pp 33–40.

Berry, L L (1983) 'Relationship marketing', in Berry L L, Shostack, G L and Upah, G D (eds), *Emerging Perspectives on Services Marketing*, American Marketing Association, Chicago, pp 25–28.

Berry, L L (1986) 'Big ideas in services marketing', *The Journal of Consumer Marketing*, Vol 3, No 2.

Bowen, D E, and Schneider, B (1988) 'Services marketing and management: implications for organizational behaviour', in Stow, B and Cummings, L L (eds), *Research in Organizational Behaviour*, Vol 10, JAI Press, Greenwich, Conn.

Buchanan, R W J (1990) 'Customer retention: the key link between customer satisfaction and profitability', Unpublished paper, Bain & Co.

Buchanan, R W T and Gillies, C S (1990) 'Value managed relationships: the key to customer retention and profitability', *European Management Journal*, Vol 8, No 4, pp 523–526.

Carlzon, J (1987) *Moments of Truth*, Ballinger, New York.

Carroll, P and Reichheld, F F (1991/92) 'The fallacy of customer retention. The truth of customer retention', *Journal of Retail Banking*, Vol 13, No 4.

Christopher, M, Payne, A F T and Ballantyne, D (1991) *Relationship Marketing; Bringing Quality, Customer Service and Marketing Together*, Butterworth-Heinemann, Oxford.

Dawkins, P M and Reichheld, F F (1990) 'Customer retention as a competitive weapon', *Directors and Boards*, Vol 14, No 4.

DeSouza, G (1992) 'Designing a customer retention plan', *The Journal of Business Strategy*, March–April.

George, W R (1986) 'Internal communications programs as a mechanism for doing internal marketing', *Creativity in Services Marketing*. in Venkatesan V et al. (eds), American Marketing Association, Chicago, pp 83–84.

George, W R (1990) 'Internal marketing and organizational behaviour: a partnership in developing customer-conscious employees at every level', *Journal of Business Research*, Vol 20, No 1.

Gronroos, C (1981) 'Internal marketing – an integral part of marketing theory', in *Marketing of Services*. Donnelly, J H and George, W R (eds), American Marketing Association, Chicago, pp 236–238.

Gronroos, C (1982) 'An applied service marketing theory', *European Journal of Marketing*, Vol 16, pp 30–41.

Gronroos, C (1985) 'Internal marketing – theory and practice', in *Services Marketing in a Changing Environment*, Bloch, T M *et al.* (eds), American Marketing Association, Chicago, pp 41–47.

Gronroos, C (1989) 'Defining marketing: a marketing-oriented approach', *European Journal of Marketing*, Vol 23, pp 52–60.

Gronroos, C (1990) 'Relationship approach to marketing in service contexts: the marketing and organisational behaviour interface', *Journal of Business Research*, Vol 20, No 1.

Gronroos, C and Gummesson, E (1986) 'Service orientation in industrial marketing', in *Creativity in Services Marketing. What's New, What Works, What's Developing*, American Marketing Association, Chicago.

Gummesson, E (1987a) 'The new marketing – developing long-term interactive relationships', *Long Range Planning* Vol 20, No 4, pp 10–20.

Gummesson, E (1987b) *A Long-Term Interactive Relationship Contribution to a New Marketing Theory*, Marketing Technique Center, Stockholm, Sweden.

Hakansson, H (ed.) (1982) *International Marketing and Purchasing of Industrial Goods*, Wiley, New York.

Helman, D and Payne, A F T (1991) *Internal Marketing: Myth Versus Reality*, Cranfield School of Management Working Paper.

Intindola, B (1991) 'Customer retention: now more than just quality', *National Underwriter*, Vol 95, No 22.

Jackson, B B (1985) 'Build customer relationships that last', *Harvard Business Review*, November–December.

Levitt, T (1983) 'After the sale is over', *Harvard Business Review*, 61, September–October.

Lewis, R C (1989) 'Hospitality marketing: the internal approach', *Cornell Hotel and Restaurant Administration*, Vol 30, No 3.

McKenna, R (1992) *Relationship Marketing*, Century Business, London.

Reichheld, F F and Kenny, D W (1990) 'The hidden advantages of customer retention', *Journal of Retail Banking*, Vol 12, No 4.

Reichheld, F and Sasser, W E (1990) 'Zero defections: quality comes to services', *Harvard Business Review*, September–October, pp 105–111.

Rosenberg, L J and Czepiel, J A (1984) 'A marketing approach for customer retention', *The Journal of Consumer Marketing*.

Schlesinger, L A and Heskett, J L (1991) 'Breaking the cycle of failure in services', *Sloan Management Review*, pp 17–28(b).

Schneider, B (1973) 'The perception of organisational climate: the customer's view', *Journal of Applied Psychology*, Vol 57, No 3.

Schneider, B (1980) 'The service organisation: climate is crucial', *Organisational Dynamics*.

Schneider, B (1986) 'Notes on climate and culture', in Venkatesan, M *et al.* (eds), *Creativity in Services Marketing.* American Marketing Association, Chicago, pp 63–67.

Schneider, B and Bowen, D E (1985) 'Employee and customer perceptions of service in banks: replication and extension', *Journal of Applied Psychology*, Vol 70, pp 423–433.

Schneider, B, Parkington, J J and Buxton, V, M (1980) 'Employee and customer perceptions of service in banks', *Administrative Science Quarterly*, Vol 25, pp 252–267.

3

ACHIEVING LONG-TERM CUSTOMER LOYALTY: A STRATEGIC APPROACH*

Moira Clark and Adrian Payne

INTRODUCTION

The concept and underlying philosophy of relationship marketing has been receiving increasing attention in recent years. More practitioners and academics are shifting their interest from the conventional focus of attracting new customers, to a new focus on retaining existing customers. Marketing is now increasingly concerned with relationship marketing – the business of attracting, retaining and enhancing long-term client relationships.

There has been little previous academic work in the area of developing integrated customer retention strategies. This chapter seeks to draw together a wide range of research and contemporary literature on the subject and develop a strategic approach to gaining long-term customer loyalty. The chapter commences with a review of the literature in the evolving area of relationship marketing and customer retention and examines the impact of improved customer retention on profitability. A framework to assist organisations operationalise and improve their customer retention and loyalty is then developed.

THE EVOLVING RELATIONSHIP MARKETING CONCEPT

Increasing activity is being directed towards the area of relationship marketing. Two books on the topic have now been published (Christopher, Payne and Ballantyne, 1991 and McKenna, 1992) and articles and presentations at academic conferences are starting to grow in number. The area has increased in importance to a degree where it has

---

* A version of this chapter was presented to the Annual Conference of the Marketing Education Group, July 1994.

been chosen as the sole topic, amongst considerable competition from many other areas of marketing, for the American Marketing Association's 1994 Annual Faculty Consortium.

The concept of relationship marketing was first introduced by Berry (1983) in a service context to describe a longer-term approach to marketing. Since then it has attracted considerable attention (Levitt, 1983; Rosenberg and Czepiel, 1984; Jackson, 1985; Crosby, Evans and Cowles, 1990; Christopher, Payne and Ballantyne, 1991; McKenna, 1992). A similar approach has also emerged in what has been called the 'Nordic School' of services. This has also been labelled interactive marketing (Gummesson, 1981 and 1987; Gronroos, 1978, 1990a and b; Hakansson, 1982). Research undertaken in the 'Nordic School' over the past decade in the area of industrial and services marketing has concluded that 'the most important issue in marketing is to establish, strengthen and develop customer relationships – where this can be done at a profit, and where individual and organisational objectives are met' (Gronroos, 1990a).

The relationship marketing concept encompasses a number of complimentary perspectives (Christopher, Payne and Ballantyne 1991), including:

- emphasis on customers is moving from a transaction focus to a relationship focus with the aim of long-term customer retention;
- in addition to customer markets, the organisation also becomes concerned with the development of relationships with other external markets including supplier, recruitment, referral and influence markets, as well as internal markets;
- a recognition that quality, customer service and marketing activities need to be brought together. A relationship marketing orientation focuses on bringing these three elements into closer alignment.

Each of these three perspectives are linked to customer retention – not only the first one. The second perspective suggests that five other markets, in addition to customer markets, may need to be addressed to ensure an ultimately satisfactory relationship with customers. In particular, directing effort to internal markets is becoming more important as the strong linkage between employee satisfaction, employee retention and customer retention becomes more apparent (Buchanan, 1990). The third perspective suggests how service quality should be improved through the integration of quality, customer service and marketing. Thus relationship marketing is concerned with customer retention and how this can be achieved by developing long-term customer loyalty. This does not mean that short-term sales are not desirable – in fact, they may be very profitable (Jackson, 1985). However, if close and long-term relationships can be achieved and maintained, this can lead to long-term business success and increased profitability for the company, making market entry or share gain difficult for competitors (Buchanan, 1990).

CUSTOMER RETENTION AND ITS IMPACT ON PROFITABILITY

Much of the literature on customer retention draws on the philosophy of relationship marketing (Levitt, 1983; Berry, 1983; Jackson, 1985). There is, however, relatively little published research in the area of customer retention. The pioneers in the field are Bain & Co, a US consulting firm whose primary focus has been on the impact of retention marketing on company profitability (Buchanan and Gillies, 1990; Buchanan, 1990;

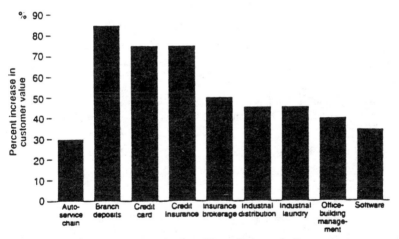

* Calculated by comparing the net present values of the profit streams for the average customer life at current defection rates with the net present values of the profit streams for the average customer life at 5% lower defection rates.

Source: Based on Reichheld, F.F. and Sasser, W.E. Jr. (1990) 'Zero Defections: Quality Comes to Services'. Harvard Business Review, September - October, pp105-111

Figure 3.1 Profit impact of a 5 percentage point increase in customer retention for selected businesses

Reichheld and Kenny, 1990; Dawkins and Reichheld, 1990; Reichheld and Sasser, 1990; Carroll and Reichheld 1991/92; Reichheld 1993).

Bain & Co have developed approaches for both measuring customer retention and modelling the impact of retention on company profitability. They have quantified the potential impact of improving customer retention for many businesses and, as shown in Figure 3.1, have identified that a five-percentage point improvement in customer retention can lead to profit improvements of between 25 per cent and 85 per cent, in terms of net present value (Reichheld and Sasser, 1990).

There are a number of factors which explain why retaining customers can have such a dramatic impact on profits. These include: retained business; the sales, marketing and set-up costs are amortised over a longer customer lifetime; satisfied customers are likely to cost less to service, provide free word-of-mouth advertising and referrals, purchase additional products and services and may be willing to pay a price premium. Improved customer retention can also lead to increased employee retention which feeds back into even greater customer longevity and increased profitability.

Bain & Co's work has been criticised by Carroll (1991/92) who argues that customer retention does not result in significant profitability improvement – it only appears to because of faulty cross-sectional analysis of data. In response to these criticisms Reichheld (1991/92) points out that Bain & Co have never suggested that by simply increasing retention rates, profits will automatically increase. They point out that 'foolish investment to retain hopelessly unprofitable customers would destroy profits'. Therefore, marketing efforts must be directed towards profitable customers. It should, however, be recognised that unprofitable customers may eventually become profitable and that they may well provide a contribution towards fixed and variable costs.

This debate raises the role of customer segmentation in retention analysis (although it is not specifically described in this way in the above authors' work). Appropriate segmentation analysis is essential to ensure efforts are directed at the most profitable segments. The issue of segmentation is further developed within the next section of this chapter.

The issue of retention needs to be seen in the context of the existing level of customer loyalty. It is clearly more important in those or-ganisations where customers do not have a strong commitment to their suppliers. Our work with a wide range of service organisations suggests opportunities for improvement may be considerable. For example, research into the banking sector undertaken by the Forum for Private Business (Nash, 1993) illustrates the low overall commitment of

Table 3.1: Percentage of customers who have considered changing their bank

	%
Barclays	50.6
Lloyds	58.7
Midland	55.8
National Westminster	53.0
Bank of Scotland	37.3
Clydesdale Bank	38.6
Royal Bank of Scotland	41.2
Sample average	51.9

Source: Forum for Private Business

customers to their bank, measured by the percentage of customers who have considered changing their banks, as shown in Table 3.1.

Table 3.1 illustrates that, on average, over 50 per cent of customers have considered changing banks. This highlights just how important building improved long-term customer loyalty is within industries such as the financial services sector. This can be achieved through the development of a strategic approach to customer retention. The key elements and a framework for developing such an approach are now examined.

A FRAMEWORK FOR CUSTOMER RETENTION IMPROVEMENT

Given the dramatic effect that improved customer retention can have on business profitability, organisations need an approach that leads to greater customer loyalty and results in enhanced retention and profitability. A framework for customer retention improvement is now developed. The framework, shown in Figure 3.2, involves three major steps: measurement of customer retention, identification of root causes of defection and related key service issues, and the development of corrective action to improve retention. Each of these steps consists of a number of critical tasks and elements which are now examined.

Step 1: Measurement of Customer Retention

Measurement of existing customer retention rates is the first critical step in the task of improving loyalty. This involves two major tasks – measurement of retention rates and profitability analysis by segment. The customer retention rate can be defined, at its most simple level, as the

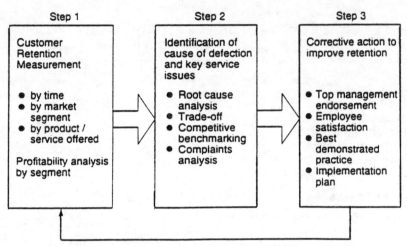

Figure 3.2 Customer retention improvement framework

percentage of customers at the beginning of a period that still remain customers at the end of the period. However, it should be recognised that other dimensions need to be addressed and that relevant segmentation analysis is essential.

Dimensions of customer retention measurement

To measure customer retention and identify changes in it, a number of dimensions need to be analysed in detail. These include measurement of customer retention rates – over time, by market segment and by product/service offered.

As some customers will buy all their products or services from one company whereas other customers will be serviced by many suppliers, it is necessary to weight customers by the amount they spend. Otherwise high apparent customer retention rates can hide a serious problem. For example, there are many banks who boast high levels of customer retention but which, in fact, have high levels of account dormancy, where customers have defected to other banks but have not closed their accounts.

Segment profitability analysis

It must not, however, be assumed that companies will wish to retain all their customers. Some customers may actually cost too much money to service and may never prove to be worthwhile and profitable. Further investment in these customers clearly would be undesirable.

Instead, companies should segment their market by level of profitability and identify which groups of customers the company wishes to retain and which are likely to provide the most profitable returns. This will help identify the type and frequency of the marketing activity which should be directed towards the different segments. For example, a large insurance company discovered that it was not high net worth individuals, to whom they were targeting most of their selling effort, that were providing them with their largest profit streams, but school teachers whom they had completely ignored. Previously this group had never been considered a worthwhile market segment.

Step 2: Identification of Cause of Defection and Key Service Issues

The second step in Figure 3.2 involves the identification of the underlying causes of why customers defect. Four analytical approaches are useful in undertaking this task. These include: root cause of defection analysis, trade-off analysis, competitive benchmarking and complaints analysis.

Root cause of defection analysis

Traditional marketing research into customer satisfaction does not typically provide answers as to why customers defect. For example, a questionnaire for a major high street bank asked customers why they were closing their account. One of the alternative answers provided was that 'the account was no longer required'. Not surprisingly the vast majority of people ticked that box because it was a safe and easy answer and none of the other alternative answers adequately addressed the real issues that caused defection.

Instead, the root causes for customer defections must be determined. Root cause of defection analysis should be undertaken by specially trained researchers who are able to probe in detail for the reasons why customers defect. For example, a customer may say that they no longer patronise a particular supermarket because the prices are too high. But in reality the root cause may be unhelpful staff, long queues, difficulty in finding products on the shelves, etc.

Trade-off analysis

It is also important to undertake research to identify the key customer service issues which result in customers being retained. This can be undertaken through 'trade-off' analysis (Christopher, 1992). This enables companies to evaluate the implicit importance that a customer attaches to the specific elements of customer service.

Competitive benchmarking

Competitive benchmarking enables companies to rate their performance and that of their competitors on critical elements of customer service in terms of their perceived importance. It is then possible to establish standards for the service encounter. For example, what is the maximum length of time a customer should be left waiting in a queue? Should employees be expected to answer the telephone within a given time? What level of product knowledge should employees be expected to have about the products and services that they sell?

Customer complaint analysis

Another useful way of identifying key service issues is to analyse customers' complaints. This not only highlights those areas which may eventually be the cause of customer defections but also acts as an early warning system to the company to enable them to resolve a problem with a customer before it is too late. Some companies are now developing 'recovery teams' which move into action immediately a likely defector is identified. The recovery team is charged with identifying the real reasons for customers' dissatisfaction and are empowered to resolve these problems.

Step 3: Corrective Action to Improve Retention

The third and final step involves undertaking corrective action aimed at generating improved customer loyalty. At this point plans to improve retention become highly specific to the organisation concerned. We can, however, outline broad issues which should be addressed in any plan to improve retention. These include ensuring visible top management endorsement, generating employee satisfaction and commitment to building long-term customer relationships, utilising best demonstrated practice techniques to improve performance and the development of an implementation plan.

Visible top management endorsement

Visible top management endorsement is vital to the success of customer retention programmes. If employees see that management are genuinely enthusiastic, supportive and involved in a new retention initiative, it is more likely that employees will be inspired to follow management's example and take the retention programme seriously. However, if the employees see that this is just another management fad they will not adopt the practices necessary to implement an effective retention programme. They will make the superficial changes essential for survival, but underneath the facade nothing will have fundamentally changed. Employees will just wait for the novelty to wear off and revert to their old routines. The level of enthusiasm, involvement, effort and visibility that top management put behind such programmes is, therefore, often seen by employees as indicative of the amount of support that they should give such programmes.

Customer retention and employee satisfaction

A major key to customer retention improvement, it can be argued, is the extent to which an appropriate climate can be established whereby employees see, as their main priority, the satisfaction and retention of customers. There is certainly a strong link between the internal customer service climate and its impact upon employee satisfaction and customer retention (Schneider, 1973; Schneider, Parkington and Buxton, 1980; and Schlesinger and Heskett, 1991). Happy employees will make for happy customers. The happier the customers, the more likely it is that the employees will find their work satisfying and rewarding and wish to stay with the company for a long time. This improved employee retention is likely to deliver improved internal and external service quality.

The selection and recruitment of customer contact staff who have the appropriate interpersonal skills to build relationships with customers is also necessary. These people must then be trained by the company to acquire the knowledge and skills necessary to identify and meet customer needs and expectations and exceed the service standards already specified. Staff performance must then be monitored against these standards. Finally, it is also important to adapt the company's reward and recognition systems so that staff who perform well are rewarded by the organisation.

Utilising best demonstrated practice

Best demonstrated practice is a useful technique for disseminating superior practices throughout a company (Buchanan, 1990; Reichheld and Kenny, 1990). In this context it involves identifying the best retention performers in the industry and within the organisation. Teams of managers then examine these organisations to see how they are managed and then develop new approaches to raise customer satisfaction and increase retention in their own businesses. Sometimes it is worthwhile looking outside the company's own industry for best practice. There may well be more likelihood of achieving competitive advantage if practices are borrowed from other industries.

Development of an implementation plan

In addition to the usual procedural steps that form the basis of any implementation plan, several additional opportunities to create customer loyalty are now discussed.

A good retention strategy should try to identify and build barriers that stop customers from switching to the competition no matter what inducements the competition is offering. *Strategic bundling* is an example of building a barrier to customer defections. Groups of associated products or services are offered to the customer with the advantage of convenience and/or cost savings. Bank accounts are a good example of this, where customers often use their bank for mortgages, insurance policies, as well as the more usual standing orders and direct debits. Bain & Co's research in financial services suggests retention rates are significantly greater where customers use two or more of the organisation's services, than where they use only one service. However, if the customer feels that the company is taking advantage of past loyalty, attempts to offer bundled products and cross-selling will be resented.

Team-based relationship management can create a very effective barrier to customer defections. The relationship with the customer is managed by an account manager who manages a team-based approach to relationship building. The aim is to make the relationship more enduring by building as many links as possible between the customer and supplier. Figure 3.3a illustrates the establishment of multiple contacts between, for example, the supplier's production team and the customer's

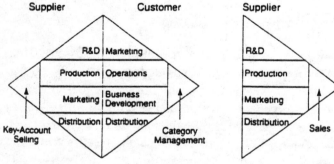

(a) Building Stronger Partnerships Through Multiple Linkages

(b) Traditional Buyer / Supplier Relationship

Source: Christopher 1994

Figure 3.3 Team based relationship marketing

operations team; and with the supplier's marketing team and the customer's business development team; and so on. This is in contrast to Figure 3.3b which shows a traditional buyer–seller relationship dependent on the sometimes fragile and fairly limited connection between a supplier's key account executive and a retailer's buyer (Christopher, 1994).

EDI (electronic data interchange) can also be a 'tie that binds'. Getting customers to invest in sharing information about sales and inventories can provide a powerful disincentive to switch supplier. The benefits are reduced system costs, efficiency and increased customer and consumer satisfaction. Unfortunately, from the supplier's point of view many smaller organisations have been forced by their larger customers to make investments in EDI at their own expense.

In many industries switching barriers should only be built if they are in the best interests of both customer and supplier. This suggestion is not based on philanthropism or morality. Bad publicity, generated by disgruntled customers locked into unsatisfactory supplier relationships, can significantly reduce profits. This is especially true in consumer markets where, if things go wrong, switching barriers mean that customers find themselves in a system from which it is difficult to leave. Customers may feel trapped, helpless and even cheated. For example, bank customers who feel dissatisfied with the service they receive often find the task of moving their account too onerous to carry out. The result is very unhappy customers who go out of their way to tell others of their negative experiences and who warn others of the pitfalls that await them should they deal with these organisations.

CONCLUSIONS

This chapter addresses customer retention in a relationship marketing context and the need companies have for a strategic approach to achieving improved customer loyalty. The customer retention framework developed in the chapter provides an approach for identifying the key elements which need to be addressed in order to achieve long-term customer loyalty. Implementing this framework requires commitment, enthusiasm and dedication, not only from senior executives, but also from all company employees. The emerging relationship marketing paradigm is able to help crystalise these key issues for managers and, as such, provides guidance on how to leverage business performance and profitability in an increasingly competitive environment.

We have argued that most companies could be doing more to cultivate business from their existing customers. However, our discussions on the importance of customer retention do not imply that this is essential for all organisations. For example, during our research we have identified a small number of companies who are placing too much attention on existing customers and not enough effort on attracting new customers. Instances of this are, nevertheless, relatively rare. Discussions with managers from over 180 companies have indicated that less than 10 per cent of these companies fall into this category. It is essential, therefore, that managers are aware of the importance of achieving the appropriate balance, in terms of expenditure and managerial time, between retaining and acquiring customers and that appropriate strategies are adopted to achieve the most cost-effective use of scarce marketing resources.

References

Berry, L L (1983) 'Relationship marketing', in, Berry, L L, Shostack, G L and Upah, G D (eds), *Emerging Perspectives on Services Marketing*, American Marketing Association, Chicago, pp 25–28.

Buchanan, R W J, (1990) 'Customer retention: the key link between customer satisfaction and profitability', Unpublished paper, Bain & Co.

Buchanan, R W T and Gillies, C S (1990) 'Value managed relationships: the key to customer retention and profitability', *European Management Journal*, Vol 8, No 4.

Carroll, P and Reichheld, F F (1991/92) 'The fallacy of customer retention: The truth of customer retention', *Journal of Retail Banking*, Vol 13, No 4.

Christopher, M (1992) *The Customer Service Planner*, Butterworth-Heinemann, Oxford.

Christopher, M (1994) 'Customer service and logistics strategy', in Baker, M (ed.), *The Marketing Book*, Butterworth-Heinemann, Oxford.

Christopher, M, Payne, A F T and Ballantyne, D (1991) *Relationship Marketing: Bringing Quality, Customer Service and Marketing Together*, Butterworth-Heinemann, Oxford.

Crosby, L A, Evans, K R and Cowles D (1990) 'Relationship quality in service selling: an interpersonal influence perspective', *Journal of Marketing*, Vol 54, July, pp 68–81.

Dawkins, P M and Reichheld, F F (1990) 'Customer retention as a competitive weapon', *Directors and Boards*, Vol 14, No 4.

Grönroos, C (1978) 'A service-oriented approach to marketing of services', *European Journal of Marketing*, Vol 12, pp 588–601.

Grönroos C (1990a) 'Marketing redefined', *Management Decision*, Vol 28, No 8, pp 5–9.

Grönroos, C (1990b) *The Marketing Strategy Continuum: Towards a Marketing Concept for the 1990s*, Meddelanden Fran Svenska Handelshogskolan, Working Paper 201.

Gummesson, E (1981) 'Marketing costs concepts in service firms', *Industrial Marketing Management*, No 3.

Gummesson, E (1987) 'The new marketing – developing long-term interactive relationships', *Long Range Planning*, Vol 20, No 4, pp 10–20.

Hakansson, H (ed.) (1982) *International Marketing and Purchasing of Industrial Goods*, Wiley, New York.

Jackson, B B (1985) 'Build customer relationships that last', *Harvard Business Review*, November–December.

Levitt, T (1983) 'After the sale is over', *Harvard Business Review*, Vol 6, No 1, pp 87–93.

McKenna, R (1992) *Relationship Marketing*, Century Business, London.

Nash, T (1993), 'A clear alternative?', *Director*, May.

Reichheld, F F (1993), 'Loyalty-based management', *Harvard Business Review*, March–April.

Reichheld, F F and Kenny, D W (1990) 'The hidden advantages of customer retention', *Journal of Retail Banking*, Vol 12, No 4.

Reichheld, F F and Sasser, W E (1990) 'Zero defections: quality comes to services', *Harvard Business Review*, September–October, pp 105–111.

Rosenberg, L J and Czepiel, J A (1984) 'A marketing approach for customer retention', *The Journal of Consumer Marketing*.

Schlesinger, L A and Heskett, J L (1991) 'Breaking the cycle of failure in services', *Sloan Management Review*, Spring, pp 17–28.

Schneider, B (1973), 'The perception of organisational climate: the customer's view', *Journal of Applied Psychology*, Vol 57, No 3, pp 248–256.

Schneider, B, Parkington, J J and Buxton, V M (1980), 'Employee and customer perceptions of service in banks', *Administrative Science Quarterly*, Vol 25, pp 252–267.

PART TWO

INTERNAL MARKETING

4

INTERNAL MARKETING: MYTH VERSUS REALITY *

Deborah Helman and Adrian Payne

INTRODUCTION

Internal marketing is concerned with turning traditional marketing techniques inwards; focusing on the internal customers and suppliers of the internal market-place, with the aim of improving internal market relationships, quality and customer service and ultimately corporate effectiveness. Internal marketing represents one of the key markets addressed in relationship marketing (Christopher, Payne and Ballantyne, 1991) and is emerging as a topic of increasing interest to both academics and practitioners. This interest is reflected in a growing literature on the topic reporting the development and implementation of internal marketing programmes in organisations. Much of the existing literature takes one of two predominant forms: it either details the experience of a specific organisation or it is largely prescriptive in nature with little or no reference to the realities of the organisational context. Currently, no real theory has emerged and no attempt has been made to contrast internal marketing in different organisations to determine the characteristics of good internal marketing practice. Internal marketing is said to be a 'good thing', but we do not understand exactly what it is, who in the organisation has responsibility for it, nor what its effects are.

This chapter reports preliminary findings of an exploratory study to determine the nature and extent of internal marketing activity across a range of organisations, in an attempt to dispel some of the myths associated with it and explain the reality of its practice. Interestingly the prompt for the current research came from the realisation that practitioners were some way ahead of academics in addressing the internal marketing issue.

In the literature, as we found in practice, internal marketing encom-

---

* This chapter is based on Helman, D and Payne, A F T (1992) 'Internal Services Marketing' working paper, Cranfield School of Management. Reprinted with permission. © Cranfield School of Management.

passes a broad range of activities. To confuse matters internal marketing is also closely associated with the concept of the 'internal customer' and is often otherwise defined as 'inner marketing' or 'internal communications'. There are at least four interesting approaches to internal marketing in the literature. The first relates to Gronroos's (1981, 1985) pioneering work on the integrative marketing concept and perceived service quality, where internal marketing facilitates improvements in service quality. The second is concerned with Flipo's (1986) alignment of external and internal marketing strategies and the resolution of functional conflicts; internal marketing must support and be aligned with external marketing efforts to ensure the latter's success. The third approach relates to Berry's (1981) and Gummesson's (1987) concept of the internal customer, which is closely linked to the issue of quality management. And fourthly, recent work integrates the earlier work on internal marketing, where internal marketing is seen as a means of effecting organisational change and implementing marketing strategies (Piercy and Morgan, 1990a and 1990b).

Marketing usually focuses on external exchanges. With internal marketing the argument is made for the efficacy of marketing in exchanges between employees and organisations. Berry (1981) suggests there are several forms of internal marketing, but they have in common a focus on the customer inside the organisation. For instance, he considers the employee as customer where jobs are internal products and the organisation endeavours to offer jobs – internal products that will satisfy internal customers in keeping with the objectives of the organisation. For example, Berry suggests by satisfying internal customers a bank upgrades its capability for satisfying the needs and wants of its external customers. Marketing research, segmentation and advertising are applied to internal markets providing a marketing solution to managing people. He suggests internal marketing is of great importance in service industries where employee performance is the 'product'; it provides a means to differentiate from competitors, via the quality of people – it is an investment in 'people quality' as opposed to 'product quality'. Collins and Payne (1991) examine the use of internal marketing in the human resource management function.

Internal marketing may not be as nebulous and ill-defined as it might appear at first glance, for at the core of most of this work are the interrelated themes of people, quality, and managing relationships. An argument could be made that internal marketing encompasses more than the proper sphere of marketing and does not have as its central focus the (internal) customer.

A consideration of the literature and discussions with executives in companies raises two perspectives that are often in the form of questions: Is internal marketing some formalised 'cure-all', enabling smooth operations, superior communication and implementation of strategies? Or does internal marketing, in reality, describe a unique set of loosely related activities, aimed at improving the effectiveness of operations and relationships within the organisation?

SOME QUESTIONS ANSWERED ABOUT INTERNAL MARKETING

The following observations of internal marketing in practice come from discussions with senior marketing managers from a range of large service and manufacturing organisations that have undertaken internal marketing programmes.

Managers were asked in semi-structured interviews to describe the internal marketing programmes established in their organisations. Specific questions were asked in relation to the length of time an internal marketing programme had been running, whether the programme was formal, if it had a specific name, the job title of the person in charge of internal marketing, whether this was a full-time or part-time appointment and the size of the internal marketing staff, and whom the staff reported to. Additionally, respondents were asked to describe the critical success factors of the internal marketing programme and to describe modifications to the programme, employee perceptions and potential future developments.

Three forms of internal marketing identified in the literature were discussed in the interviews:

1. Marketing to employees – motivating employees to better performance and improved relationships with internal and external customers.
2. Marketing of an internal function – eg marketing the marketing department, so that marketing is perceived as investment not expenditure, or other functional areas/departments marketing their roles within the organisation.
3. Marketing the organisation's products and services to employees – for example, where a bank would encourage employees to use the bank's own services.

As far as internal marketing as a discrete activity is concerned no clear pattern emerges in terms of a distinct set of activities. The concept of internal marketing is used to define a range of both formally organised activities and a range of *ad hoc* initiatives. In relation to the three forms of internal marketing identified above, we have observed in practice, that 'marketing to employees' is the most common form of internal marketing. Internal marketing has evolved in organisations to facilitate the implementation of quality initiatives and a diverse range of activities targeted at customer contact staff to improve performance and employee/customer relations. In relation to 'marketing of a functional department', less use of this form of internal marketing is found, although where it is used, the need to market the marketing function may be especially important. 'Marketing the organisation's products and services to employees' is only sometimes considered by managers as a form of internal marketing, even though most organisations offer their own products and services at discounted prices to employees.

Internal marketing has evolved alongside the development of customer-driven thinking in organisations. A variety of claims are made for internal marketing ranging from the suggestion that internal marketing is not a new concept, but is rather a new label attached to internal communication projects, to claims that internal marketing performs an important new role in changing the structure of the organisation enabling the creation of autonomous units which display a greater sense of ownership, accountability and responsibility. We now consider the responses to our questions in more detail below.

What is the Scope of Internal Marketing?

Internal marketing primarily takes two main forms in the organisations reviewed: marketing to employees – motivating employees to better performance and improved relationships with internal and external customers; and marketing the marketing department, such that marketing is perceived as an investment rather than an expenditure, and encouraging other functional areas to market themselves within the organisation.

Organisations tend to do one or the other depending on the specific objectives of the internal marketing programme. Internal marketing may be focused on specific groups within the organisation – for example customer contact staff, the sales force; or have a wider audience – for example an education programme from the board downwards. Internal marketing may involve a communication programme throughout the organisation, thus involving everyone in the organisation in internal marketing.

The marketing of an internal function is an important form of internal marketing. It may be necessary to demonstrate internally the skills and competences of a newly formed marketing function to justify its existence. Internal marketing may even be a wholly defensive action to safeguard the survival of a marketing department. Internal marketing is also used to internally sell strategic marketing initiatives and objectives.

How Long have Organisations been doing Internal Marketing – and Why?

Internal marketing has been introduced by organisations over the past decade. It has often been initiated as part of a Total Quality Management programme or similar activities. In the past few years internal marketing has emerged as a separate task, in many cases representing the coordination of a range of disparate activities.

Internal marketing is introduced for a variety of reasons connected with the realisation that the organisation has to be better integrated and directed towards the customer; thus internal marketing forms part of broader business objectives. Internal marketing is used to develop interfunctional relationships, to improve understanding and minimise conflict (including those between sales and marketing functions). Internal marketing has also been used to assist in cultural change as part of a post-merger integration process. Internal marketing is often recognised as an important task by key individuals in a company who then champion its introduction. Internal marketing has been used to raise the profile of marketing departments, to make them more responsive, and to improve their internal credibility where they have suffered from poor image or performance.

Are Internal Marketing Programmes Formalised?

Internal marketing programmes tend not to be highly formalised, in the sense of having a distinct set of plans, policies and documents. Rather internal marketing involves a range of activities some of which are structured and others *ad hoc*. Formal aspects of internal marketing programmes tend to originate from head office, which may provide a formal framework or skeleton of a programme. For example, in one company specific activities are labelled the 'Sales and Marketing Programme'. This involves a range of activities which collectively constitute internal marketing, but are not expressly described as such. An internal marketing programme tends to be subtle; it exists and it has manifestations everywhere but is not explicit. Whilst in many cases very little would have to be done to actually formalise the programme, there is a strong belief in the companies surveyed that formalising internal marketing programmes may undermine their credibility and effectiveness.

What are the Specific Objectives of Internal Marketing?

In relation to marketing the marketing function, the objectives of internal marketing are to improve internal perceptions of the marketing department, and more broadly to remove (or reduce) interfunctional conflicts and develop a more integrated organisation.

Internal marketing often forms part of quality and service initiatives with the objective of getting everyone in the organisation oriented towards the same direction, to develop awareness of internal and external customers and to foster a team spirit within business units.

In some organisations the objective of internal marketing is to promote a greater degree of innovation. In response to ever shortening product lifecycles, internal marketing is being used to generate greater responsiveness at every level. Internal marketing in promoting leadership in innovation involves the empowerment of all staff towards making a contribution. Related to this, internal marketing may be used to market new technologies internally, to market a new corporate image, to change the ethos of the organisation and, importantly, to communicate strategic market issues.

Internal marketing may be used as a competitive weapon to differentiate the organisation externally, giving the organisation an externally perceived competitive advantage in terms of responsiveness.

Who Organises the Internal Marketing Effort?

Responsibility for organising internal marketing often rests with marketing managers, and in some cases involves direct board level representation as part of the marketing director's brief. 'Internal marketing managers' *per se* are rare, but internal marketing may exist as part of the internal communications unit's remit. However in some cases responsibility is delegated to an external consultant, or may be considered the responsibility of everyone in the organisation. In other cases responsibility falls to the individuals responsible for implementing specific programmes and these often come under the auspices of personnel or human resource departments. In very large firms with autonomous business units, each unit tends to 'do its own thing' within head office guidelines, therefore some units may have internal marketing appointments and others not. Often responsibility lies with the whole marketing department who seek to diffuse an internal marketing message throughout the organisation. Those responsible for internal marketing report variously to their CEOs, commercial directors or sales VPs who tend to be the champions of the internal marketing programme.

A lack of formality and structure in the organisations examined is evident in the absence of specific plans, policies and documentation, and appointments that are formulated and implemented in internal marketing.

What Range of Activities Comprise Internal Marketing?

Internal marketing is achieved by a broad range of activities. These fall into two basic forms of communication exercises: internal publications, and briefing sessions and educational programmes. Internal marketing tends to use different messages and forums for discussion for different groups of employees. It is important to identify the target customer and determine if it is all employees, specific groups of customer contact staff, or decision-makers who will influence adoption of proposals.

In relation to internal publications, information is circulated throughout the organisation to raise awareness concerning how the business is doing and understanding customer relationships. This typically involves monthly marketing reports, in-house magazines, and quarterly and monthly newsletters. Videos are also used to convey the internal marketing message in much the same way. Internal marketing related issues are often discussed in workshops and monthly meetings and reported back through internal magazines.

Briefing sessions and educational programmes are designed to transmit the internal marketing message. Additionally they provide the opportunity to collect ideas and feedback from employees, and to publicise the organisation's successes. These may involve:

- a package of exercises involving workshops and incentives for all employees;
- team briefings and awareness programmes that 'cascade' down the organisation accumulating more local issues at each stage;
- regular workshops for staff and managers;
- quarterly briefings to senior managers, which are corporate strategy oriented – in turn these senior managers brief their own line managers;
- meetings for product marketing managers to establish sales guidelines and discuss product development. This can provide a feedback mechanism, where managers also attend the meetings of other departments.

Educational programmes may be designed for all employees. Programmes are tailored for the needs of key customer contact staff. Internal marketing, as mentioned above, is an inherent part of quality and service initiatives such as TQM.

The following four examples demonstrate some contrasting approaches to internal marketing:

Case 1

The sales and marketing effectiveness programme of one organisation had as its objective the diffusion of the customer orientation message throughout the organisation, based on the belief that customer needs are best met by a fully functionally integrated organisation. It was the marketing department's responsibility to define what customers want and help the other functions in the organisation understand this. As such it was largely an exercise in persuasion. The programme had top-level commitment, but was organised by an external consultant. Essentially the programme's activities involved multifunctional problem-solving teams. Participants in the projects also served as change agents and conveyed the message throughout the organisation. Projects were identified in areas where the customer had not been satisfactorily serviced. The process has involved writing case histories of successes and failures, based on the belief that there is something to be learnt even in failure. Indeed, the organisation rewards individuals who have tried, irrespective of the result. The programme has broken down functional barriers and as a result the focus of many jobs has changed and value has been added to them.

Case 2

A large organisation provides a contrasting approach to internal marketing. Following the British Airways customer care programme model 18,000 employees attend a half-day session programme. Employees pass through in small groups and the programme is designed to foster a team spirit; it has an extrovert quality and a customer orientation. Working parties of employees are also formed to deal with specific issues. The programme has involved a substantial investment and has evolved through three stages.

Case 3

A business unit of a large hotel group with a substantial degree of autonomy operates its own internal marketing programme. Activities are organised around an internal marketing plan. Emphasis is placed on teams within the business unit developing a thorough knowledge of the organisation. This is achieved by quality circles which communicate with one another, by a staff magazine in which teams compete for space, and by a newsletter. Employees' knowledge of the organisation is also developed by visits to other parts of the organisation, which in this instance involves free stays at other hotels in the group. Internal marketing also performs an important role in developing the company's local reputation as a good employer which is seen as critical in a labour-intensive service business.

Case 4

A recently privatised company has used internal marketing to develop customer and competitor awareness. An internal communications programme includes an in-house journal which covers product development, customer initiatives and performance results. This is sent to all employees' homes. Other publications are targeted at different divisions and levels within the organisation. Regular team meetings are held which convey the corporate or division message, the roles of individuals and specific local issues are discussed. Corporate videos presented by celebrities are also used to transmit specific corporate messages.

What are Employee Perceptions of Internal Marketing?

Companies are finding their employees are responding to internal marketing both positively and with a degree of scepticism. In organisations where the reaction is positive, internal marketing is helping significantly to improve quality of work and developing a deeper involvement and cross-fertilisation amongst staff. Responses are more positive in those organisations which have a supportive culture. Employees in such companies are less cynical than they might otherwise be of internal marketing activities. This suggests the right organisational climate is highly desirable prior to developing an internal marketing programme.

What Problems are Encountered with Internal Marketing?

Some problems are encountered in establishing internal marketing as a priority, although once a small group of individuals become involved the programme can run itself. Relying on the internal marketing message to diffuse through the organisation can be problematic, even where a good grapevine exists, as the message may not get through to the right people. Many internal marketing activities, for example getting people together to celebrate the organisation's successes, may be difficult to implement because of the company's geographic spread. When 'selling' internal marketing by written form, it is seen as important to recognise that you are competing for the readers' time; as a consequence written materials and reports must be attractively 'packaged' to gain attention.

With internal marketing activities measurement is difficult. However, organisations may impose formal measures on specific initiatives which affords some measure of control. There is a general feeling that introduction of tight financial controls may endanger the effectiveness of internal marketing.

What Results have been Achieved?

The results of internal marketing efforts are largely qualitative. Examples given by respondents include:

- 'Relationships have improved between functions in organisations by the establishment of two-way communications. For example, the marketing department is now told if product specifications are changed, where in the past they would not have been told.'
- 'General levels of information and communication have increased.'
- 'Employees are becoming aware of the objectives of internal marketing initiatives, and encourage others to become aware of the direction the organisation is following.'
- 'Success breeds confidence in initiatives and bolder approaches are being adopted.'
- 'Internal marketing is seen to be paying off in the creativity it has inspired.'
- 'Internal marketing is helping solve some of the problems of being a large company.'

What are the Critical Success Factors?

Successful internal marketing programmes appear to be dependent on a number of factors:

- Foremost, programmes rely on communications, good communication systems and strong messages. The message must get through to the people who need to hear it.
- Internal marketing depends on factors associated with the organisation's culture, including commitment at all levels, cooperation, an open management style, general awareness of the need to make cultural changes and recognition that the customer comes first. This involves a recognition that everyone in the organisation must be pointing in the same direction towards the customer.
- Internal marketing must be accepted as a mainstream responsibility. Internal marketing must be 'customer-led'.
- Recipients of the internal marketing message need to see the benefits for themselves. This leads to ownership of the process.
- Internal marketing has to be consistent, balanced, maintained and built upon as an ongoing resource. This in turn is reliant upon feedback and continued interest – the internal marketing message should also be enjoyable.

INTERNAL MARKETING IN THE FUTURE?

Internal marketing will continue to evolve as a concept. Many changes have occurred in the past ten years including changes in attitudes and changes in the problem-solving techniques used in internal marketing. Employees are now more aware of who the customer is. In some organisations it is difficult to anticipate future changes because the internal marketing programme is still in the early phase of development.

Internal marketing is seen as an ongoing process, with motivation, time and financial constraints determining its future. The success of many programmes are tied to the individuals who run them; as a consequence they may lapse if these individuals move on. It is also possible that the formal aspects of programmes will be discontinued, because the informal aspects are working well enough. Internal marketing could become more formalised, profit oriented and professional, although formalisation may undermine its effectiveness. Functional areas such as human resource management must learn to market themselves and head office departments such as computer operations will increasingly be concerned with developing the appropriate service orientation.

Internal marketing will have a more central role and will form an important part of the relationship marketing strategy. Organisations will continue to strive towards their current internal marketing objectives: for everyone in the organisation to understand the mission and the part they have to play as individuals and to enjoy their jobs more because they see the whole picture.

CONCLUSIONS

Internal marketing in all its forms is recognised as an important activity in developing a marketing oriented organisation. In practice, internal marketing is concerned primarily with communications, with developing responsiveness, responsibility and unity of purpose. Fundamental aims of internal marketing are to develop internal and external customer awareness and remove functional barriers to organisational effectiveness.

The following points emerge from this preliminary study.

- Internal marketing is generally not a discrete activity, but is implicit in quality initiatives, customer service programmes and broader marketing and business strategies.
- Internal marketing typically comprises some formal structured activities accompanied by a range of less formal *ad hoc* initiatives.
- Communication is critical to successful internal marketing.
- Internal marketing has evolved out of customer-driven thinking.
- Internal marketing has the potential to perform a significant role in the creation of competitive differentiation.
- Internal marketing has an important role to play in reducing interfunctional conflict within the organisation.
- Internal marketing is an experiential process, leading employees to arrive at conclusions themselves.
- Internal marketing is evolutionary; it involves the slow erosion of barriers.
- Internal marketing has considerable potential as a force to help facilitate an innovative spirit within the organisation.
- Internal marketing is more successful when there is commitment at the highest level, the cooperation of all employees and an open management style.
- Overt packaging of the internal marketing concept may be less successful than a more subtle approach which permeates the organisation and becomes a shared value.
- Imposing profit goals and measurement on internal marketing could endanger the benefits derived from it.

- Internal marketing is concerned with getting all employees to understand the organisation's mission statement.

From a strategic perspective internal marketing provides considerable value. Firstly, where internal marketing is concerned with the development of a customer orientation, the alignment of internal marketing and external marketing ensures a coherent strategy. Secondly, internal marketing plays an important role in employee motivation and retention. Expansion of the service sector and demographic changes will continue to increase the pressure on organisations to compete in the labour market and increase the attractiveness of employee retention.

This initial study suggests a set of issues to explore in future research, in particular: the barriers to successful implementation in terms of structures, systems and people; measurement and control; internal marketing as part of developing a marketing orientation; and marketing effectiveness and internal marketing. The effectiveness of programmes would be better understood by investigating 'customer' perceptions. More can be learnt of how internal marketing within firms is organised and to what extent marketing techniques and tools are actually applied internally.

We conclude that there is considerable variation in the ways in which internal marketing is practised due to differences in organisational culture and needs, but typically internal marketing involves using traditional marketing techniques inside the organisation. Good communications and top management support are the critical success factors. The benefits arising from internal marketing are seen to be increased organisational effectiveness through more effective implementation of marketing strategies and, specifically, in implementing the marketing concept and getting everyone in the organisation to become involved in marketing.

This preliminary investigation has revealed that whilst internal marketing does exist as more than a theoretical concept, there remains a myth about its formalisation and benefits. The reality is that internal marketing is not a 'cure-all' but like all marketing requires vision, energy, commitment and hard work to make it work. For those internal marketing programmes that are imaginatively and sensitively created and implemented the result will be an improvement in both internal efficiency and external effectiveness of the company's marketing efforts.

In contrast to accepted wisdom, it was found that the widespread existence of highly formalised and structured internal marketing programmes was a myth. The reality is internal marketing programmes typically constitute a diverse range of activities and are often relatively unstructured.

References

Berry, L (1981) 'The employee as customer', *Journal of Retail Banking*, Vol 3, No 1.

Bloch, T *et al.* (eds) (1985) *Services Marketing in a Changing Environment*. American Marketing Association, Chicago.

Christopher, M, Payne A F T and Ballantyne, D (1991) *Relationship Marketing; Bringing Quality Customer Service and Marketing Together*, Butterworth-Heinemann, Oxford.

Collins, B and Payne A F T (1991) 'Internal marketing', *European Management Journal*, Vol 9, No 3.

Donnelly, J H and George, W R (1981) *Marketing of Services*, American Marketing Association, Chicago.

Flipo, J (1986). Service firms: interdependence of external and internal marketing strategies. *European Journal of Marketing*, Vol 20, No 8.

Gronroos, C (1981) 'Internal marketing – an integral part of marketing theory', in Donnelly, J H and George, W R (eds), *Marketing of Services*, American Marketing Association, Chicago.

Gronroos, C (1985) 'Internal marketing – theory and practice', in Bloch, T *et al.* (eds), *Services Marketing in a Changing Environment*, American Marketing Association, Chicago.

Gummesson, E (1987) 'Using internal marketing to develop a new culture – the case of Ericsson quality', *Journal of Business and Industrial Marketing*, Vol 2, No 3.

Piercy, N and Morgan, N (1990a) 'Internal marketing: making marketing happen', *Marketing Intelligence and Planning*, Vol 8, No 1.

Piercy, N and Morgan, N (1990b), 'Internal marketing: strategies for implementing organisational change', *Long Range Planning*, Spring.

5

BUILDING CUSTOMER RELATIONSHIPS THROUGH INTERNAL MARKETING: A REVIEW OF AN EMERGING FIELD*

Helen Peck

INTRODUCTION

Much has been written about relationship marketing and the benefits of customer retention in recent years, so much so that the terms relationship marketing and retention marketing are common currency among marketing practitioners and academics alike. The notion that it is a good idea for a business to keep its customers – and that the quality of service that those customers receive will have some bearing on the likelihood of them staying – is also widely accepted within the service sector and beyond. Less widely understood are the implementation issues surrounding the improvement of customer service, particularly the role of internal marketing in achieving these ends. The term internal marketing is itself unhelpful, as it smacks of a marketing function based concern. Other synonyms exist for the concept but tend to have equally territorial or functionally biased overtones.

This chapter reviews a wide range of writings relating to service quality improvement, and the role of internal marketing (in its broadest interpretation), within the context of the relationship marketing concept. A distillation of this literature is presented as a conceptual overview against which service improvement and customer retention programmes in automotive and computer business, and in other industries, can be examined. First, though, the chapter considers why a new marketing paradigm is necessary at all.

---

* A version of this chapter was presented to the Annual Conference of the Marketing Education Group, July 1993.

LIMITATIONS OF THE TRADITIONAL MODEL OF MARKETING

The development of marketing theory, as it has been most widely accepted, is based on two central concepts. The first is the concept of exchange – the exchange of goods, services, money or anything of value – between any two parties, be they buyer and seller or an organisation and its client (Bagozzi, 1975; Kotler, 1984). The second core concept is a framework for marketing decision-making, which is based on the work of Borden during the 1960s. Borden isolated twelve factors or elements which, when combined, would produce a 'marketing mix' that serves to influence demand. The concept was quickly simplified and popularised by its distillation into the 'Four Ps' (product, price, place and promotion). This model of marketing became the basis of marketing theory taught and (less widely) practised around the world (Christopher, Payne and Ballantyne, 1991).

Throughout the 1980s this traditional model was frequently reappraised. There is now a growing body of literature expressing doubts over its relevance to international, industrial and services marketing (de Ferrer, 1986; Gummesson, 1987a; Gronroos, 1990a). The Four Ps model was developed upon assumptions derived from the huge US market for consumer goods. Critics claim that although the traditional combination of the exchange concept and the Four Ps is appropriate for consumer marketing – where the exchange is a brief, single transaction – the model is inappropriate in the industrial or services contexts where relationships with the customers are often ongoing, and of critical importance (Hakansson, 1982; Gummesson, 1987a; Gronroos, 1990b, c). Furthermore, Gummesson goes on to point out that the traditional US model has been found wanting when applied to international marketing, as it makes no provision for the fact that trade barriers and politics may deny access to the market altogether.

Academics have also long been aware of four central characteristics of a service which dictate that services marketing is different from the marketing of consumer goods (Levitt, 1981; Parasuraman, Zeithaml and Berry, 1985; Schneider, 1985; Webster, 1990). Services are, by their nature, intangible and perishable because production and consumption are simultaneous, and, because services are often labour intensive and high contact, they tend to be heterogeneous. This is partly because those people delivering the service are individuals – so the service varies – and partly because buyers usually participate in the service delivery and therefore affect its quality (Parasuraman, Zeithaml and Berry, 1985).

These shortcomings have, to some extent, been recognised by marketing writers in the United States, where attempts have been made to extend the model to encompass some of the issues relating to the non-FMCG areas of marketing. The result has been a proliferation of 'Ps', as process, people and physical evidence, power and public relations have been added to the mix (Booms and Bintner, 1982; Kotler, 1986).

As the model of marketing itself has become more complex, definitions of marketing have emerged to try and reflect these changes. In acknowledgement of the increasing sophistication of marketing theory, the American Marketing Association revised its definition of marketing in 1985. The result:

> Marketing is the process of planning and executing the conception, pricing, promotion and distribution of ideas, goods and services to create exchange and satisfy individual and organizational objectives.
> (*American Marketing Association 1985*)

However, this definition is still seen as inadequate by some Nordic academics, who maintain that the approach remains *product* rather than *market* led (Gummesson, 1987a; Gronroos, 1990c).

THE EMERGENCE OF A SECOND PARADIGM – RELATIONSHIP MARKETING

During the 1980s an alternative approach to marketing was emerging, much of it based on findings from studies of the marketing function (not the marketing department) as viewed by the customers of companies operating in the industrial and service sectors of Northern Europe, ie studies which concentrated on customers' perspectives of marketing – what matters and what makes it work (Gronroos, 1990c). The findings from both sectors suggested the existence of a second marketing paradigm, labelled 'interactive marketing' or 'interactive relationships' in the industrial arena (Hakansson, 1982), and the 'Nordic School' when applied to services. A number of American writers had also developed an interest in a longer-term approach to marketing, and were examining more closely the role of relationships in the industrial marketing and services contexts (Berry, 1983; Jackson, 1985; Crosby and Stephens, 1987). It was they who introduced the term 'relationship marketing'. Whichever name is chosen, customer relationships lie at the centre of these concepts, and from this body of research several key findings have consistently emerged:

- the existence of interactive networks;

- the critical importance of promises;
- the existence of part-time marketers;
- the identification of internal markets.

The Existence of Interactive Networks and Relationships

The successful development of a customer relationship is likely to be dependent on the successful management (by all parties) of a number of other supporting and interlocking relationships within the participating organisations, and externally. In industrial markets in particular, a number of individuals with assorted roles or functional backgrounds can be involved in new product development or tailoring the product or service offering.

The influence of external networks is sometimes equally evident, eg the relationships between a supplier and its suppliers or bankers, and perhaps trade unions, politicians or public bodies. The involvement and support of several or all of these groups may be required in order for a transaction to be effected. These relationships are themselves cemented and strengthened by successful exchanges between the parties involved. The exchanges are likely to be in the form of exchanges of information, collaboration on product development or social exchanges – exchanges which ultimately build trust between the parties – rather than simply the exchange of goods or services for money (Hakansson, 1982; Gummesson, 1987a; Biemans, 1990; Gronroos, 1990c).

Importance of Promises

Maintaining and strengthening trust is essential to the longer-term success of a relationship. Writers from the Nordic School emphasise the pivotal role of promises in a relationship and the assurance of commitment from both parties. Levitt (1983) also stressed the need for promises and commitment when he likened sustaining quality long-term customer relationships to sustaining the quality of a marriage. The demonstration of commitment, and fulfilment of these promises is crucial. If promises between businesses and their customers are not fulfilled, then trust diminishes, and the quality of these relationships too will deteriorate, eventually ending the relationship and eliminating future opportunities (Crosby, Evans and Cowles, 1990).

'Part-Time Marketers'

In many industrial markets, and in most services, the customer interacts with members of an organisation who are not principally employed as marketers. Customers often have more frequent and ongoing contact with front-line service, support, R&D or production employees than with marketing department personnel. Yet the development and sustained quality of the relationship is likely to depend on its management by these front-line employees or 'part-time marketers' (Gummesson, 1987a; George, 1990). Market-oriented management is required to grasp that many workers have dual responsibilities (operational and marketing), and to maintain support for the part-time marketers in both aspects of their work, ensuring that they understand fully their dual roles. Under this second paradigm marketing ceases to be a narrow, discrete function – the preserve of the marketing department:

> Marketing is not a function, it is a way of doing business ... marketing has to be all pervasive, part of everyone's job description, from the receptionists to the board of directors.
>
> *(McKenna, 1991)*

Gummesson and Gronroos predict that the traditional style marketing departments of many organisations will be reduced in size, or disappear altogether, as marketing becomes a cross-functional activity, involving integration into planning, production, operations and human resource policies (Gronroos, 1990d).

'Internal Markets'

To further the cross-functional theme, the concept of internal customers is gaining credibility; often as a by-product of total quality initiatives, non-customer contact support staff are encouraged to view colleagues who depend on their services as their customers. The internal marketing concept is advocated as a means of introducing and developing these service-orientated practices, and as an aid to creating and sustaining a customer service culture (Gummesson, 1987b).

New Definitions of Marketing

New definitions based on the second marketing paradigm reflect some of these core concepts:

> The most important issue in marketing is to establish, maintain and

enhance long-term customer relationships at a profit, so that the objectives of the parties involved are met. This is done by a mutual exchange and fulfilment of promises.

(Gronroos, 1990c)

Alternatively:

Relationship marketing is attracting, maintaining and – in multi-service organisations – enhancing customer relationships.
(Berry, Shostack and Upah, 1983)

Or, to quote Christopher, Payne and Ballantyne (1991):

The Relationship Marketing concept is emerging as a new focal point, integrating customer service and quality with a market orientation.

APPROPRIATENESS OF THE MARKETING PARADIGMS

Gronroos (1990b) explores the suitability of marketing strategies based on the two paradigms when applied in the contexts of consumer packaged goods, consumer durables, industrial goods and services. He concludes that the paradigms are not mutually exclusive alternatives, but represent the two ends of a continuum (see Figure 5.1). A company marketing consumer packaged goods is likely to adopt a strategy which is towards the transaction end of the continuum, while a strategy which is towards the relationship marketing end is likely to be more effective for a service or industrial marketer. Towards the middle of this continuum the marketing strategy of an organisation will contain elements of both paradigms, one contributing factor, perhaps, to the rather confusing array of interpretations of the term relationship marketing. For example, US-based consultants Copulsky and Wolf (1990) described relationship marketing (applied in a consumer goods context) in the following, and arguably product-led, way:

Relationship marketing combines elements of general advertising, sales promotion, public relations and direct marketing to create more effective and more efficient ways of reaching customers. It centres on developing a continuous relationship with customers across a family of related products.

Customer behaviour is also a determinant of the appropriateness of a transactional vs relationship marketing approach because a relationship will be almost impossible to sustain profitably if the customer is distinctly transaction orientated – a situation common when the product is

MARKETING PARADIGMS

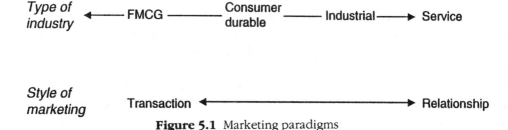

Figure 5.1 Marketing paradigms

considered a commodity – and switching costs are low (Levitt, 1983; Jackson, 1985; Coggan, 1991).

THE LOGIC OF CUSTOMER RETENTION

Increased international competition, sluggish growth rates in the developed markets of the Western world, and ongoing deregulation have encouraged many companies to revise their marketing practices. This is particularly true in the marketing of services (Berry, Shostack and Upah, 1983; Roach, 1991).

In 1980 Schneider remarked that:

> What is surprising is that (1) researchers and businessmen have concentrated far more on how to attract consumers to products and services than on how to retain those customers, (2) there is almost no published research on the retention of service consumers, and (3) consumer evaluation of products or services has rarely been used as a criterion or index of organisational effectiveness.

In the years since the publication of Schneider's article the attention of both the academic and business communities have focused on all of these issues. Research and literature on the subjects have proliferated. There are also some signs that marketers' traditional preoccupation with winning new customers could be waning, as the importance of maintaining and protecting existing customer bases has become apparent. While it is acknowledged that very close relationships between buyers and suppliers are not without risk (Jackson, 1985; Yovovich, 1991), and that with even the best care and attention, the life expectancy of a relationship may be finite (Crosby and Stephens, 1987), there are, however, often sound financial as well as competitive incentives for extending the lifespan of customer relationships. Studies of a cross-section of service industries by management consultants Bain & Co support received wisdom (eg Berry and Gresham, 1986) that existing customers are often more profitable than new ones. Established customers tend to buy more, are more predictable and usually cost less to service than new customers. Furthermore, a company's own customer base may be increased – at very little cost – through referrals by satisfied customers, while simultaneously reducing opportunities for competitors. Findings of the studies also demonstrated that by increasing service quality, and consequently customer satisfaction, a higher percentage of customers were retained. The resulting increase in average lifespan of the relationships was accompanied by a dramatic increase in profitability (Reichheld and Sasser, 1990; Buchanan and Gillies, 1990). This link between service quality, customer satisfaction and customer retention has been drawn before by several other writers (Berry and Gresham, 1986; Heskett, 1987). Bain & Co advanced the discussion through to measurement and implementation.

CUSTOMER SATISFACTION AND SERVICE QUALITY

Many attempts to define service quality have been made in recent years, some focusing on meeting the needs of the customer. Lewis (1988), for example, described service quality as:

> providing the customer with what he wants, when he wants it, and at acceptable cost, within the operating constraints of the business.

A second and growing group of definitions emphasise the concept of perceived quality; these include the much quoted interpretations of Gronroos (1982), and Parasuraman, Zeithaml and Berry (1985, 1988). All of these definitions stress that service quality is deeply subjective and, like beauty, it is very much in the eye of the beholder. However, Parasuraman, Zeithaml and Berry (1985) noted that while the precise determinants of quality were undefined – partly through difficulties individuals encounter when asked to articulate their requirements – there is universal acceptance that quality is important. Parasuraman *et al.* go on to say that they believe that perceived quality is largely determined by the gap between customers' expectations of service and perceptions of the actual experience. In a later article they summarise the concept as:

> Customers assess service quality by comparing what they want or expect to what they actually get or perceive they are getting.
> *(Berry, Parasuraman and Zeithaml, 1988)*

In other words, if customers find the experience disappointing it is likely to cause dissatisfaction, but if the experience met expectations (providing they were not negative to start with) or exceeded them, the result is likely to be satisfaction. The validity of the concept has been corroborated by practitioners (eg Dixon, 1991).

Dimensions of Service Quality

Customers' expectations of service quality have risen in recent years (Lewis, 1991) and are unlikely to remain static. Competition is likely to mean that service providers will have to raise the quality of their services progressively in order to retain their customers and to stay in business. Academics have sought ways to identify the dimensions of service quality and means of measuring customer satisfaction against these key dimensions.

Gronroos (1982, 1983) suggested a two-dimensional model, using 'technical' and 'functional' determinants, technical being the outcome of the service (ie whether its nominal purpose had been achieved) and the functional dimension related to the manner in which the service was delivered. A third dimension – 'corporate image' – was included later, as this too was thought to influence the perception of quality. Parasuraman (1987) used a similar two-dimensional model in which the terms 'outcome' and 'process' equate roughly with the 'technical' and 'functional' descriptions used by Gronroos.

More frequently quoted is 'SERVQUAL', an instrument developed by Parasuraman, Zeithaml and Berry (1988). Originally a set of ten determinants were identified which they believed impacted on a customer's perception of services (Parasuraman, Zeithaml and Berry, 1985). Subsequent research reduced the ten down to five core dimensions, described in the following way:

- *Tangibles* – physical facilities, equipment and appearance of personnel;
- *Reliability* – ability to perform the promised service dependably and accurately;
- *Responsiveness* – willingness to help customers and provide prompt service;
- *Assurance* – knowledge and courtesy of employees and their ability to inspire trust and confidence;
- *Empathy* – caring, individualised attention the firm provides its customers.

Measurement and Monitoring of Service Quality

For management to implement and monitor a programme of quality improvement, it must first find a yardstick or benchmark to measure its performance against. 'Competitive benchmarking' is such a system – used to great effect by the Xerox Corporation – whereby key aspects of the product and service offering (as determined by the customers) are measured and monitored against examples of (cross-)industry best practice. These aspects of service or product performance are unlikely to be of equal value and importance to the customer but, by using a process of trade-off analysis, weightings to establish the relative importance of each service attribute can be identified. From this information individual customer's service requirements can be established, offering the service provider the opportunity to pitch its offering to the needs of a single customer, or a defined segment of the market (see Christopher, Payne and Ballantyne, 1991).

Impact of Service Changes on Customer Attitudes

Less well explored is the impact of improved service on customers' overall attitudes toward service quality. Given that a perception of service quality is drawn from overall expectations and perceptions of performance, whereas satisfaction tends to be transaction specific (Tansuhaj, Randall and McCullough, 1988), a longitudinal study by Bolton and Drew (1991) has thrown some light on the impact of service changes on customer attitudes towards the quality of telephone services. The researchers worked on the assumptions that attitudes and perceptions of quality were based on a combination of three factors: prior attitude to the service; performance (particularly current and recent performance); and disconfirmation (how much experience varies, either favourably or unfavourably, from expectations). The study revealed that the balance and relative impact of each of the three influences became unstable during a period of change. Customers did perceive an improvement in service quality quite quickly, but there was some time lag before a change in attitude to the service occurred.

Improving the Perceived Quality of Service Delivery

Bearing in mind the intangible nature of services, one relatively simple way to improve perceived quality is by 'managing the evidence' (Berry,

1980; Levitt, 1981). Levitt points out that if customers do not know what they are getting, they are not likely to appreciate it. Managing the evidence is the art of leaving strategically placed, physical clues which indicate that a service has been performed successfully, where no visible or tangible proof would otherwise exist. In these circumstances the quality of the physical surroundings, or the 'evidence' itself, are taken as quality indicators by the customers. The tangible clues to service quality are relatively easy to manipulate because – for the most part – such improvements can be bought. It should be noted though that tangible clues, although easy to produce, tend to carry less significance for customers than other people-related quality determinants (Parasuraman, Zeithaml and Berry, 1988). Parasuraman (1987) noted that for some maintenance services (such as car engine tuning) customers may be unable to identify, let alone evaluate, the outcome or technical quality of the service. In this situation Parasuraman claimed that it was the process or functional aspects of the service delivery – particularly the nature of the customer–employee interactions – that dominated customers' evaluations of service quality.

The Industrialisation of Services

Improving the performance of service delivery personnel is widely believed to be the key to greater customer satisfaction, and consequently improved customer retention, ultimately leading to increased profitability (Levitt, 1972; Berry, Shostack and Upah, 1983; Schlesinger and Heskett, 1991a).

The industrialisation of services is one approach (Levitt, 1972, 1976, 1981). Levitt (1972) argued that the service sector was inefficient because – unlike manufacturers who think technocratically – service providers think humanistically. This he believed to be the fatal flaw:

> Service looks for solutions in the performer of the task. This is a paralysing legacy of our inherited attitudes: the solution to improved service is viewed as being dependent on improvements in the skills and attitudes of the performers of the service ... While it may pain and offend us to say so, thinking in humanistic rather than technocratic terms ensures that the service sector of the modern economy will be forever inefficient and that our satisfaction will be forever marginal.

In his series of classic articles on the subject, Levitt explained that by adopting a manufacturing approach to service through the design of systems that eliminated the most unpredictable and inconsistent element of service – discretion – service of a high and uniform standard could be delivered. Through the adoption of new technology and meticulously detailed planning, the traditional, inefficient and erratic model of service delivery could be replaced by an efficient, automatic, capital-intensive system supplemented, occasionally, by people. Furthermore, skilled workers could be replaced by low paid, unskilled workers. Training and motivation would cease to be necessary if a system was sufficiently well designed and implemented.

The fast-food chain, McDonald's is possibly the best known example of an organisation which embraced the industrial philosophy of service delivery. The approach has, however, been adopted throughout the services sector.

The Cycle of Failure

The industrial approach to services is now increasingly under attack. It has been criticised for its inflexibility and blamed for a steady decline in service quality (Schlesinger and Heskett, 1991a, b; Roach, 1991). Schlesinger and Heskett (1991b) claim that the industrial model fails because it is based on a set of assumptions and practices which have created and perpetuated what they describe as 'a cycle of failure'. Human resource practices are based on, and justified by, assumptions about the labour pool and technology. But these assumptions fly in the face of older received wisdom, and have been shown to be false by recent academic and practitioner research on customer service and satisfaction.

The industrial approach is based on an assumption of surplus labour: on a continuing and plentiful supply of passive and undemanding workers. The demographic profiles of many developed countries indicate that labour shortages are likely to occur by the end of the decade (Atkinson, 1989). This will leave companies with two choices: either they increase their dependency on technological solutions; or they compete for employees by becoming a favoured employer, an 'employer of choice'.

Technology was heralded as the deliverer of high volume, high quality, low cost service, potentially an almost universal panacea for the ills of the service sector (Levitt, 1976). The service sector has become technology intensive, yet massive investment in technology has failed to deliver the desired increase in productivity (Roach, 1991) or solve the problems of customer dissatisfaction. Heavy use of technology can lead to impersonal service, loss of personal contact, and with it, a reduction in customer satisfaction and a loss of customer loyalty. Even as a differentiator, the benefits of technology are likely to be short term and expensive, as anyone with enough money can acquire them (Schlesinger and Heskett, 1991b). Service organisations would do well to remember that customers *like* a personal service as well as expecting technological efficiency (Lewis, 1991). Research undertaken by Berry, Parasuraman and Zeithaml (1988) indicated that 'human performance plays a major role in customers' perceptions of service quality'. Three of the five dimensions for service quality, identified by Parasuraman, Zeithaml and Berry (1988) – responsiveness, assurance and empathy – were directly dependent on *human* performance.

Counterproductive Management Practices

Managers, though, are not always aware of what constitutes good service in the eyes of their customers. Worse still, when they *are* aware of customers' service quality criteria, they may consider it desirable, but not necessary or practical to satisfy these requirements (Parasuraman, Zeithaml and Berry, 1985). Schlesinger and Heskett (1991b) point to an abundance of excuses available to managers which, seemingly, exempt them from taking action to improve the quality of service delivery and performance. Evidence from self-fulfilling prophecies convinces them that their low expectations of service worker performance are justified, and that time and money spent on training and retaining badly educated, poorly motivated and uncommitted staff is wasted. Consequently turnover of service workers remains high, training is minimized, few have opportunities for advancement, hours are long, and wages are low.

Any will to change human resource practices in order to improve employee retention is further undermined by shorter-term fluctuations in the availability of the workforce (through economic restructuring and recession). Commitment to change is undermined further still through the short-termism fuelled by accounting systems, systems which are preoccupied by costs – known and easy to cut costs such as wages, training and recruitment. They fail to monitor *opportunity costs*, such as the value of increased customer satisfaction and retention, or the impact of high staff turnover on customers' perceptions of the service quality (Schneider, 1980; Hart, Heskett and Sasser, 1990). As Roach (1991) observed:

> Traditional accounting standards are orientated toward the needs of factories and are woefully inadequate in measuring white-collar productivity.

Thinking Humanistically Again

During the 1980s, a number of academics and practitioners turned their attention back to the human element in the service delivery system as the source of possible advantage (Solomon *et al.*, 1985; Carlzon, 1987; Gummesson, 1987a; Gronroos, 1990d; Lewis, 1991). The potential – though not always the value – of customer contact employees as 'part-time marketers' was recognised, partly through the realisation that customer satisfaction rested on the dyadic service encounters at the customer interface. Carlzon described these encounters as 'moments of truth'. Employees may be given formal written guidelines as to what constitutes the desired form of behaviour during these dyadic encounters (see for examples Hochschild, 1983 or Ogbonna and Wilkinson, 1990), but Parasuraman (1987) believes that it is the organisational culture which exerts a greater influence on employees' behaviour and productivity.

At the American Marketing Association's Third Services Marketing Conference in 1984, a focus group consisting of experts in the services sector discussed the determinants of success in services marketing. The group identified the '3 Cs' – customer orientation, consistency – 'key attributes of an organisational culture that is appropriate for service firms', and the third factor – creed – as an integral part of organisational culture.

Culture and Climate

The terms organisational culture and climate are often used interchangeably in management literature. The term 'culture' is used predominantly by academics and practitioners in management or industry, while 'climate' is the preferred term for writers on interpersonal practices and social climates (Webster, 1990). Webster confirms that the two terms do refer to different constructs, and draws the following distinction between them:

> Whereas climate researchers have been concerned with the facets of policies that characterise particular organisational phenomena, culture scholars attempt to understand the systems (values and norms) that dictate the policies or activities and the modes by which the beliefs are communicated and transmitted.

However, establishing the subtle differences between the two constructs is not a primary concern of this chapter.

Work by Schneider in 1973, and in subsequent studies, indicated that customer perceptions of an organisation's climate were linked to customer retention in a service business (retail banking). Schneider noted that:

> Climate perceptions of an organisation (e.g. how warm and friendly it is) may be summary perceptions of events or experiences perceived by people who interact with it ... Climate perceptions are more strongly related to switching behaviour than are the perceptions of specific events and experiences.

A later study by Schneider and Bowen (1985) – also in banking – found a direct relationship between well designed service encounters, enhanced customer satisfaction and employee satisfaction. In short: happy employees = happy customers.

In the latter half of the 1980s this line of logic was translated into a rash of customer satisfaction 'smile' initiatives in the 'non-professional' services sector. These behavioural management initiatives may have produced a degree of improvement in customer behaviour and perceptions of service (Luthans, 1991), but studies have shown that they were unlikely to improve employee satisfaction and retention (Ogbonna and Wilkinson, 1990), making long-term and sustained improvements in customer service all the more difficult to effect (Schlesinger and Heskett, 1991b). Ogbonna and Wilkinson reported on a study which monitored attempts by management of three British supermarkets to change corporate cultures in line with changing corporate strategies. All were attempting to introduce a customer orientation in order to compete on service instead of price. Despite enthusiasm from supervisory staff and compliance from front-line employees, researchers revealed that there was no significant increase in staff loyalty or job satisfaction amongst customer contact staff. Staff had changed their behaviour but did not internalise the espoused values and assumptions of the management. The researchers concluded that the changes in behaviour were due to coercion rather than satisfaction or enthusiasm. They concluded that the programmes' longer-term success was likely to be limited by the nature of the work, which was described as 'unglamorous, monotonous, and frequently intense'. It seems that the work in question failed on most of the dimensions identified by Smith, Kendall and Hulin (1969) as constituting to the overall feeling of job satisfaction, namely: satisfaction with the work itself, satisfaction with pay, satisfaction with promotion prospects, satisfaction with supervision and satisfaction with co-workers.

The study by Ogbonna and Wilkinson also highlights a problem earlier identified by Hochschild (1983): the high levels of stress experienced by customer contact personnel whose employers insist that they must perform their services with a smile. This commercialisation of emotional labour in order to meet marketing objectives has brought bitter condemnation from Mundie (1987), who questions whether marketing has a legitimate role to play in the context of service employees. There is also a substantial body of work which describes how a lack of role clarity can be a major source of stress for service employees, (eg Parkington and Schneider, 1979; Solomon *et al.*, 1985; Kelly, 1990). Schneider (1980) points out that service employees are, to a greater or lesser degree, self-selecting. They choose service jobs in profit-making organisations because they want to give a good service, and are probably concerned with the organisation's success. If service employees then perceive management to be less service-orientated than themselves, ie management places greater emphasis on adhering to rules than serving the customers, employees are likely to have to perform to conflicting criteria, causing dissatisfaction and prompting them to seek alternative employment (Parkington and Schneider, 1979).

If the 'cycle of failure' is to be reversed, and improvements in customer service, satisfaction and retention are to be achieved, Schlesinger and Heskett (1991b) suggest that this requires a change in underlying assumptions of management: firstly, the assumptions which determine human resource practices. Employees must be recognised as a valuable and finite resource. In their role as part-time marketers they are a potential source of competitive advantage. The process of creating this competitive advantage is likely to start with careful recruitment and development of staff whose own values and motivations are compatible with those of the organisation. Schlesinger and Heskett insist that the decisions about the suitability of an employee should be based on innate psychological characteristics rather than technical skills which can be taught later if necessary. The researchers also recommend that prospective employees should be given an accurate preview of the job and the organisation as a whole before joining, and that training should be comprehensive at induction and part of an ongoing development programme. If employees are to remain motivated and committed to service excellence, they must feel valued by the organisation, and their efforts should be recognised and rewarded.

Research by Kelly (1990) indicates that poor job design is yet another avoidable pitfall. Managers may recognise that employees enjoy performing a range of duties, but careful thought should be given to avoid the combination of conflicting tasks and performance indicators. Above all employees must be given the opportunity to serve the customers well.

Today customers are demanding increasingly varied and flexible solutions to their service requirements, but – despite the best efforts of companies like McDonald's – organisations cannot plan for every eventuality (Schlesinger and Heskett, 1991a). By acknowledging the role of customers as co-producers (Gummesson, 1987a), and consequently the fact that, even if employees' behaviour could be standardised, the behaviour and expectations of its customers cannot (Schneider and Parkington, 1980), companies are on their way to recognising the need for an alternative approach to the management of human resources in services businesses.

Empowerment and Involvement

By training and empowering front-line employees to go beyond the usual requirements of their job, organisations are once more authorising their employees to use their discretion to deliver a better quality of service to their customers (Armstrong, 1991; Schlesinger and Heskett, 1991b), a radical reversal of the philosophy that declared discretion to be 'the enemy of order, standardisation and quality' (Levitt, 1972).

Researchers Bowen and Lawler (1992) have taken a closer look at what empowerment of employees means in a practical sense. They concluded that there are four empowerment criteria, all of which require enlightenment or involvement of front-line employees. Employees must receive:

- information about the organisation's performance;
- rewards based on the organisation's performance;
- knowledge that enables them to understand and contribute to organisational performance;
- power to make decisions that influence organisational direction and performance.

Bowen and Lawler believe that a growing number of service businesses are likely to attempt to empower their front-line workers in the future as the advantages of empowerment reach a wider audience. However, they caution managers that all-out empowerment may not be the best or the only route to improved quality for every service organisation. They propose that managers should first assess the pros and cons of empowerment. The advantages of empowerment can include a quicker and more flexible response to customers' needs by better informed and confident employees. Studies have shown front-line employees to be much more attuned than senior management or a distant marketing department to the needs of their customers, and have a greater awareness of what constitutes quality and satisfaction in the eyes of the customers (Schneider, Parkington and Buxton, 1980; Parasuraman, Zeithaml and Berry, 1985). Therefore front-line employees represent a valuable source of intelligence for the development and implementation of new and improved service offerings, and provide an early warning system when things are amiss. Service failures happen though, even in organisations where the most scrupulous care has been taken. If front-line employees are trained and empowered to take prompt, on-the-spot, corrective action, the situation is unlikely to be irretrievable, and the customer is unlikely to be lost. A satisfactorily resolved incident may even raise the customers' perception of service quality (Hart, Heskett and Sasser, 1990). The sentiment echoes Parasuraman (1987) when he said that:

> A service firm must be willing to tolerate, and perhaps even encourage, a certain degree of departure from written policies at the individual customer–employee transaction level, *if such a departure is deemed necessary for customer satisfaction*. Such flexibility is especially important, and can reap handsome benefits for the firm, during the process of handling non-routine transactions.

Bowen and Lawler, also note that empowerment can improve employee motivation and job satisfaction, with the knock-on benefits for customer satisfaction and retention. However, they note that the advantages of empowerment must be offset against increased labour, recruitment and training costs. Empowerment clearly calls for a longer-term investment in employees which is likely to preclude the use of a 'hire and fire' solution to seasonal or other short-term fluctuations in business. There is also the issue of even-handedness, with the possibility that special treatment for one customer may cause resentment among others waiting (possibly longer as a result) in a queue for the same service.

Bowen and Lawler indicate that limited empowerment of service workers may be appropriate in some organisations. In its mildest form it may be limited to 'suggestion involvement' where employees can offer suggestions, but the decision-making power remains with management. 'Job empowerment' is another alternative. Jobs are redesigned so that employees can apply a wider range of skills and employ greater discretion over how they work (usually) within a team assigned responsibility for a whole and identifiable piece of work. In its most radical form empower-ment is the antithesis of the control model of management. It expects employees to manage their own work, develop problem-solving and teamwork skills, and be directly involved in the decisions which affect the operations and profitability of the business. The researchers believe that empowerment is not an either/or choice. Its appropriateness as a method of management is dependent on a range of variables: the business strategy of the firm, whether low cost or highly differentiated; customer behaviour, ie whether they are transaction or relationship orientated; the degree to which the work is technology dependent; the stability of the business environment; and the availability of employees who actually want to manage their own work (many do not), and management who will provide support and encouragement, but stand back and let them get on with it. Finally, Bowen and Lawler stress that the whole subject of empowerment of service workers is much less understood than the industrialisation approach to service delivery, mainly because the industrial approach utilised the well-developed control model of organisational design, whereas the empowerment approach is part of a still evolving commitment model (see for examples Walton, 1985; Charan, 1991; Wheatley, 1992). Indeed, successful implementation of the commitment model of management may require radical redesign of the organisation's structure and work flows to remove organisational constraints on empowerment and facilitate cross-functional or team-based working (Gronroos, 1983; Ostroff and Smith, 1992).

THE ROLE OF INTERNAL MARKETING

Development of an alternative and more integrated approach to human resource management and marketing has in fact been underway since the early 1980s, under the banner of 'internal marketing'. Internal marketing is in fact a 'broad church' concept (ie one which currently tolerates many interpretations) with cross-functional origins and implications. To George and Gronroos (1989) it represents 'a philosophy for managing the organisation's human resources based on a marketing perspective'. Gronroos (1990d) and other writers describe the two related roles that internal marketing appears to perform (George, 1990; Collins and Payne, 1991). In the first, it is a tool to help individuals to understand the significance of their roles, and to create an awareness of how their roles relate to others within the organisation. This encourages and improves cross-functional working and cooperation (Christopher, Payne and Ballantyne, 1991; see also Gupta and Wilemon, 1988, 1990). The second role is to promote, develop and sustain the ethos of customer service for internal as well as external customers.

Internal marketing covers a diverse range of activities, some to be executed on a strategic level, and some on a tactical level. Gronroos (1981a) classed the following activities which motivate employees or create a customer-conscious corporate culture as strategic elements of internal marketing: the adoption of supportive management styles and personnel policies (recruitment, job and career planning, etc); customer service training which focuses on how the customer should be treated; and planning procedures which ensure that all personnel understand and support the systems, mission, goals and strategies of the organisation. On the tactical level, informal and ongoing internal training, the encourage-ment of informal interactive communication, periodic newsletters or updates, internal market segmentation and internal market research all fall within the internal marketing remit (Gronroos, 1981b). Other writers describe similar groups of activities as components of internal marketing. Although there is broad agreement among writers that an internal marketing programme should be executed on strategic and tactical levels (Richardson and Robinson, 1986; Morgan, 1990; Tansuhaj, Randall and McCullough, 1991), the demarcation between strategic and tactical activities is blurred (see Richardson and Robinson, 1986; Tansuhaj, Randall and McCullough, 1991). Tansuhaj, Randall and McCullough (1991), while acknowledging the strategic importance of internal market-ing, point out that some business units have very little control over their marketing efforts, and that while funds and support for a formal internal marketing programme may not be available at the overall strategic level, they believe that many of the 'strategic' internal marketing activities like recruitment, training and management support can be adopted success-fully at a tactical level.

The effectiveness of internal marketing (whether strategic or tactical) can be measured through internal marketing research in much the same ways as market research is conducted in the external environment (Gelb and Gelb, 1991). Tansuhaj, Randall and McCullough (1988) and Collins and Payne (1991) describe how internal marketing research can also be used to identify the needs, wants and attitudes of internal customers (see also Thomas, Farmer and Wallace, 1991). However, care should be taken to ensure that employees understand the purpose of the research at the outset, and that appropriate (quantitative and/or qualitative) methods of data collection are applied. If the purpose of the research is undertaken simply to measure trends, then employee expectations should be managed to convey an understanding that measurement is the purpose of the exercise. Action may then follow, but not necessarily. In this situation organisations should not expect high levels of in-depth and time consuming involvement from employees or expect them to sit through long and detailed presentations of the results. The danger is that a measurement survey may inadvertently raise expectations of change, where none was intended. If on the other hand the purpose of the research is to provide insights for strategic or tactical decision-making (ie when change is intended), a high level of employee input is desirable and in-depth presentations of the results and proposed courses of action are in order (Pounsford, 1992). Most importantly, action must be taken to deal with issues raised in the research. Failure to do so is likely to demotivate employees and undermine the credibility of the internal marketing programme.

With the aid of internal marketing research, viable internal marketing plans can be constructed to support and facilitate the successful implementation of external marketing plans. In the opinions of Piercy and Morgan (1990, 1991) the internal marketing plan is nothing less than the missing half of the marketing programme. Morgan (1990) has, however, explored the not inconsiderable difficulties of implementing internal marketing plans within professional service businesses (accountancy and legal firms). He concludes that the culture of these organisations, with their emphasis on the paramount importance of technical excellence, and the prevalence of a 'the way we do things here' attitude towards clients, makes cultural and organisational change – geared towards improved customer service – particularly problematic. This single-minded pursuit of technical service quality – though not an altogether bad thing – tends to be developed at the expense of other skills, such as marketing and communication. The result tends to be the isolation of the marketing department, which has little or no say over the content, price or manner of the service offering, and therefore tends to be equated with selling, advertising and public relations. Similarly entrenched attitudes to marketing and customer service were revealed by Wilson (1991) in his descriptions of central government departments, local authorities and the internal services departments of large businesses. All were faced for the first time with the prospect of having to market their services proactively in internal markets suddenly opened up to external competition. Recession, creeping privatisation and a growing trend towards profit centre management indicate that these organisations may eventually have no option but to embrace internal marketing as a means of delivering a customer-orientated culture.

SERVICE BEYOND THE SERVICE SECTOR – THE CONVERGENCE OF MANUFACTURING AND SERVICES

The conceptual overview outlined in this chapter is built from research and literature on service improvement as a customer retention device within overtly service businesses. This is because most of the rigorous empirical research on service quality/improvement and customer retention has been conducted in businesses which are unambiguously service sector organisations – usually financial service companies – most noticeably the retail banks. However, revision of the function of marketing is not confined to these traditional service industries. In fact, the delineation between manufacturing and services has been breaking down for some time (Levitt, 1972, 1976; Canton, 1988; Quinn, Baruch and Paquette, 1988; Vandermerwe and Rada, 1988; McKenna, 1991). As McKenna observed:

> The line between products and services is fast eroding. What once appeared to be a rigid polarity now has become a hybrid: the servicization of products and the productization of services ... In fact, the computer business today is 75% services ... The point applies just as well to less grandiose companies and to less expensive consumer products ... what customers frequently want most from a product is often qualitative and intangible; it is the service that is integral to the product.

Service businesses are seeking to make their offerings more tangible through repetitive routines, standard and customised packages and events, or by creating special packages for frequent users of services. Meanwhile, the move towards competition through service in the manufacturing sector is now clearly visible across a wide range of industries, not least in the computer and automotive businesses (see for examples Guiniven and Grossman, 1991; Lawless, 1992). In the developed economies of the Western world economic necessity is driving change. Market maturity, recession and global overcapacity have reduced margins on computer hardware and new cars to a point where they have all but disappeared. Motor industry experts predict that with little growth in prospect, European car manufacturers can anticipate margins of around 1 per cent on new car sales in 1993, from over 9 per cent in 1989 (Michelson, 1992). After-sales and peripheral services, spares and accessories are now the principle source of profits for the motor manufacturers and their franchised dealer networks (see Sherman, Moran and Wormald, 1990). Customer retention suddenly matters a great deal, especially retention of the lucrative after-sales service business.

The motor industry has been maturing gradually, but for the computer industry maturity came overnight. Technological advances reduced the cost of computing power by once unimaginable degrees. The availability of ever smaller, cheaper and more powerful machines permanently lowered margins on hardware and as a result revenues imploded. The introduction of open systems and the move towards industry standards freed increasingly knowledgeable and pragmatic customers from the grip of a single supplier, freeing them – if they wished – to source hardware from a host of low cost suppliers. Hardware is increasingly viewed as a commodity, and the industry as a whole is slipping down the commodity slide with gathering velocity (Stone, 1991). In the computer industry, as in the motor industry, value-added services have become an increasingly important source of profits, while service quality has become a device for building customer loyalty and a principle means of differentiation. Meanwhile, manufacturers in both industries are having to contend with the growing influence of reputable, specialist, third-party service suppliers (Sherman, Moran and Wormald, 1990; Bohlin and Guiniven, 1991).

Lessons from The Service Sector

For the large computer manufacturers and their counterparts in the car industry and elsewhere, there are many lessons to be learned from the service sector – witness the appalling state of customer relations in the British retail banking industry, where standardisation and 'improved efficiency' have been pursued at the expense of customer relations. Successive customer care initiatives have failed to bridge the widening chasm between the banks and their increasingly alienated customer bases (Hunter, 1992; Feuchtwanger, 1992; Hidaloo, 1993). However, bank customers rarely leave their banks. The inertia is partly due to the enormous inconvenience of changing banks, and possibly due in part to a perception that bank service is universally abysmal. The rehabilitation

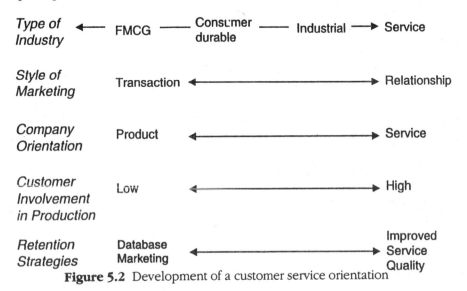

Figure 5.2 Development of a customer service orientation

of the banking sector requires the rediscovery of first principles – the revival of a customer service orientation. For the big car and computer manufacturers the service challenge is in many ways much greater, and even more immediate. As producers of consumer durable or industrial products, their marketing strategies would traditionally have placed them towards the centre of Gronroos's continuum (Figure 5.1). They are businesses with strong product and technology orientations, businesses that have grown and prospered by selling 'boxes'. The development of a customer service orientation in such settings requires not a rediscovery of first principles but a quantum leap in thinking (characterised by the accommodation of a shift to the right along all the dimensions of Figure 5.2). Such quantum leaps, though, are notoriously difficult to achieve. In the words of Berry, Parasuraman and Zeithaml (1985):

> Service can be improved only through a systematic, step-by-step journey that enhances employees' ability and willingness to provide service by creating an organisation that supports quality service in every area ... A long-term view is essential for service quality. There are no ways to change habits, knowledge, and skills of human beings quickly. It is more useful to think in terms of organisational evolution than revolution.

Whether corporate culture is changed through evolution, revolution or a series of spurts interspersed with periods of consolidation – 'punctuated equilibria' (Tsun-Yan, 1992) – the lessons from the service sector indicate that there can be no shortcuts to achieving long-term competitive advantage through customer service quality. Few would argue that the likes of IBM and Digital should abandon their quests for ever more powerful technology to become wholly service businesses (see Rappaport and Halvi, 1991; Guiniven and Grossman, 1991), or that the product attributes of a car – or indeed its brand appeal – will not be significant considerations for customers for many years to come. The reality is that these are now hybrid industries, and as such manufacturers can learn much from the current best practice and the marketing mistakes of the service sector.

References

American Marketing Association (1985) 'AMA board approves new marketing definition', *Marketing News*, No 5.
Armstrong, L (1991) 'Beyond may I help you', *Business Week*. 2 December, pp 58–60.

Atkinson, J (1989) 'Four stages of adjustment to the demographic downturn', *Personnel Management*. August, pp 20–24.

Bagozzi, R P (1975) 'Marketing as exchange', *Journal of Marketing*, October, pp 32–39.

Berry, L L (1980) 'Service marketing is different', *Journal of Marketing*. October, pp 32–39.

Berry, L L (1983) 'Relationship marketing', in Berry, L L, Shostack, G L and Upah G D, (eds), *Emerging perspectives on Services Marketing*, American Marketing Association, Chicago, pp 25–28.

Berry, L L and Gresham, L G (1986) 'Relationship retailing: transforming customers into clients', *Business Horizons*, November/December, pp 43–47.

Berry, L L, Parasuraman, A and Zeitham, V A (1988) 'The service quality puzzle', *Business Horizons*, Vol 31, No 5, September/October, pp 35–43.

Biemans, W G (1990) 'The managerial implications of networking', *European Management Journal*, Vol. 8, No 4, December pp 529–540.

Bohlin, R and Guiniven, J (1991) 'Challenges for the computer industry in the 1990s', *McKinsey Quarterly*, No 1, Winter, pp 106–116.

Bolton, R N and Drew, J H (1991) 'A longitudinal analysis of the impact of service changes on customer attitudes', *Journal of Marketing*, Vol 55, January, pp 1–9.

Booms, B H and Bitner, M J (1982) 'Marketing strategies and organisation structures for service firms', in Donnelly, J H and George, W R (eds), *Marketing of Services*, American Marketing Association, Chicago, pp 47–51.

Bowen, D E and Lawler, E E (1992) 'The empowerment of service workers: what, why, how and when', *Sloan Management Review*, Spring, pp 31–39.

Buchanan, R W T and Gillies, C S (1990) 'Value managed relationships: the key to customer retention and profitability', *European Management Journal*, Vol 8, No 4, pp 523–526.

Canton, I D (1988) 'How manufacturers can move into the service business', *Journal of Business Strategy*, July/August, pp 40–44.

Carlzon, J (1987) *Moments of Truth*, Ballinger, New York.

Charan, R (1991) 'How networks reshape organizations – for results', *Harvard Business Review*, September/October, pp 104–115.

Christopher, M, Payne, A and Ballantyne, D (1991) *Relationship Marketing: Bringing Quality, Customer Service and Marketing Together*, Butterworth-Heinemann, Oxford.

Coggan, P (1991) 'Bank relations: the banks reply', *The Treasurer*, January, pp 17–18.

Collins, B and Payne, A (1991) 'Internal services marketing', *European Management Journal*, Vol 9, No 3, September, pp 261–270.

Copulsky, J R and Wolf, M J (1990) 'Relationship marketing: positioning for the future', *The Journal of Business Strategy*, July/August, pp 16–20.

Crosby, L A and Stephens, N (1987) 'Effects of relationship marketing on satisfaction, retention, and prices in the life insurance industry', *Journal of Marketing Research*, Vol. 24, pp 404–411.

Crosby, L A, Evans, K R and Cowles, D (1990) 'Relationship quality in services selling: an interpersonal influence perspective', *Journal of Marketing*, Vol 54, pp 68–81.

Dixon, S (1991) *Making Quality Cars*, Conference paper: National Consumer Council, 15 May.

de Ferrer, R J (1986) 'A case for European management', *International Management Development Review*, Vol 2, pp 275–281.

Feuchtwanger, A (1992) 'Services are "not to blame" as bank complaints go up', *Daily Telegraph*, 13 December, p 8.

Forge, S (1991) 'Why the computer industry is restructuring now', *Futures*, November, pp 960–977.

Gelb, B D and Gelb, G M (1991) 'What research inside the organization can accomplish', *Marketing Research*, Vol 3, No 4, December, pp 44–51.

George, W R (1990) 'Internal marketing and organisational behaviour: a partnership in developing customer conscious employees at every level', *Journal of Business Research*, Vol 20, pp 63–70.

George, W R and Gronroos, C (1989) 'Developing customer-conscious employees at every level – internal marketing', in Congram, C A and Friedman, M L (eds), *Handbook of Services Marketing*, AMACOM.

Gronroos, C (1981a) 'Internal marketing – an integral part of marketing theory', *Services Marketing Conference Proceedings*, American Marketing Association, Chicago, pp 236–238.

Gronroos, C (1981b) 'Internal marketing – theory and practice', *Services Marketing Conference Proceedings*, American Marketing Association, Chicago, pp 41–47.

Gronroos, C (1982) *Strategic Management and Marketing in the Services Sector*, Swedish School of Economics and Business Administration, Helsinki.

Gronroos, C (1983) 'Innovative marketing strategies and organizational structures for service firms', in Berry, L L, Shostak, G L and Upah, G D (eds), *Emerging Perspectives on Services Marketing*, American Marketing Association, Chicago.

Gronroos, C (1990a) 'Marketing redefined', *Management Decision*, Vol 28, No 8, pp 5–9.

Gronroos, C (1990b) *The Marketing Strategy Continuum: Toward a Marketing Concept for the 1990s*, Meddelanden Fran Svenska Handelshogskolan, Working Paper 201.

Gronroos, C (1990c)) 'Defining marketing: a market-oriented approach', *European Journal of Marketing*, Vol 23, No 1, pp 52–60.

Gronroos, C (1990d) 'Relationship approach to marketing in services contexts: the marketing and organisational behaviour interface', *Journal of Business Research*, Vol 20, pp 3–11.

Guiniven, J and Grossman, E (1991) 'Should the US abandon computer manufacturing?', *Harvard Business Review*, September –October, pp 156–157.

Gummesson, E (1987a) 'The new marketing – developing long-term interactive relationships', *Long Range Planning*, Vol 20, No 4, pp 10–20.

Gummesson, E (1987b) 'Using internal marketing to develop a new culture – the case of Ericsson quality', *Journal of Business and Industrial Marketing*, Vol 2, No 3, pp 23–28.

Gupta, A K and Wilemon, D (1990b) 'The credibility–cooperation connection at the R&D–marketing interface', *Journal of Product Innovation Management*, Vol 5, pp 20–31.

Hakansson, H (ed.) (1982) *International Marketing and Purchasing of Industrial Goods: An Interaction Approach*, Wiley, Chichester.

Hart, C W L, Heskett, J L and Sasser, W E Jr (1990) 'The profitable art of service recovery', *Harvard Business Review*, July–August, pp 148–156.

Heskett, J L (1987) 'Lessons in the service sector', *Harvard Business Review*, March–April, pp 118–126.

Hidaloo, L (1993) 'Banks' conduct code fails to halt rise in customer complaints', *The Times*, 5 March.

Hochschild, A R (1983) *The Managed Heart*, University of California Press.

Hunter, T (1992) 'Withdrawal threat to banks in campaign on complaints', *The Guardian*, 12 November, p 12.

Jackson, B B (1985) 'Build customer relationships that last', *Harvard Business Review*, November–December, pp 120–128.

Kelly, S W (1990) 'Customer orientation of bank employees and culture', *International Journal of Bank Marketing*, Vol 8, No 6, pp 25–29.

Kirkpatrick, D (1992) 'Breaking up IBM', *Fortune*, No 15, pp 112–121.

Kotler, P (1984) *Marketing Management*, Prentice Hall, New Jersey.

Kotler, P (1986) 'Megamarketing', *Harvard Business Review*, March–April, pp 117–124.

Lawless, J (1992) 'Ford imports American know-how to keep UK customers satisfied', *The Times*, 16 December, p 23.

Levitt, T (1972) 'Production-line approach to service', *Harvard Business Review*, September–October, pp 41–52.

Levitt, T (1981) Marketing intangible products and product intangibles', *Harvard Business Review*, May–June, pp 94–102.

Levitt, T (1983) 'After the sale is over ...', *Harvard Business Review*, September–October, pp 87–93.

Lewis, B R (1988) *Customer Service Survey: A Major UK Bank*, Financial Services Research Centre, Manchester School of Management, UMIST.

Lewis, B R (1991) 'Service quality: an international comparison of bank customers' expectations and perceptions', *Journal of Marketing Management*, Vol 7, pp 47–62.

Luthans, F (1991) 'Improving the delivery of quality service: behavioural management techniques', *International Journal of Bank Marketing*, Vol 9, No 3, pp 17–20.

McKenna, R (1991) 'Marketing is everything', *Harvard Business Review*, January–February, pp 65–79.

Michelson, M (1992) 'Europe car makers cut jobs as Japan opens UK plants', Textline/Reuter News Service, 17 December.

Morgan, N A (1990) 'Implementing marketing: key issues for professional service firms', *Journal of Professional Services Marketing*, Vol 6, No.1, pp 7–16.

Mundie, P M (1987) 'Internal marketing: cause for concern', *Quarterly Review of Marketing*, Spring/Summer, pp 21–24.

Ogbonna, E and Wilkinson, B (1990) 'Corporate strategy and corporate culture: the view from the checkout', *Personnel Review*, Vol 19, No 4, pp 9–15.

Ostroff, F and Smith, D (1992) 'The horizontal organization', *McKinsey Quarterly*, Winter, pp 148–167.

Parasuraman, A (1987) 'Customer-orientated corporate cultures are crucial to services marketing success', *Journal of Services Marketing*, Vol 1, No 1, pp 39–46.

Parasuraman, A, Zeithaml, V A and Berry, L L (1985) 'A conceptual model of service quality and its implications for future research', *Journal of Marketing*, Vol 49, pp 41–50.

Parasuraman, A, Zeithaml, V A and Berry, L L (1988) 'SERVQUAL: a multiple-item scale for measuring consumer perceptions of service quality', *Journal of Retailing*, Vol 64, No 1, pp 12–40.

Parkington, J P and Schneider, B (1979) 'Some correlates of experienced job stress: a boundary role study', *Academy of Management Review*, Vol 22, No 2, pp 270–281.

Piercy, N and Morgan, N (1990) 'Internal marketing: making marketing happen', *Marketing Intelligence and Planning*, vol 8, No 1, pp 4–6.

Piercy, N and Morgan, N (1991) 'Internal marketing – the missing half of the marketing programme', *Long Range Planning*, Vol 24, No 2, pp 82–93.

Pounsford, M (1992) 'When employee research is a waste of time', *Internal Communication Focus*, February, pp 17–18.

Quinn, J B, Baruch, J J and Paquette, P C (1988) 'Exploiting the manufacturing–services interface', *Sloan Management Review*, Summer, pp 45–56.

Rappaport, A S and Halvi, S (1991) 'The computerless computer company', *Harvard Business Review*, July–August, pp 69–8.

Reicheld, F F and Sasser, W E Jr (19900) 'Zero defections: quality comes to services', *Harvard Business Review*, September–October, pp 105–216.

Richardson, B A and Robinson, C G (1986) 'The impact of internal marketing on customer service in a retail bank', *International Journal of Bank Marketing*, Vol 4, No 5, pp 3–30.

Roach, S S (1991) 'Services under siege – the restructuring imperative', *Harvard Business Review*, September–October, pp 82–91.

Schlesinger, L A and Heskett, J L (1991a) 'The service-driven company', *Harvard Business Review*, September–October, pp 71–81.

Schlesinger, L A and Heskett, J L (1991b) 'Breaking the cycle of failure in services', *Sloan Management Review*, Spring, pp 17–28.

Schneider, B (1973) 'The perception of organisational climate: the customer's view', *Journal of Applied Psychology*, Vol 57, No 3, pp 248–256.

Schneider, B (1980) 'The service organisation: Climate is crucial', *Organizational Dynamics*, Autumn, pp 52–65.

Schneider, B and Bowen, D E (1984) 'New services design, development and implementation and the employee', in George, W R and Marshall, C E (eds), *Developing New Services*, American Marketing Association, Chicago, pp 82–101.

Schneider, B and Bowen, D E (1985)) 'Employee and customer perceptions of service in banks: replication and extension', *Journal of Applied Psychology*, Vol 7, pp 423–433.

Schneider, B, Parkington, J J and Buxton, V M (1980) 'Employee and customer perceptions of service in banks', *Administrative Science Quarterly*, Vol 25, pp 252–267.

Sherman, L, Moran, U and Wormald, J (1990) 'Automotive retailing in the 1990s', *European Motor Business*, May, pp 97–124.

Smith, P C, Kendall, L M and Hulin C L (1969) *The Measurement of Satisfaction in Work and Retirement*, Rand-McNally, Chicago.

Solomon, M R, Surprenant, C, Czepiel, J A and Gutman, E G (1985) 'A role theory perspective on dyadic interactions: the service encounter', *Journal of Marketing*, Vol 49, pp 99–111.

Stone, D L (1991) 'Should the US abandon computer manufacturing?', *Harvard Business Review*, September–October, pp 158–159.

Tansuhaj, P, Randall, D and McCullough, J (1991) 'Applying the internal marketing concept within large organisations: as applied to a credit union', *Journal of Professional Services Marketing*, Vol 6, No 2, pp 193–202.

Tansuhaj, P, Marshall, D and McCullough, J (1988) 'A services marketing management model: integrating internal and external marketing functions', *Journal of Services Marketing*, Vol 2, No 1, pp 31–38.

Taylor, A (1992) 'More power to J.D. Power', *Fortune*, 18 May, pp 75–78.

Thomas, R K, Farmer, E E and Wallace, B (1991) 'The importance of internal marketing: the case of geriatric services', *Journal of Health Care Marketing*, Vol 11, No 1, pp 55–58.

Tsun-Yan, H (1992) 'The road to renewal', *Mckinsey Quarterly*, No 3, pp 28–36.

Vandermerwe, S and Rada, J (1988) 'Servitization of business: adding value by adding services', *European Management Journal*, Vol 6, No 4, pp 314–325.

Walton, R E (1985) 'From control to commitment in the workplace', *Harvard Business Review*, March–April, pp 77–84.

Webster, C (1990) 'Toward the measurement of the marketing culture of a service firm', *Journal of Business Research*, Vol 21, pp 345–362.

Wheatley, M (1992) 'The gospel according to Schonberger', *Management Today*, June, pp 74–76.

Wilson, A (1991) 'The internal marketing of services – the new surge', *Management Decision*, Vol 29, No 5, pp 4–7.

Witcher, B J (1990) 'Total marketing: total quality and the marketing concept', *Quarterly Review of Marketing*, Winter, pp 1–6.

Yovovitch, B G (1991) 'Hand in glove relationships', *Business Marketing*, April, pp 20–21.

6

INTERNAL MARKETING: A NEW PERSPECTIVE FOR HRM*

Brett Collins and Adrian Payne

INTRODUCTION

Over the past few years the term *internal marketing* is increasingly being used to describe the application of marketing internally within the organisation. There are two dimensions relevant to our discussion of internal marketing. Firstly there is the notion that every department and every person within an organisation is both a supplier and a customer. The second aspect relates to the organisation's staff and involves ensuring they work together in a manner supporting the company strategy and goals. This has been recognised as being especially important in service firms where there is a close relationship between production and consumption of the service. It is thus concerned with both quality management and customer service and involves coordinating people and process improvement strategies.

Internal marketing relates to all functions within the organisation, but it is vitally concerned with the management of human resources. However, the traditional personnel department and the more advanced human resources department have frequently been oriented towards control and administrative activities rather than the alignment of human resources towards achieving strategic organisational purposes and goals. In this chapter we explore the marketing of a particular internal service within the organisation – the human resource function. Our purpose is to illustrate how internal marketing concepts and methods used by marketing managers can provide the basis of a new perspective on meeting the opportunities and challenges faced by human resource managers. A market-oriented human resource manager is more likely to make an impact on the success of a company, through being more effective in both demonstrating the relevance of human resource

* This chapter was first published in the *The European Management Journal*, Vol 9, No 3, September 1991, pp 261–269, and is reproduced with permission.

management (HRM) to all management team members, and helping other managers to increase their productivity.

Our approach is to first consider the nature of the challenges and opportunities confronting human resource (HR) managers. A view of what is seen to be a central task for the HR management professional is then outlined. The congruence between marketing function activities and the HR management activities is then described. Finally, we consider how the HR manager can utilise the philosophy, ideas, and tools of the marketing function to make a more effective contribution toward the organisation's objectives.

CHALLENGES FACING THE HR MANAGER

The managers in a company who deal with the 'people' issues are now recognised as having an increasingly strategic role in the success of many businesses. Regardless of whether the function these managers perform is called personnel, human resources, industrial relations, or training and development, it collectively now represents a business role similar in importance to the areas of finance, marketing and operations management. This trend has been driven by a more intensely competitive business environment, increased use of technology in some industries, and the shift in corporate philosophy from asset management to operations management.

A focus on operations management has forced chief executive officers (CEOs) to understand the need for skilled HR executives if they are to successfully cope with change. An organisation able to adapt to change is generally found to be more able to sustain competitive advantage in an environment of increasing uncertainty. The constant stress of corporate takeovers, new ventures, the restructuring of companies, rationalisation of existing operations, new technology introduction and staff layoffs, means that the success of basic strategic decisions increasingly depends on 'matching skills with jobs, keeping key personnel after a merger, and solving the human problems that arise from introducing new technology or closing a plant' (*Business Week*, 1985). The dramatic turnaround of SAS by Jan Carlzon was driven through people rather than through an expensive investment in equipment and assets (Carlzon, 1987).

Increasing attention is being focused on the area of external customer retention and the enormous potential for improved profitability (Reichheld and Sasser, 1990; Buchanan and Gillies, 1990). Top management should also seek to obtain improved organisational performance through effective HRM strategies aimed at improving personnel retention.

The baseline benefits are cost savings on retraining in a rapid turnover job market and cutting down the equally expensive knowledge drain. Companies able to manage this issue will reap the rewards which go with a team of committed, active individuals at a time when under-training is sapping productivity among competitors.

Increased usage of technology in some industries has led to the assumption that the quality of people performance will become a less important issue as technology becomes more pervasive. However the maintenance of reliable performance by competent employees is becoming *more* crucial. For example, we are now in an era where electronic banking means fewer face-to-face encounters between the bank and its customers. Consequently the importance of handling these interactions, and the 'costs' of not making the most of opportunities are greater. In a relatively homogeneous industry such as banking, a key opportunity for banks to gain a competitive edge over competitors lies in the quality of its people. In an era of electronic fund transfer there is opportunity for a bank to position itself as one that has good people, not just good machines (Berry, 1981). Many of the key challenges facing retail banking involve the employee: the need to sell and cross-sell, unionisation, electronic banking, affirmative action, service quality management and technology management.

It has been argued that HR professionals have failed in the past to reach their full potential within the corporate framework because they devoted themselves to the creation of ever more sophisticated programmes and forgot the whole purpose of the business (Baird and Meshoulam, 1986). HR managers have had a role in organisations dealing with outside pressures such as government, unions, and safety, but their active involvement and collaboration is also needed with the production, marketing and finance functions. They have been responsible for fending off interruptions, handling the reporting requirements of regulatory bodies, and dealing with social responsibility issues, but often are not involved in activities perceived by other managers to be fundamentally important to the business.

Managing a corporation is complex, and CEOs find it necessary to simplify their task by concentrating on what appear to be the most important strategic issues. Because of resource limitations, it is necessary to focus senior management's attention and time on those aspects of the business process with the highest expected payoff. This means that some areas with extremely high potential impact, but a very low perceived probability of delivering significant results, must get less attention than one might really wish. Strategic HRM requires a significant investment of organisational resources, which directly and immediately affects profits, and can thus make it unattractive to managers under pressure for short-term results. Further, any real understanding of what competent HRM could contribute to the success of a business has only been popularised fairly recently (Peters and Waterman, 1982). For these reasons senior management has often failed to grasp why HRM was relevant to business strategy, business performance and the cost management function.

Clearly the central task of HRM must be to gain the support of senior management, secure the commitment of the CEO, and ensure HRM makes the most effective contribution possible to the organisation's objectives.

The HRM function in a company is never likely to be valued unless it convinces management it can provide significant payoffs, and is part of the key interactions between the organisation and environment. HRM will become established as an integral part of a business through helping other managers to increase their productivity. Managers do not require more sophisticated programmes. They require someone who understands their problems, can actively contribute to the more effective and efficient management of human resources, and who has a good understanding of the business. We will now consider how the roles of marketing managers and HR managers are linked.

THE MARKETING–HRM ANALOGY

The HRM function has three distinct client groups, or markets, with which it must deal effectively:

- employees within the organisation;
- other managers involved with the senior management tasks including the CEO; and
- external groups such as prospective employees, government, unions, and regulatory bodies.

Consideration of the challenges faced by HR managers indicates that they are similar to those challenges faced by other senior managers, and requirements for success correspond to those needed by good marketing managers. The use of marketing ideas does not need to be narrowly confined to products and markets. Marketing has been defined as 'a social process by which individuals and groups obtain what they need and want through creating and exchanging products and value with others' (Kotler, 1984:4), and implies two voluntary parties with unsatisfied needs, an expectation of mutual benefit, a means of communication, and a medium to complete the exchange.

People who buy goods and services are involved in the same type of exchange process as people who seek employment that is satisfying, interesting, and more than a well-lit work space. The relationship between buyer and seller in a labour market is such that the employee must sell labour to earn an income. A company must create goods or services and exchange them in order to earn profits. Clearly there are times when one party to an exchange has much more bargaining power than the other party. The manager who seeks mutual benefit through working closely with the HRM department is involved in a similar exchange process to that which takes place between consumers and companies everywhere.

A source of interdepartmental conflict can be the need for a marketing manager to represent the interests of a customer against the needs of other managers. We do not lack examples of conflict between the marketing and accounting functions. For example, while the sales department are properly concerned with maintaining a good relationship and un-disrupted supply to the customer, the accounts department is concerned with administering credit control. Accounts may seek the withholding of supply, because credit guidelines have been exceeded at a time when sales is trying to service a sudden increase in demand, resulting in open conflict (Collins, 1985). Similarly, an HR manager can become involved in interdepartmental conflict through a need to represent the interests of an employee against the needs of another manager. Like marketing, HRM is a function where success requires close cooperation with other functions, but there can be significant potential for conflict. The coalitions of power and politics at the core of fundamental conflicts such as this can be used to maximise business performance, or detract from it. The task for the HR manager is made more difficult because the quality of management performance is difficult to quantify – there is no bottom line responsibility. This can leave the HR manager without the defence available to managers of profitable business units who have tangible evidence of performance in their regular financial reports, bottom line results.

Marketing performs a valuable role in that it creates utility, the capacity to satisfy needs (Murphy and Enis, 1985). The HR manager is similarly concerned with the creation of utilities. The marketing philosophy or concept states that, in serving market-place needs, the entire organisation should be guided by thinking that centres around the consumer. For our purposes the concept has three key elements:

- The HR manager requires a thorough knowledge of the needs, wants, and problems of the CEO, other managers and employees. Ideally the HR manager should start with a knowledge of client needs and work backwards to developing products and services to satisfy them.
- The second element requires that the cost, design, implementation and follow up on HR projects should be carefully planned so all features are consistent with project goals, and the process coordinated with other functions in the organisation.
- Finally, in our definition of marketing we recognise individuals or groups engaging in the marketing process have diverse goals and objectives. If the organisation itself does not gain utility from an exchange then this element of the philosophy is not met. Consequently we would expect that if an HR activity did not lead to organisational gain the activity would be discontinued.

Quantification of performance plays a crucial role in the success of the marketing function, and the performance audit guides corrective action, while providing measurements essential to supporting access to resources for projects. HR managers have sometimes been characterised by a lack of willingness to work with performance measures. Marketing strongly depends on techniques developed in the behavioural sciences for quantification of the needs, wants and perceptions of consumers. These tools can be readily adapted to the requirements of the HR manager. While measures employed by marketing managers are not always of high precision, they are essential to the building of credibility through measurement and performance against explicit goals. Management performance in functions other than marketing and HRM are generally more amenable to performance measurement.

An HR manager with a market orientation would have good knowledge of the needs and wants of the client groups served, and would develop a coordinated approach to servicing those requirements consistent with organisation goals, and with the expectation of achieving organisational gain from any exchange process. In contrast, a product-oriented HR manager would place primary emphasis on the products or services the HRM department offers, and how these are provided. It is instructive to consider the differences between these two opposing views. Consider training programmes for example; the difference between a product-oriented, and a market-oriented manager, is shown in Table 6.1. This

Table 6.1 Stereotypical differences between market-oriented and product-oriented HR managers with respect to training programmes

Attitudes and procedures	Product orientation	Market orientation
Attitudes towards clients:	They should be glad we exist. Trying to cut costs and bring out better programmes.	Client needs determine training programmes.
Programme offerering:	Department provides courses that fit our skills and interests.	Schedule programmes we know the clients need.
Interest in innovation:	Focus in on technology and cost cutting.	Focus on identifying new opportunities.
Importance of costs:	A number in the budget we cannot exceed.	A critical objective.
Number of programmes scheduled for the year:	Set with the delivery requirements in mind.	Set with client needs and costs in mind.
Role of marketing research:	To determine client reaction if used at all.	To determine client needs and if they are being met.
Attendance at programmes:	Fill all available places – repeating is good revision.	Select attendees according to their needs and coordinate this with other managers.
Promotion of programmes:	Advise managers when their staff is to attend the next course.	Demonstrate need-satisfying benefits of course to clients.

example is stereotypical in that the model represents two extreme positions. No one person would be expected to exhibit all of the characteristics presented for a specific orientation, but an HR practitioner would be expected to possess several if they were either market- or product-oriented and the distinction between two very different management philosophies are illustrated.

We have found it a useful exercise, in workshops with senior managers, to discuss the role of conflicting philosophies and how they affect the achievement of a marketing orientation. This can be addressed in the context of both external customers (Payne, 1988) and internal customers (Vandermerwe and Gilbert, 1989). Although it has been accepted for many years that a market orientation is essential to the success of a business, it has not been proven in all contingent situations. Monopoly or regulated markets provide examples of non-market orientation. As the difference between a market orientation, and any one of many conflicting orientations possible, is accepted as the difference between unstable short-term success and stable long-term growth, it becomes of considerable importance to senior managers to push a market orientation within their company. Similarly, the importance of HRM has gradually gained credibility and importance, as managers have come to understand how it can contribute to the achievement of business success. There exists an increasing number of well known companies where superior HRM is believed to be a key factor in their success.

We have seen the similarity in roles of the marketing and HR managers. The marketing and HRM processes both involve the creation and exchange of utilities. A need to represent the interests of a client, against the narrow interests of another manager, may be conducive to the well-being of the company but a source of open interdepartmental conflict. This conflict is difficult to manage and can detract from the effectiveness of the function and the organisation. Both functions require commitment and support from the CEO to succeed, and performance measurement is seen to be an important tool for building credibility within the company. The market orientation can be applied equally to either the marketing or HR functions when it is accepted that success is achieving organisational goals through delivering customer satisfaction. We will now consider how the HR manager can harness the ideas and tools of the marketing function to more effectively contribute toward the organisation's objectives.

THE HRM–MARKETING FUNCTION

We are concerned here with internal marketing – that form of marketing where both the 'customer' and the 'supplier' are inside the organisation. In this context we consider employees as customers or clients. These classifications are quite broad, and could be further divided into such groupings as the board, managers, supervisors, foremen, clerical staff, etc. The HRM–marketing function can be described in terms of seeing managers and employees as in-house customers, viewing the tasks and activities performed by the HRM function as in-house products or services, and offering in-house services that satisfy the needs and wants of managers and employees, while addressing the objectives of the organisation (Berry, 1981).

The reasons for believing marketing provides a useful framework for HRM depend largely on the congruences we have demonstrated between essential activities of the two functions. In addition to these congruences, there is a strong similarity in the constraints and difficulties facing either marketing or HR managers. Concepts and tools proven to be useful to the marketing function can also be applied to the benefit of HRM.

The HRM function provides services or programmes to employees and management, which means it sells performances that directly influence business productivity. Internal marketing can help an HR manager to attract and hold the type of people a company wants, and get the best of in-house customers, the HR function can upgrade the capability of a company to satisfy the needs and wants of its external customers.

Marketing management is the process of increasing the effectiveness and/or efficiency by which marketing activities are performed. Effectiveness refers to the degree to which organisational objectives are attained, while efficiency is concerned with the expenditure of resources to accomplish these objectives. This difference is eloquently expressed in the view that it is more important to do the *right things* (improve effectiveness) than to do *things right* (improve efficiency) (Drucker, 1974). An organisation that is doing the right things wrong (effective but not efficient), can outperform organisations that are doing the wrong things right. Effectiveness and efficiency are also a concern of the HR manager seeking improved performance.

MARKETING ACTIVITIES

The marketing function in any organisation is concerned with a number of related activities which include:

- understanding of the market and competitive environment;
- definition of the firm's Mission;
- determination of the target market segments to be emphasised;
- developing integrated marketing mix strategies to accomplish this Mission in the selected segments;
- implement marketing mix strategies and control marketing activity.

This well known model of marketing function activities, which involves the above steps, is used as a basis for a discussion on internal HRM marketing.

Market and Competitive Environment

The starting point is for HR managers to gain a good knowledge of the needs and wants of the client groups served and the significant factors influencing the HR department's operations, and to identify the 'publics' which interact with the company. This process is market analysis and involves collecting information on the different client markets into a database.

Market research should be used to identify internal client needs, wants and attitudes just as it can be used to identify the needs, wants and attitudes of external consumers or industrial buyers. For example, 'climate surveys' concerning perceptions of remuneration packages, employment conditions and performance appraisal, and opinions of quality improvement programmes, provide direct benefits for the redesign and improvement of key policies, processes and programmes. There is also the positive effect on morale that flows from taking an interest in the views of employees.

This channel of communication provides an early means for pinpointing organisational breakdowns and problem areas. An important requirement before undertaking data collection is to adopt a commitment to face the issues uncovered, no matter how unpalatable. It is an ongoing process requiring that issues be resolved in order to maintain the credibility of the HR department at all levels within the company. To raise the expectations of client groups without delivering can generate strongly negative effects. Finally, market research can also provide a basis for monitoring the impact of programmes on employees, and check whether HR programmes are achieving what they were designed to achieve.

This market research process sometimes suffers from a condition referred to as the 'no-full-disclosure disease' (Weinshull, 1982). It manifests itself through people within the management hierarchy who fear the things threatening them may become known to others, and then used to their personal detriment. The extent of this problem depends on survey design and content. People interviewed tend to speak freely when given a chance to express their thoughts and opinions on HRM issues. However undertaking not to reveal the content of an interview under any circumstances, without prior approval from the person interviewed, is sometimes necessary in order to get at the real problems and issues. Whether use is made of questionnaires, personal interviews, informal meetings of managers, or group discussions, market research provides a clear means of identifying client needs and wants. It also provides the means for tracking performance.

Mission

The second step involves the development of a mission for the HR department. The corporate mission statement for an organisation is too

To develop and promote the highest quality human resource practices and initiatives in an ethical, cost effective and timely manner to support the current and future business objectives of the organisation and to enable line managers to maximise the calibre, effectiveness and development of their human resources.

This will be achieved through working with managers and staff to:

- Develop an integrated human resource policy and implement its consistent use throughout the organisation.
- Enhance managers' efficient use of human resources through the provision of responsive and adaptable services.
- Be the preferred source of core strategic HR services.
- Provide high quality tailored HR consultancy.
- Introduce methods to plan for the provision of the required calibre and quantity of staff.
- Ensure consistent line accountability throughout all areas within the organisation.
- Assist the organisation in becoming more customer aware and responsive to changing needs.
- Define and encourage implementation of an improved communications culture throughout the organisation.
- Maintain an innovative and affordable profile for HRM.

Figure 6.1 Human resource mission statement

broad to be meaningful for a specific business function, and consequently a mission statement should be specifically developed for the HRM function. It involves asking the questions – 'what is our role within the organisation?' and 'what should our role be within the organisation?'. Figure 6.1 provides an example of an HR mission statement based on one developed with a leading British service organisation.

At the HRM level the definition of mission does not have to be complex. It should provide a framework for explaining the HR department's role and how it can help the different levels and units of an organisation to coordinate their efforts to achieve the overall objectives of the organisation.

Once the mission statement has been adopted objectives need to be formalised. Because objectives are not equally important, a hierarchy of potential services, programmes and projects should be put together. If possible these objectives should be operationalised – stated in terms that are specific, and which will lead to measurable end results. It is important to understand what needs to be accomplished, when the task should be completed, and how it will be decided that the task is completed. This process links very closely with the market research function which can be used to demonstrate performance against specific objectives. A function which provides a service, and deals predominantly in intangibles, requires tangible evidence of success in order to demonstrate competent performance and help build credibility.

Market Segmentation

The third step is deciding which market groups should be emphasised. Market segmentation is a process by which we divide the total, heterogeneous group of clients into smaller, more homogeneous groups with similar needs and wants that the HR function can successfully satisfy. By developing specific services we can generally improve the effectiveness of our performance in satisfying clients. It may cost more to serve smaller groups or handle problems requiring customised solutions. Because of this, there is sometimes a need to balance the level of customisation required to adequately solve a problem, against the benefits which might accrue to the organisation. This is very much a cost–benefit exercise. The characterisation shown in Figure 6.2 can be helpful for sorting problems into classes, each of which require different capabilities.

At a high degree of customisation, there is increased demand for resources from the HR function. The HR cost to the organisation increases with an increase in the level of customisation. Programmes or projects undertaken by HR typically involve long-term benefits with short-term costs and, given limited resources, this has direct impact on the HR department's effectiveness.

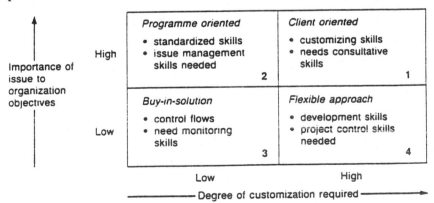

Figure 6.2 Characterising HR marketing problems

Quadrant 1 in Figure 6.2 represents the situation where there is need to fit a key programme to the specialised needs of a client group. A major company wishing to run an in-house strategic management seminar, enabling senior management to review and discuss current management thinking and practice, is an example. The CEO would perceive this to be of high value to the organisation, while requiring this process to fit closely with the business context.

The programme-oriented task found in quadrant 2 is characterised by the opportunity for a high quality but standardised approach to be taken. For example, consider a betting agency involved in the conversion of operations from a manual to a computerised telephone betting system. There is a need to develop and implement a programme at low cost which will enable a smooth transition to the new system. Due to the large group of operators requiring new skills there is an opportunity to seek savings through standardisation. The importance of this issue means effective performance by the HR department is more critical.

In quadrant 3 the degree of customisation required for a task is low – for example where factory staff are being given first-aid training. The content of a first-aid training programme will be fairly standard across a range of industries. Such a programme is not central to achievement of organisation objectives, and represents a situation where service delivery can readily be obtained from outside the organisation. Once the training programme was in place, knowing who had attended the course and monitoring the training process would be the key tasks.

An increase in the degree of customisation required corresponds to an increase in the level of organisation-specific content, as shown in quadrant 4. Consider a retail tyre organisation which needs to train shopfloor staff in the testing and servicing of car batteries. This more specialised course requires company-specific input, and an in-house programme is the best solution. In this quadrant the need is for course development skills, a flexible approach, and the ability to manage the development process. Other examples are custom-designed employee retirement programmes, or surveys of work group satisfaction where there is a need to design and implement a project with the specific needs of a client group in mind.

Obviously most impact can be made by HRM focusing efforts in those quadrants involving problems of high importance to the organisation, but not involving significant short-term investment. This type of problem area, identified because the issues involved are considered central to the achievement of business objectives, will often be more able to attract support and adequate funding. Working in areas requiring a high level of customisation, which are also critical to business success, is the challenge facing HR. This is the direction in which HR requirements have moved due to the increased complexity of business, changing technology, and the shift from an asset management to operations management philosophy.

Segmentation of employees on the basis of their needs and wants, as opposed to the segmentation of management clients, recognises the need to accommodate individual differences. This is the basis for concepts such as negotiable remuneration packages, employment contracts, flexible working hours, and job sharing. The techniques used for consumer segmentation by marketers can be applied directly here. It provides opportunity for companies to 'lessen the influence of unions by placing greater emphasis on direct employee communication, in addition to, or instead of, industrial relations conducted in the traditional representative way' (Cupper, 1987).

Developing and Implementing the Marketing Mix

Once the tasks of determining the mission of the HR department and the target market segments to be emphasised have been undertaken, a marketing-oriented HR function will focus on the 'marketing mix'. The marketing programme is developed based upon a decision on marketing mix variables over which the HR manager has some control: designing the product or service, costing it, setting up a service delivery system, promotion of the product to clients, and gaining commitment for proposals from management. Table 6.2 illustrates the four elements of the marketing mix which need to be addressed. Whilst all elements need to

Table 6.2 The four elements of the marketing mix

Elements of the marketing mix for a company	Equivalent elements for the HRM function
1. Products or services	1. 'Products' (services, courses, etc)
2. Place (distribution)	2. The location and delivery means of services and courses
3. Promotion (mainly through advertising and personal selling)	3. Communications with client groups (primarily through discussion and documentation)
4 Pricing	4 Transfer pricing and expense allocation

Introducing the new product (1 to 3 year cycle)	Resolving a complex HR issue (1 to 3 year cycle)
DETERMINE NEED FOR NEW PRODUCT Who will buy it and why? How much will they spend on it? What need will it satisfy?	**DETERMINE NEED FOR NEW PROJECT/PROGRAMME** What is the cost of not resolving this issue? What will be its impact on norms and values? What is cost-benefit value to internal clients?
SCREEN NEW PRODUCT IDEA What impact will it have? Will it be profitable? Is it compatible with existing products?	**EVALUATE POSSIBLE SOLUTIONS FOR CLIENTS** What impact will it have on operations? Who will manage and use the project? How does it fit with current projects/priorities?
TEST MARKET THE PRODUCT How do prospects view the product? What needs does it satisfy? Have we designed the right product?	**CONDUCT A PILOT PROJECT** Do internal clients find it useful? Will they support/pay? To what extent? Who will oppose it? Why?
EXPAND TO OTHER TEST MARKETS Are findings consistent? Are there logistic/quality problems? Did promotions result in expected sales?	**ADVANCE TO OTHER POTENTIAL USERS** Is the project valid/reliable? Does it meet the needs of all company locations? Have the benefits been properly communicated?
ANALYSE, MEASURE, PROJECT What impact on other functions? Detailed budget and plans. Have all implications been considered?	**ASSESS OUTCOME IN ADVANCE** Which functions are affected and how? Will it cause confusion? Have times, resources and costs been detailed?
EXPAND TO A NATIONAL LAUNCH Does the potential outweight the risks? Are promotions and follow-up planned? Are logistics and supply lines ready? Have we means for identifying service problems and dissatisfactions?	**IMPLEMENT COMPANY-WIDE** Does project add to HR's credibility? Who will train whom to do what, where, when? Have we an effective audit/evaluation system? Will the issue really be resolved?

Figure 6.3 Comparing product development to resolving a complex HR issue

be considered, two key variables – the design of the 'product' (ie courses or services) and communications are especially important. These two key variables and their relevance for the HR manager are now reviewed.

Designing the 'product'

It has been pointed out that the process of a marketing department introducing a new product, and the resolution of a complex long-standing problem by the HR function are very similar. Figure 6.3 illustrates this, and is based on Desatnick (1983:52) who argues that 'as the contribution of HRM is less tangible and more difficult to measure in terms of end results, it is even more important to market it effectively. This implies taking the time to reflect, to position, to package, to merchandise, and to sell.' Thus the HR manager must get the maximum impact from each situation through careful management of those elements he can control. Developing a product or service for a client group is an activity over which the HR manager has a great deal of control, and consequently provides an area where management attention can be rewarded with maximum impact.

Communication

Communication represents promotional activity in the form of advertising, indirect publicity, and face-to-face selling which is employed by marketers to influence potential or existing customers to behave in desired ways, such as to undertake the trial purchase of a product the firm has just launched onto the market. Promotion can also be used to influence employees to reconsider attitudes, to inform managers, or alter the way in which a particular programme is perceived by the clients to whom it is directed. The use of 'publicity' through internal publications and other documentation can be used to provide feedback to employees on current issues, as well as enhance and reinforce the credibility of the research process. A well-conceived internal promotional programme can have very positive effects on employees. It can motivate, educate or help provide a sense of belonging. The famous Avis Rent-a-Car slogan suggesting that Avis employees 'Try harder' was as effective for their employees as it was for the public image of Avis. This type of corporate advertisement primarily seeks to influence the perceptions of external publics, but management tends to forget these campaigns are also critically viewed by employees at all levels within the organisation. A campaign which lacks credibility with employees is not consistent with the development of a positive organisational culture. Management should develop corporate communications which are consistent with the HRM objectives of the organisation. Simpler, less ambitious projects can also produce significant impact for the HR function.

Personal interaction with other functional areas can contribute significantly to HR marketing efforts. In situations where a service or programme is either partly or fully dependent on the performance of employees for success, the communications and promotional activity should be concerned not only with encouraging clients to buy, but with encouraging employees to perform. Success in business requires the commitment of both employees and management.

The implementation and control processes represent the final step which involves the measuring of effectiveness and efficiency, taking corrective action, and iteration through the marketing planning processes. The well-established marketing planning literature (McDonald, 1989) provides a framework to follow in undertaking this task.

CONCLUSIONS

The 1980s saw the start of a new emphasis on the HRM function. It has been pointed out that the reality is that a firm adopting 'HRM' may simply involve a retitling of the old personnel department with no obvious change in its functional role, or it may be 'strategic HRM' which represents a fundamental re-conceptualisation and re-organisation of personnel roles and departments (Guest, 1987, 1989). The focus of strategic HRM encompasses all those decisions and actions which concern the management of employees at all levels within the organisation and which are directed towards creating and sustaining competitive advantage (Miller, 1989), but recent European research suggest that 'strategic HRM' is still not widespread. Findings from the Price Waterhouse/Cranfield HR research project shows that in many European organisations HR strategies follow on behind corporate strategy rather than making a positive contribution to it; and although HR representation at board level is becoming more common, this does not necessarily bring with it involvement in key decisions (Brewster and Smith, 1990; Burack, 1986). Some firms have been able to integrate HR and strategy but to achieve this it usually requires a concentrated and multidimensional effort (Buller, 1988).

The scope of marketing has traditionally been limited to the exchanges that take place between organisations and their customers. More recently this scope has been expanded to encompass the field of 'relationship marketing' (Christopher, Payne and Ballantyne, 1991), which suggests that marketing principles can be applied to a number of other key markets, including internal markets within the firm. We argue that there exist compelling reasons for bringing the internal marketing concept to bear on problems faced by all HR managers, but the greatest value will be obtained in those firms adopting 'strategic HRM'.

The shift in organisational philosophy from asset management to operations management, the introduction of new technologies to some industries, and the increased strategic importance of managing people resources effectively and efficiently has meant the role performed by HR managers demands a much higher level of competence and professional skills. Marketing provides an action framework, and a practical approach by which the HR manager can provide effective solutions to key corporate problems. This fresh perspective will bring market-oriented HR managers significant benefits.

In spite of emphasis in this chapter on the need for HR managers to deal effectively with the challenges they face, it must be recognised that much opportunity for the future status of HRM lies with the CEOs. Their task is to provide organisational vision, and many have still failed to recognise the value of strategic HRM in the present business environment. In spite of this, the HR manager must share the responsibility through not having convinced top management that HRM is strategically relevant to business success. Adopting a market orientation requires the HR manager to focus on the needs and wants of internal customer groups and to stimulate internal service. An investment in the marketing approach is an investment in people.

References

Baird, L and Meshoulam, I (1986) 'A second chance for HR to make the grade', *Personnel*, Vol 63, No 4, pp 45–48.

Berry, LL (1981) 'The employee as customer', *Journal of Retail Banking*, Vol 3, No 1, pp 33–40.

Brewster, C and Smith, C (1990) 'Corporate strategy: a no-go area for personnel?' *Personnel Management*, July, pp 36–40.

Buchanan, R W J and Gillies, C S (1990) 'Value managed relationships: the key to customer retention and profitability', *European Management Journal*, Vol 8, No 4, pp 523–526.

Buller, P F (1988) 'Successful partnerships: HR and strategic planning at eight top firms', *Organizational Dynamics*, Vol 17, No 2, pp 27–43.

Burack, E H (1986) 'Corporate business and human resource planning practices: strategic issues and concerns', *Organizational Dynamics*, Vol 15, No 1, pp 73–87.

Business Week (1985) 'Human resource managers aren't corporate nobodies anymore', 2 December, p 58.

Carlzon, J (1987) *Moments of Truth*, Ballinger.

Christopher, M, Payne, A F T and Ballantyne, D (1991) *Relationship Marketing: Bringing Quality, Customer Service and Marketing Together*, Butterworth-Heinemann, Oxford.

Collins, B A (1985) 'The friction between marketing and finance', *The Australian Accountant*, Vol 55, No 4, pp 45–48.

Cupper, L G (1987) 'An employer's viewpoint on the use of dialogue in industrial and employee relations', *Melbourne University Business School Association Journal*, Vol 10, No 1.

Desatnick, R L (1983) 'Marketing HRD: the credibility gap that's got to go', *Training*, Vol 20, No 6.

Drucker, P F (1974) *Management: Tasks, Responsibilities, Practices*, Harper & Row.

Guest, D E (1987) 'Human resource management and industrial relations', *Journal of Management Studies*, Vol 24, No 5, pp 503–521.

Guest, D E (1989) 'Personnel and HRM: can you tell the difference?', *Personnel Management*, Vol 13, No 1, pp 48–51.

Kotler, P (1984) *Marketing Management*, 5th edn, Prentice-Hall, Englewood Cliffs, NJ.

McDonald, M (1989) *Marketing Plans: How to Prepare Them; How to Use Them*, 2nd edn, Heinemann, Oxford.

Miller, P (1989) 'Strategic HRM: what it is and what it isn't', *Personnel Management*, February, pp 46–51.

Murphy, P E and Enis, B M (1985) *Marketing*, Scott, Foresman.

Payne, A F T (1988) 'Developing a marketing oriented organisation', *Business Horizons*, Vol 31, No 3, pp 46–53.

Peter, T J and Waterman, R H Jr (1982) *In Search of Excellence: Lessons from America's Best Run Companies*, Harper & Row.

Reichheld, F F and Sasser, W E Jr (1990) 'Zero defections: quality comes to services', *Harvard Business Review*, September–October, pp 105–111.

Vandermerwe, S and Gilbert, D (1989) 'Making internal service market driven', *Business Horizons*, Vol 32, No 6, pp 83–89.

PART THREE

MANAGING RELATIONSHIPS BEFORE, DURING AND AFTER THE SALE

7

KEY ACCOUNT MANAGEMENT IN BUSINESS-TO-BUSINESS MARKETS

Tony Millman

INTRODUCTION

The latter half of the 1990s is expected to be a period in which academics and managers focus increasingly on operationalising the concept of relationship marketing. This is already evident in business-to-business markets where there is burgeoning interest in customer retention/development strategies against a background of centralised purchasing, supply base rationalisation and unprecedented levels of foreign competition.

One of the most popular and successful approaches to customer retention/development is key account management (KAM). Interpretations of the nature and appropriateness of KAM systems, however, vary across companies and industries, and care must be exercised in assessing the way contextual factors shape buyer/seller relationships and in distilling the elements of best practice.

The purpose of this chapter, therefore, is to explore the nature of KAM in business-to-business markets, with particular emphasis on four interrelated conceptualisations, namely: KAM as an approach to customer segmentation; as the basis of a customer retention strategy; as a growth/development strategy; and as an organisational process. These conceptualisations have been elicited from two main sources: first, empirical research on relational aspects of KAM in selected buyer/seller dyads; second, observations from running management development programmes for account managers at Cranfield School of Management. The chapter then goes on to examine the training/development implications for managers occupying boundary-spanning roles.

KAM AS AN APPROACH TO CUSTOMER SEGMENTATION

What is a Key Account?

For the purpose of this chapter we define a key account as a customer in a business-to-business market identified by a selling company as of strategic importance (Fiocca, 1982; Campbell and Cunningham, 1983; Yorke and Droussiotis, 1993; Millman, 1994). We offer this definition because the term 'key account' tends to be used interchangeably with 'national account' and 'major account', both in the literature and in practice.

Definitions of national accounts and major accounts typically focus upon the geographical spread and size of customers, emphasising such criteria as: sales turnover, profitability, centralised purchasing systems, requirements of special treatment, and so on (Shapiro and Posner, 1976; Platzer, 1984; Colletti and Tubridy, 1987; Barrett, 1986; Cooper and Gardner, 1993). National accounts, we would argue, are a sub-category of key accounts, which may require particular attention and specific ways of managing them, but to suggest that key accounts (and major accounts) are necessarily national is to ignore the importance of other accounts within the seller's customer portfolio.

Campbell and Cunningham (1983) classified customers as yesterday's customers, today's regular, today's special and tomorrow's customers, suggesting that long-term profitability may well depend on the cultivation and management of customers who do not represent a large proportion of present sales turnover/profit, but whose *future potential* renders them of strategic importance. Sellers may wish to consider some customers as key accounts, for example for their prestige or reference value, or because they facilitate access to new markets and technologies.

Key accounts, therefore, may be small or large by comparison with the seller; operate locally, nationally or globally; exhibit a willingness to forge close long-term relationships with sellers; or operate at arm's length and be brutally opportunistic in their dealings. What is critical in classifying customers as key accounts is that they are considered by the seller to be of strategic importance.

Key Account Profitability as a Segmentation Variable

If KAM is to be successful, there is an urgent need to develop reliable measures of performance and customer value which support strategic marketing decisions. Of these measures, the most promising involves attempts to segment individual customers or groups of customers in terms of their profitability.

Unfortunately, one of the major obstacles to implementing customer account profitability analysis is the inability of most management accounting systems to cope with cost allocation, or more precisely, defining what attributable costs should be included in the analysis at different levels of aggregation. On the one hand, it is important to avoid merely spreading direct costs across the customer base in some arbitrary way; and on the other, it is desirable to include the real cost of servicing particular customers. Every account manager or sales administration manager knows intuitively what a 'good' customer looks like. The point is that different customers invariably have different sales mixes, order patterns, locations, levels of sophistication, etc. What is required is a means of capturing the incremental costs above and beyond routine order processing and service support.

A particular problem in some engineering and manufacturing companies is to ensure that the costs incurred in 'customisation' are included, together with any special requests for stockholding, technical service, maintenance, etc. Making these costs visible is important because in an effort to please and retain customers, we have found numerous key account managers making loose promises and concessions which erode profitability. Similar promises are frequently made by technical managers, who are outside the direct control of the key account managers, resulting in 'specification drift' and cost/time overruns, both before and after a price has been agreed. Product/project cost monitoring should pick up these items, but by then it is often too late.

Sellers face a multitude of decisions related to their portfolio of key accounts: Which accounts are growing, for example, and is growth in profit commensurate with growth in sales? When should a customer be regarded as a key account? Are some customers claiming more than their fair share of service/support? What might be the impact of losing part or all of the business from a key account? When should the level of relational activity be raised? Computer systems offer plenty of scope for improving customer account profitability analysis: first, to generate financial performance reports on a regular basis; and second, to assess the future profit impact of key account decisions and changes in the trading environment. At the time of writing, few seller companies in our sample had installed sophisticated systems of this kind, and for most such investment seemed a long way off.

KAM AS A CUSTOMER RETENTION STRATEGY

Seller and Buyer Perspectives

Relationship marketing is often conceptualised as involving migration along a continuum from the 'transactional' (seeking and acquiring new customers) to the 'relational' (developing and enhancing relationships to secure repeat business and moving towards full partnership) – see Jackson (1985), Gronroos (1990), Christopher, Payne and Ballantyne (1991), Payne (1993), Millman (1993).

Retaining customers, therefore, at least from the seller's perspective, is seen primarily as a cumulative process of building customer loyalty and achieving higher levels of customer satisfaction. The merit of a segmented model or continuum of this kind is that it allows identification of the value placed on long-term relationships by particular customers and groups of customers – a useful starting point for tailoring customer retention strategies and setting up key account management systems.

The greatest danger in formulating/implementing customer retention strategies lies in the one-sided approach adopted by some academics and practitioners. This is reflected in the literature. Marketing academics, for example, have laid claim to the emerging concept of relationship marketing and are vigorously constructing/testing integrative models of customer retention which encompass such areas as customer service, branding, public relations, database management, consultative selling and, of course, key account management. In contrast, purchasing academics are examining relational aspects of supply chain management, supplier development, total quality management, electronic data interchange, supply partnerships, etc. While professional self-interest is likely to perpetuate separate seller and buyer perspectives, hopefully common sense will prevail and researchers will not lose sight of the marketing/purchasing interface. Hence the focus on buyer/seller dyadic relationships in the Cranfield KAM research programme.

Receptivity to Key Account Management Systems

The notion of *receptivity* is central to relationship development. No matter how appropriate KAM systems may appear in particular buyer/seller situations, it is clear from our research that different companies are often at different stages of readiness to adopt KAM.

Senior managers in both buyer and seller companies may extol the virtues of getting closer to suppliers/customers, but in reality many either do not wish to migrate the whole way to full partnership or they wish to do so at a different rate than the other partner would like. This potential mismatch in objectives/aspirations has emerged as a critical issue in our research on buyer/seller dyads and is best illustrated by reference to two examples.

The first example involved divisions of two supposedly customer-oriented multinational companies agreeing to develop jointly an advanced pigmentation system. The seller perceived the arrangement as 'moving towards a long-term partnership' with good prospects for broadening into other product/market areas, whereas the buyer (user) regarded it as a 'single project opportunity'. When the buyer recommended termination after two years, with no resulting sales volume, the seller was shocked and disappointed initially, and later, rather bitter about the way they had been treated.

Not only was the project terminated, it was disclosed that the buyer had been 'backing two horses', ie running a similar project in parallel with another supplier which turned out to be more promising. A 'lost opportunity' analysis conducted by the seller revealed that there was minimal top management involvement and the relationship was largely operational and based on technical exchanges and sales forecasts.

A second, more successful approach to KAM, based on a deep understanding of customer behaviour, is being pursued by a supplier of cleaning equipment and consumables to the food/drink industry. Two of their key accounts compete in the global market with similar product ranges, processing facilities and distribution networks. Their attitude towards building closer buyer/seller relationships, however, could not be more polarised. The first account (the acknowledged market leader) tends to prefer an 'arms's length' relationship with all the suppliers, using its purchasing power to focus tightly on price, specified performance and delivery criteria. In contrast, the second account has demonstrated a desire for close long-term relationships by setting up mechanisms for information sharing and joint applications development. Pricing is competitive, but kept continually under review and open to adjustment as the business environment changes.

In essence, the seller company handles both key accounts effectively because it recognises that *receptivity* to KAM is a major segmentation variable – each segment (account) requiring a different allocation of resources to the relational mix as part of an account plan.

KAM AS A GROWTH/DEVELOPMENT STRATEGY

Faced with the trend towards centralised purchasing and supply base rationalisation, many selling companies focus their KAM activities on customer retention in order to bring a measure of stability to their operations. While this is a laudable aim, particularly in companies for which survival is threatened by foreign competition, it is seldom sufficient as a response to medium/long-term structural change in the business environment.

Most selling companies believe that by adopting KAM systems they are 'customer driven'. Often, they exhibit all the trappings of KAM and offer proof of effectiveness in the form of customer satisfaction ratings, competitor benchmarking, etc. Less evident is their ability to assess, and capitalise upon, the 'potential' of key accounts, ie the scope for increasing the share of profitable customers. Shortcomings in this entrepreneurial approach to growth/development may be attributed as much to a lack of in-depth understanding of their customers' business and how they add value as to the inadequacies of diagnostic support tools mentioned earlier. Our research has shown repeatedly that combining customer retention with building customer share is an essential feature of successful KAM.

KAM AS AN ORGANISATIONAL PROCESS

The Key Account Relational Development Cycle

Relationships evolve over time, with each specific transaction being affected by the history of the relationship, and the relationship modified by each specific exchange (Ford, Hakansson and Johanson, 1986). Individual transactions will not only be affected by market considerations, but also by relational or process factors (Symanski, 1988) which demand that different key account selling and management strategies are adopted as the relationship develops.

Our six-stage model of key account relational development (Millman and Wilson, 1994) provides a useful tool for examining sources of competitive advantage and characterising managerial behaviour. The various stages of the model will now be outlined.

Pre-KAM

Not all customers are key accounts. The task facing the sales and marketing function in the pre-KAM stage is to identify those with the potential for moving towards key account status and to avoid wasteful investment in those accounts which do not hold that potential. Pre-KAM selling strategies are concerned with making basic product or service offerings available, whilst attempting to gather information about the customer in order to determine whether or not they have key account potential.

Early-KAM

Early-KAM is concerned with exploring opportunities for closer collaboration by identifying the motives, culture and concerns of the account; with targeting competitor strengths and weaknesses; and with persuading customers of the potential benefits they might enjoy as 'preferred' customers. A detailed understanding is required of the decision-making process and the structure and nature of the decision-making unit, as well as the buyer's business and the problems that relate to the value adding process.

At this stage, tentative adaptations will be made to the seller's offer in order to more closely match buyer requirements. The focus of the sales effort will be on building trust through consistent performance and open communications.

Sales people will need to demonstrate a willingness to adapt their offering to provide a bespoke solution to the buyer's problems. High levels of uncertainty about the long-term potential of the relationship may mean that they will need to promote the idea of non-standard product offerings into their own company. Where these attempts are unsuccessful, then 'benefit selling' and the level of personal service provided by the sales person may serve to differentiate the seller's offer.

Mid-KAM

As the relationship develops, so do levels of trust and the range of problems that the relationship addresses. The number of cross-boundary contacts will also increase with the sales person perhaps taking a less central role.

The account review process will tend to shift upwards to senior management level in view of the importance of the customer and the level of resource allocation, although the relationship may fall short of exclusivity and the activities of competitors within the account will require constant review.

Partnership KAM

Partnership KAM represents a mature stage of key account development.

The supplier is often viewed as an external resource of the customer and the sharing of sensitive commercial information becomes commonplace as the focus for activity is increasingly upon joint problem resolution.

Synergistic KAM

At this advanced stage of maturity, key account management goes 'beyond partnership' when there is a fundamental shift in attitude on the part of both buyer and seller and they come to see each other, not as two separate organisations, but as parts of a larger entity creating joint value (synergy) in the market-place.

Uncoupling KAM

Dissolution of a KAM relationship tends to be viewed in a pejorative way, as though a 'successful' relationship is by definition one of long duration. While in most cases buyers and sellers may perceive benefits in developing long-term relationships, we have uncovered some short-term relationships deemed to be successful by the participants and many others which, with the benefit of hindsight, were ill-conceived. As Low (1994) reminds us: 'Deciding when to get out of an existing relationship and into a new one would minimise the substantial economic, political and emotional cost associated with building a relationship that was never destined to last.' In essence, many relationships are propped up beyond their relevance or some event precipitates their termination, suggesting the need for an uncoupling process and contingency planning.

The foregoing model of key account relational development implies that fundamental changes in approach to customer needs are required by selling companies. This is evident in the total offering, which tends to focus on product/service attributes and benefits in the early stages of KAM, moving towards a 'bespoke' offering as buyers become more sophisticated and seek solutions to a wider range of problems.

Organizational Integration

Adoption of KAM systems typically requires setting up dedicated teams to coordinate day-to-day interaction under the umbrella of a long-term relationship. This has significant implications for organisation structure and communications processes in support of relational strategy.

For the seller this means positioning the key account management activity within the organisation in a way which gives due regard to its boundary-spanning role and the need for a fast reporting route to top management. In practice, we have found companies organised in a variety of ways, with many organised for their own internal convenience rather than for easy access by external parties such as customers, distributors and suppliers. This is, of course, why radical approaches to business process redesign have come to the fore in recent years.

While it may be argued that the origins of KAM lie in the sales function, there is mounting evidence to question whether KAM activities should be retained under sales or set up as a separate entity at general management level. On the one hand, the mere existence of KAM activities suggests a strategic perspective and growing involvement of staff from other functions. Separation, such as we have uncovered in our research, appears to be partly rooted in the unease felt by senior executives as they struggle to balance short-term and long-term demands, and partly a response to the external driving forces alluded to earlier. On the other hand, there is clearly a problem when accounts are upgraded to key accounts and taken out of the sales function, where they may have been nurtured by sales/service people over many years. Upgrading an account is a relatively simple operation when sales people are trained up and transferred along with the key account, but it can be disheartening for those who stay behind to grow, develop and maintain the usually larger number of accounts perceived to be of lesser strategic importance. Such channel decisions, in our experience, are seldom implemented in a sensitive way and often undermine the process of generating the key accounts of the future.

IMPLICATIONS FOR MANAGEMENT PRACTICE

Salesforce Training

Much of the traditional skills training associated with selling and sales management is of the generic 'how to do it' variety with little theoretical/empirical underpinning and paying scant attention to context. Such techniques are inappropriate in the case of key account selling and many trainers have done the profession a disservice by putting the marketing/purchasing interface in adversarial mode.

What seems to be required now is a shift from confrontational and transactional selling styles towards relational and consultative approaches, consistent with the various stages of KAM development. This extends the role of the sales person in KAM to encompass a wider set of context-specific activities which demand more of the individual sales person and of their managers. Changing the prevailing mind-set is a major challenge. As the old adage goes: 'Knowledge and skills are relatively easy to acquire. Attitudinal and cultural change takes a little longer!'

Role of the Key Account Manager

While we are not in a position to offer a tight prescription of the key account manager's role, tentative support for four main requirements is emerging from our exploratory research:

- responsibility for sales/profit growth of one or more key accounts, consistent with the business objectives of the seller's total portfolio of key accounts;
- coordination and tailoring the seller's total offering to key accounts;
- facilitating multilevel, multifunctional exchange processes;
- promoting KAM systems within his/her own company.

The key account manager, like members of the salesforce and customer service/support staff, performs the boundary-spanning role of 'relationship builder', where the incumbent is simultaneously negotiator, consultant, interpreter of customer needs/values, mediator, customer's advocate/friend, information broker, and so on (Millman, 1994). This demands the recruitment/training of high calibre people who are not only sufficiently 'rounded' to be able to diagnose/analyse complex commercial and technical situations, but also equipped to cope with highly politicised interaction, together with personal tensions and ambiguities inherent in the boundary-spanning role.

The last point is important because it spawns several penetrating questions about the apparent vulnerability of selling companies which depend heavily on one person occupying a pivotal role in achieving customer orientation. Why, for example, despite widespread awareness that multilevel, multifunctional relationships reduce the risk of total relational breakdown, do some key account managers fail to develop such relationships? Do key account managers trust their top managers and colleagues to form relationships with counterparts in the buying company? Why, and under what circumstances, do some key account managers form stronger bonds with customers than with their own employer? What set of relational skills/competencies is necessary for effective KAM? Researching these questions would yield valuable insights into how key account managers spend their time and into the influence of softer variables such as organisational culture and personal management style.

CONCLUDING REMARKS

Our ongoing study of the nature of KAM offers tentative support for the notion of a key account relational development cycle. We observe, however, that the way many selling companies have managed the overall transition from the relatively narrow focus of key account selling to the broader requirements of key account management has proved problematic. Indeed, much of what executives call KAM lacks a strategic perspective and is in most respects still in the realms of key account selling. This may be largely attributed to the strong sales orientation among top/middle managers in some companies and the uncomfortable relationship between the marketing and sales functions in others.

At top management level, recurring themes emerging from our research are: limitations on the amount of time top managers devote to key accounts, the variable quality of their exchanges with customers, and their often strained relationships with key account managers. In contrast, at middle management level we have been very cautious when attempting to interpret behaviour because so many of our sample companies were in a state of flux. Downsizing and delayering in both buying and selling companies, for example, has left many middle managers overloaded and unsure of their new roles. Few senior managers have recognised the negative impact of such internal turbulence on their company's knowledge base and long-term relationships.

The most striking observations from our work is how the presence/absence of a few enthusiastic and competent people occupying critical positions in buyer and seller companies can ease progression to a mature stage of KAM. While we have mentioned competencies and, by implication, best practice, we hesitate to prescribe 'hard' and 'soft' measures too closely, although this would be our intention ultimately. Nevertheless, our current state of understanding suggests that management training/development of seller company staff in two areas would not go amiss. The first may be summarised as a better appreciation of the process of matching the seller's total offering with increasingly dynamic supply chain developments in some industries. This requires the acquisition of knowledge of key accounts and their industry context, coupled with diagnostic and analytical skills related to customer behaviour and performance. The second is the urgent need for a systematic approach to the tricky area of relationship building. This has implications for individual, team and company level development. Much greater awareness is required, for example, of relationships as an integral part of the total product/service offering and overall positioning strategy.

References

Barrett, J (1986) 'Why major account selling works', *Industrial Marketing Management*, Vol 15, pp 63–73.

Campbell, N and Cunningham, M (1983) 'Customer analysis for strategy development in industrial markets', *Strategic Management Journal*, Vol 4, pp 360–380.

Christopher, M, Payne, A and Ballantyne, D (1991) *Relationship Marketing: Bringing Quality, Customer Service and Marketing Together*, Butterworth-Heinemann, Oxford.

Colletti, J A and Tubridy, G S (1987) 'Effective major account sales management', *Journal of Personal Selling and Sales Management*, Vol 7, pp 1–10.

Cooper, M C and Gardner, J T (1993) 'Building good business relationships: more than just partnering or strategic alliances', *International Journal of Physical Distribution and Logistics Management*, Vol 23, No 6, pp 14–26.

Fiocca, R (1982) 'Account portfolio analysis for strategy development', *Industrial Marketing Management*, Vol 11, pp 53–62.

Ford, D, Hakansson, H and Johanson, J (1986) 'How do companies interact?', *Industrial Marketing and Purchasing*, Vol 1, No 1, pp 26–41.

Gronroos, C (1990) *The Marketing Strategy Continuum: Towards a Marketing Concept for the 1990s*, Swedish School of Economics and Business Administration, Working Paper 201.

Jackson, B B (1985) *Winning and Keeping Industrial Customers: The Dynamics of Customer Relationships*, Lexington Books.

Low, D (1994) *Long-Term Relationships in Industrial Marketing: Reality or Rhetoric?*, Working Paper 2/1994, Department of Marketing, University of Western Sydney, Nepean, Australia.

Millman, A F (1993) *The Emerging Concept of Relationship Marketing*, presented at the Conference on Industrial Marketing and Purchasing (IMP), University of Bath, UK, September.

Millman, A F (1994) *Relational Aspects of Key Account Management*, presented at the Fourth Seminar of the European Network for Project Marketing and Systems Selling, University of Pisa, Italy, April.

Millman, A F and Wilson, K J (1994) *From Key Account Selling to Key Account Management*, presented at the Conference on Industrial Marketing and Purchasing (IMP), University of Groningen, The Netherlands, September.

Payne, A (1993) *The Essence of Services Marketing*, Prentice-Hall.

Platzer, L C (1984) *Managing National Accounts*, Report No 850, The Conference Board, New York.

Shapiro, B P and Posner, R (1976) 'Making the major sale', *Harvard Business Review*, Vol 54, No 2, March–April, pp 68–78.

Szymanski, D M (1988) 'Determinants of selling effectiveness: the importance of declarative knowledge to the personal selling concept, *Journal of Marketing*, Vol 52, pp 64–77.

Yorke, D and Droussiotis, G (1993) *The Use of Customer Portfolio Theory – An Empirical Survey*, presented at the Conference on Industrial Marketing and Purchasing (IMP), University of Bath, UK, September.

8

MANAGING CUSTOMER RELATIONSHIPS FOR PROFIT*

Kaj Storbacka, Tore Strandvik and Christian Grönroos

INTRODUCTION

The chain of impact of service quality on satisfaction and satisfaction on customer retention (customer loyalty), and further customer retention on profitability has been addressed by, among others, Rust and Zahorik (1993). They note that there might be some scepticism among managers about the profitability of service improvement, ie increased service quality. The dominating perspective within service quality research has been to assume that service quality has a positive correlation with satisfaction, which in turn will lead to increased purchase loyalty. However, most of the published academic studies have looked only at the link between service quality and satisfaction. A few have also included the effect on behaviour in the form of purchase intentions. Purchase intention stated at the point of time when a service episode has just occurred does not necessarily have a high predictive power. A stated intention might be seen as an ideal, which can be different from the actual behaviour, influenced by contingencies. There is a lack of studies investigating customer relationship economics, ie the link between perception measures (service quality, satisfaction, intentions) and action measures (purchase loyalty, purchase volume, word-of-mouth behaviour and long-term *customer relationship profitability*). Only the actual acts by customers influence the firm's profits and long-term profitability.

The current satisfaction paradigm is based on the assumption that customers' actions are based on their perception of quality and satisfaction, that they are free to act and choose, and that a loyal customer is more profitable than a less loyal customer. Implicitly this kind of argument contains a number of assumptions that might be debatable. Our intention

* This chapter was first published in the *International Journal of Service Industry Management*, Vol 5, No 5, 1994, pp 21–28, and is reproduced with permission.

is to pinpoint some of the assumptions which are present in the dominating line of thought.

The purpose of the chapter is to discuss factors affecting customer relationship economics and customer profitability in light of the current service quality and customer satisfaction paradigm. Our basic argument is that in the service quality literature a number of assumptions are made about how quality leads to profitability. These should be verified in empirical research. According to Storbacka (1994a) quality and profitability can be studied at both an individual level and a customer base or market level. In this chapter we are focusing on the individual level but from the firm's point of view. Examples from the financial services sector are used as illustrations in the text but the conceptual framework should be applicable to all kinds of services.

A RELATIONSHIP MARKETING PERSPECTIVE

Marketing theory has generally been oriented towards how to acquire customers – how to create a transaction. Berry (1983) contends that marketing in order to protect the customer base is becoming increasingly important in services, owing to the fact that deregulation creates situations with an increased supply of essentially similar services. Grönroos, (1990, 1994) suggests a relationship definition of marketing:

> Marketing is to establish, maintain, and enhance relationships with customers and other partners, at a profit, so that the objectives of the parties involved are met. This is achieved by a mutual exchange and fulfilment of promises.

Such relationships are usually, but not necessarily, long term. On the basis of the above definition, the profitability of relationships is one of the key goals of marketing. To illustrate the relationship marketing approach we can make a comparison with the traditional transaction marketing view (Grönroos, 1994). In a relationship perspective the focus is not on service encounters (or transactions) as such. The encounter is rather seen as an element in an ongoing sequence of episodes between the customer and the service firm. Thus marketing, service quality and customer satisfaction have to be analysed both on an episode level and on a relationship level. Second, relationship marketing tends to be more focused on keeping customers and enhancing the relationship with them.

A similar mode of thinking has been proposed by contrasting offensive marketing strategy with defensive marketing strategy (Fornell, 1992; Fornell and Wernerfelt, 1987). This approach does not have its roots in either industrial or service marketing but has emerged within traditional consumer goods marketing. Offensive marketing would focus on obtaining new customers and increasing customers' purchase frequency while defensive marketing is concerned with minimizing customer turnover. The basic argument is that the cost of obtaining a new customer exceeds the cost of retaining an existing customer. Fornell and Wernerfelt (1987) argue that in non-growth markets competition centres on more or less dissatisfied customers. Offensive marketing strives to attract competitors' dissatisfied customers while defensive marketing is geared to managing the dissatisfaction among a firm's own customers. Fornell (1992) has further developed the argument of how satisfaction is related to market share and profitability. He notes that customer satisfaction is a future-oriented indicator of the profits of a company. Customer satisfaction can therefore be seen as an important complement to traditional measures of performance such as return on investment, market share and profit. A defensive strategy has two components, customer satisfaction and switching barriers. Switching barriers make it costly for a customer to switch to another supplier. Different types of costs (search costs, learning costs, emotional costs), cognitive effort and risk factors (financial, psychological, social) constitute switching barriers from the customer's point of view. The basic argument is, in other words, that profitability is enhanced by focusing on existing customers because satisfaction leads to lower costs, higher customer retention and higher revenue.

FROM SERVICE QUALITY TO CUSTOMER RELATIONSHIP PROFITABILITY

The basic assumption is that customer satisfaction drives profitability (Gronroos, 1990). The assumption is based on the idea that by improving the quality of the provider's service, customers' satisfaction is improved. A satisfied customer creates a strong relationship with the provider and this leads to relationship longevity (or customer retention – customer loyalty). Retention again generates steady revenues and by adding the revenues over time customer relationship profitability is improved. Thus the firm can utilise potential customer relationship opportunities in a favourable way.

When analysing this logic we argue that it is based on simplifications that in many industries create practical problems. We argue that there are other aspects that influence the proposed sequence. Based on the authors' experience of empirical studies of service quality on the one hand (Liljander and Strandvik, 1993a, 1993b, 1994, 1995; Strandvik and Liljander, 1994, 1995), and customer profitability on the other hand

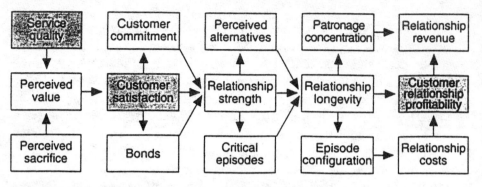

Note: The shaded boxes represent the established paradigm

Figure 8.1 A relationship profitability model

(Storbacka, 1992, 1993, 1994a, 1994b; Storbacka and Luukinen, 1994), we propose a conceptual framework as depicted in Figure 8.1. The framework incorporates the basic sequence: service quality leads to customer satisfaction, which leads to relationship strength, which leads to relationship longevity, which leads to customer relationship profitability – but it also adds new perspectives to the sequence.

In order to structure the discussion we shall examine more closely the most important of the links between the different constructs. The first link deals with the *relation between service quality and customer satisfaction.* The second link deals with the *relation between customer satisfaction and relationship strength.* The third link deals with the *relation between relationship strength and relationship longevity* and the final link deals with *how relationship longevity is connected to customer relationship profitability.* In this sequence, the static perception of service quality inherent in most conceptual and measurement models is developed towards a dynamic concept of relationship quality.

As the main purpose of the chapter is to discuss the sequence and the links we have chosen to define the constructs in Figure 8.1 in a compressed form in Table 8.1.

LINK 1: THE LINK BETWEEN SERVICE QUALITY AND CUSTOMER SATISFACTION

One important aspect in the model is that service quality and satisfaction can be experienced both at an episode and a relationship level. There has been some confusion regarding the differences between service quality and satisfaction. It is only recently that the conceptual and empirical overlap between the two concepts has raised a debate among service

Table 8.1 Description of concepts in the relationship profitability model

Concept	Definition
Perceived service quality	Customers' cognitive evaluation of the service across episodes compared with some explicit or implicit comparison standard
Perceived sacrifice	Perceived sacrifices (price, other sacrifices) across all service episodes in the relationship compared with some explicit or implicit comparison standard
Perceived value	Service quality compared with perceived sacrifice
Customer satisfaction	Customers' cognitive and affective evaluation based on the personal experience across all service episodes within the relationship
Commitment	Commitment is defined as the parties' intentions to act and their attitude towards interacting with each other. High relationship value will affect commitment positively
Relationship strength	Measured both as purchase behaviour and as communication behaviour (word of mouth, complaints). Loyalty (repetitive purchase behaviour) which is based also on positive commitment by the customer indicates a stronger relationship. The behaviour is also affected by the bonds between the customer and the service provider
Bonds	Exit barriers that tie the customer to the service provider and maintain the relationship. These are legal, economic, technological, geographical, time, knowledge, social, cultural, ideological and psychological bonds
Critical episodes	Episodes that are of critical importance for the continuation of the relationship. Episodes can be critical based on the size of the values exchanged during the episode, compared with the parties' resources and based on the experiences during the episode
Patronage concentration	The share of the customer's cash flow in a certain industry in which the customer chooses to concentrate on one provider
Relationship longevity	The length of a relationship
Episode configuration	The episode types and number of each type that occur over time in a relationship between a provider and a customer
Relationship revenue	The total revenue generated from a customer relationship during a fiscal year
Relationship cost	The total cost incurred from serving a customer relationship – including direct and indirect costs – during a fiscal year
Relationship profitability	Relationship revenue – relationship costs

quality researchers (Anderson and Fornell, 1994; Bitner and Hubbert, 1994; Bolton and Drew, 1994; Dabholkar, 1993; Liljander and Strandvik, 1993b, 1994; Oliver, 1993; Parasuraman *et al.*, 1994; Rust and Oliver, 1994). The debate has been concerned with similarities and links between the concepts and the discussion has mainly been kept on a conceptual level.

Liljander and Strandvik (1994) have suggested that perceived service quality can be seen as an outsider perspective, a cognitive judgement of a service. It need not even be experienced; it can be based on knowledge about a service provider through word-of-mouth or advertising. It is, however, usually also based on experiences with the service.

Satisfaction would, according to Liljander and Strandvik, refer to an insider perspective, the customer's own experiences of a service where the outcome has been evaluated in terms of what value was received, in other words what the customer had to give to get something. A customer could, therefore, respond on a questionnaire that a particular bank is of high quality, even if this did not mean that this customer was satisfied using the bank. It might have too high interest rates on loans or it might not fit the customer's preferences for some other reason. In the high/high and low/low boxes in Figure 8.2 there is a correspondence between the two concepts, as a function of high value, or fit between customers' preferences and the service. In this figure four combinations of service quality and satisfaction have been depicted. Low and high in the figure refer to perceived judgements. Thus, what is low for one customer may be high for another.

| | Customer satisfaction | |
	Low	High
Low Service quality	Expected outcome	Service fits the customer's restricted budget or fits the customers preferences
High	Service too expensive for the customer or does not fit the customer's preferences	Expected outcome

Source: Liljander and Strandvik (1994)

Figure 8.2 The link between service quality and customer satisfaction

In the two other boxes the paradox is visible. Service quality can be judged low but the customer is satisfied. This might be the case when the service fits the customer's budget or is priced according to the low quality. It might also be the result of low sacrifice of some other type, for example acquisition costs. Low satisfaction but high perceived service quality is also a possible outcome. The customer judges the service to be of high quality but is not satisfied because what was given (price) is not perceived to correspond to the received quality. This clearly has to do with the budget of different customers and their preferences for different attributes and alternative ways of spending their money and time. Satisfaction is thus related to perceived value.

LINK 2: THE LINK BETWEEN CUSTOMER SATISFACTION AND RELATIONSHIP STRENGTH

One way to achieve strong relationships and, thus, long relationships is to ensure that customers are satisfied. The proposition is that dissatisfied customers will defect; the relationship ends. Several researchers have proposed that this is a simplification of the matter (Liljander and Strandvik, 1993a, 1993b; Oliver, 1989; Woodruff *et al.*, 1983; Zeithaml *et al.*, 1993). Customers seem to have a zone of tolerance, which according to Zeithaml *et al.*, (1993) can be defined as the difference between an adequate and a desired level of service. According to Kennedy and Thirkell (1988), customers are 'prepared to absorb some unfavorable evaluations before expressing them in terms of net dissatisfaction.' In retail banking this would suggest that customers may be dissatisfied with a service episode and still be satisfied with the relationship. Reichheld (1993) argues that customer satisfaction may not lead to retention. He concludes that between 65 per cent and 85 per cent of customers who defect say they were satisfied or very satisfied with their former supplier.

Gronhaug and Gilly (1991) argue that dissatisfied customers may remain loyal because of high switching costs. Establishing a new relationship represents some sort of investment of effort, time and money which constitutes a significant barrier to the customer's taking action when dissatisfied with a distinct interaction during a relationship.

There are obviously aspects of *relationship strength* other than customer satisfaction. These include, for instance, the existence of *bonds* between the customer and the provider. These bonds function as switching barriers beside customer satisfaction. Another dimension relates to the customer's (and the provider's) *commitment* to the relationship. Commitment might be based on customers' intentions and plans for the future.

Within the interaction approach and network approach to industrial marketing six different types of bonds have been suggested (Dwyer *et al.*, 1987; Easton and Araujo, 1989; Ford, 1980; Hakansson, 1982; Muller and Wilson, 1988; Wilson and Mummalaneni, 1986). These are social bonds, technological bonds, knowledge bonds, planning bonds and legal/economic bonds. Although these six bonds can also be found in consumer markets, they are somewhat limited for this purpose. In addition to these bonds, Liljander and Strandvik (1995) have suggested that the consumer may also have geographical, cultural, ideological and psychological bonds to a service provider. They propose that ten different types of bond can be identified in the consumer market: legal, economic, technological, geographical, time, knowledge, social, cultural, ideological and psychological.

Liljander and Strandvik (1995) argue that the first five bonds – legal, economic, technological, geographical and time bonds – constitute effective exit barriers for the consumer. They can be seen as contextual factors that cannot easily be influenced by the customer but can be observed and managed by the service firm. They are more likely to be perceived in a negative sense than the other five bonds. It is, for example, associated with high costs for the customer to switch bank if he or she is tied up with a mortgage in one bank. These bonds can prevent the customer from switching banks even when the service given is of low quality.

The other five bonds – knowledge, social, cultural, ideological and psychological bonds – represent perceptual factors which are difficult to measure and manage by the firm. For example the cultural, ideological and psychological are directly connected to the customer's values and preferences. A psychological bond, where the customer is convinced of the superiority of a bank, is probably a very effective exit barrier. The consequence of bonds is that the customer might accept lower levels of service quality, compared with other service companies, without breaking the relationship.

An additionally interesting perspective on how relationship strength is achieved is the *commitment* of customers. Liljander and Strandvik (1993b) conclude that commitment and loyalty are related concepts, although they emanate from different research traditions. Loyalty is usually defined as observed purchase behaviour. This is consistent with the transactional perspective used within traditional consumer marketing. Commitment has been used within the interaction approach of industrial

Relationship strength

	Weak	Strong
Low	Expected outcome	Contextual or perceptual bonds outweigh the lack of satisfaction
High	Low customer commitment. The relationship is not perceived as important by the customer	Expected outcome

Customer satisfaction

Figure 8.3 The link between customer satisfaction and relationship strength

marketing. It refers to adaptation processes which are the result of the parties' intentions to act and positive attitudes towards each other. Liljander and Strandvik define loyalty as only repeat purchase behaviour within a relationship. Commitment is defined as the parties' intentions to act and their attitude towards interacting with each other. Loyalty can occur with three different types of commitment, positive, negative or no commitment. A negatively committed customer shows a negative attitude but might still buy repeatedly because of bonds. This also means that customer loyalty is not always based on a positive attitude, and long-term relationships do not necessarily require positive commitment from the customers. This distinction is important as it challenges the idea that customer satisfaction (the attitude) leads to long-lasting relationships (the behaviour).

We can conclude that customer satisfaction is only one dimension in increasing relationship strength (see Figure 8.3). Strong relationships can be dependent on perceived or contextual bonds that function as exit barriers. It is, however, important to note that the use of contextual barriers can generate latent dissatisfaction which emerges as the importance of the contextual bonds (for instance the legal bonds) decreases. In a retail banking context, for instance, a typical example of this is the defection of customers who have paid off their loans by which the banks have tied the customer.

Another important aspect that we have to consider is that the importance of the relationship for customers varies significantly. Some customers may be very committed to the relationship and for these customers the perceived satisfaction with the relationship is very important. Others may find the relationship basically unimportant and for these customers the satisfaction component is not as important.

LINK 3: THE LINK BETWEEN RELATIONSHIP STRENGTH AND RELATIONSHIP LONGEVITY

It seems plausible to assume that *relationship longevity* is of great importance to the provider both from an efficiency and profitability point of view. Assuming that we have a profitable customer relationship, a third question that we therefore have to ask – in addition to how to increase the relationship revenue and decrease relationship cost – is how can we ensure that the customer relationship lasts for as long a time as possible?

One way of analysing relationship longevity is to structure the analysis according to where the driving force for longevity has its origin. When analysing the customer relationship dyad it becomes obvious that longevity can originate from *relationship extrinsic factors* such as the market structure in which the relationship exists, and the possible geographical limitations (the customer moves to a geographical location in which the provider does not have a presence). Longevity can also originate in *relationship intrinsic factors* such as the relationship strength and the handling of critical episodes during the relationship.

An important relationship extrinsic factor relates to *market concentration*. A relationship in a monopolistic or oligopolistic market is obviously different from a relationship in a highly competitive market. The number of alternative providers, as perceived by the customer, influences her or his interest and the possibilities of evaluating alternatives. According to Campbell and Cunningham (1983), we can characterize relationships on the basis of the situation in the market, ie on the numbers of providers and customers in the market. Relationships are characterised by dependence when either the provider or the customer dominates. For instance, in a retail bank context, there are far fewer providers than customers, a particular customer's share of the provider's business is usually very limited, the customer usually buys a substantial proportion of all services from one provider, the customer needs the provider's skills, and the customer does not necessarily need customised services. In a retail banking environment, power and dependence in relationships are very much a function of the relative importance of the relationship to both parties. Small-volume customers have little power in the relationship, since bank survival does not depend on their business. High-volume customers, on the other hand, have considerable power, which they exercise especially in price negotiations. We can, nevertheless, conclude that from the point of view of power and dependence the relationship is not mutual in the sense that the parties are interdependent. Additionally we can conclude that the degree of differentiation in provider strategies seems to be inversely dependent on the degree of market concentration. In an oligopolistic market there are seldom major differences between the providers.

It is important to note that there are two aspects related to the market situation. First, there is the 'objective' market concentration which is easy to measure. The second aspect relates to the customer's perception of the market situation. The customer may perceive that there are few alternatives in the market because of the fact that some of the alternatives, in fact, are not a part of the customer's evoked set. The customer may, hence, be loyal to the relationship because of lack of perceived alternatives ('all banks are the same'), regardless of relationship strength.

When analysing relationship intrinsic factors we also have to consider how *critical episodes* are handled (Storbacka, 1994b). It is important to note that every episode does not carry the same importance or weight in the customer's evaluation of the relationship. Some of the episodes can be labelled routine episodes, whereas others can be labelled critical episodes. Routine episodes are characterised by low levels of mental involvement and routine behaviour. The customer can be said to play a large role in the production of a routine episode. The customer usually has a clear script guiding her or his behaviour during the episode. The script is acquired either by experience of the same or similar episode or by distinct guidance during the episode.

A critical episode can be defined as an episode that is of great importance for the relationship. The continuation of the relationship is dependent (both in a negative and positive way) on critical episodes. A successful critical episode can strengthen the relationship so that it may withstand several unsatisfactory routine episodes. On the other hand an unsuccessful critical episode may end the relationship abruptly although it may have been preceded even by years of satisfactory routine episodes and although the relationship has been judged to be strong.

Strandvik and Liljander (1994) have shown that one of the most critical episodes in a retail bank relationship is the negotiation of mortgages in connection with the acquisition of an apartment. A successful negotiation creates legal bonds that may last for 10–15 years, whereas an unsuccessful negotiation may end the relationship at once.

The definition of a critical episode is customer and situation specific. Customers have different backgrounds in terms of their experience of specific types of episode and in terms of their knowledge of a certain industry. This difference affects the customer as he or she enters the production process of a specific episode type. The difference in experience is clearly visible, for instance, when new episode patterns in the form of episode instruments (such as bank cards) or automatons are introduced. Even experienced customers feel insecure when confronted with the new expectations that the changed episode pattern puts on their behaviour during the episode. Hence the customer is mentally highly involved in the situation and the episode can be of critical significance for the relationship.

A routine episode can become a critical episode if, according to the customer, the adequate level of performance is not met. The episode then becomes what Bitner *et al.* (1990) call a 'critical incident' which makes the customer very involved and may end the relationship.

It is obvious, based on the above discussion, that relationship longevity is not always a function of relationship strength. There are many random factors that influence the development of a relationship. Most of the relationship extrinsic factors are such that the provider cannot influence them.

In the matrix in Figure 8.4 we have depicted some alternative links between the constructs. Although the relationship is weak it may last for a long time because of perceived lack of alternatives. It is important to note that relationship longevity may be a result of the fact that the episodes in the relationship have all been routine episodes. Thus the customer may feel that the relationship is not very important – or at least

	Relationship longevity	
	Short	**Long**
Weak	Expected outcome	Relationship continues due to bonds, and/or objective or perceived lack of alternatives
Strong	Poorly managed critical episode or insufficient service recovery ends relationship	Expected outcome

Relationship strength

Figure 8.4 The link between relationship strength and relationship longevity

not important enough to motivate the investment of time required to end the relationship. As soon as there is a poorly managed critical episode in the relationship the customer may become involved enough to take the time to choose another provider.

The importance of critical episodes is evident. Even strong relationships may end because of poorly managed critical episodes. This way of arguing can be related to the ideas about the importance of 'service recoveries' (Albrecht and Zemke, 1985; Hart *et al.*, 1990; Johnston, 1994).

Finally, we would like to conclude that obviously there are interdependencies between the constructs suggested above. An excellently managed critical episode naturally influences relationship strength, deepens the bonds and influences the customer's commitment to the provider.

LINK 4: THE LINK BETWEEN RELATIONSHIP LONGEVITY AND CUSTOMER RELATIONSHIP PROFITABILITY

Customer retention-based strategies are suggested by several researchers (Fornell, 1992; Reichheld, 1993; Rust and Zahorik, 1993; Rust, *et al.*, 1994). The proposed value of increased relationship longevity is based on the idea that keeping existing customers is cheaper than acquiring new ones and that the positive cash flow of the customer increases the value of long-lasting customer relationships.

The logic is, however, a simplification of the reality in many industries. The logic relies on the assumption that a customer relationship is profitable. Seeking to retain a hopelessly unprofitable customer in industries with continuous customer relationships cannot make business sense. It has been shown that it is not uncommon for approximately 50 per cent of the customers in a retail bank's customer base to be unprofitable (Storbacka, 1994a, 1994b; Storbacka and Luukinen, 1994). Storbacka (1994b) has shown that a very limited number of customers stand for a major part of the customer base's profits (10 per cent of customers may stand for 100 per cent of the profits). It is important to note that if it is impossible to enhance an unprofitable customer relationship in order to make it profitable there is no logic to strive towards relationship longevity. It is not self-evident that a provider should aim at long-term relationships with all customers.

Additionally, Storbacka and Luukinen (1994) report that, in a study of retail banking, customer satisfaction was higher among the most unprofitable customers in the customer base. They also conclude that customer satisfaction seemed to be a function of the relationship volume, ie the amount of deposits and lending that the customer had in the bank under consideration. We can, hence, speculate whether high volume, in fact, drives customer satisfaction rather than the opposite.

In order to understand the relation between relationship longevity and *customer relationship profitability* we need to understand how customer relationship profitability is achieved. Measuring customer profitability is a difficult task. Storbacka (1993, 1994b) has developed a framework which enables the analysis of profitability of particular relationships. The relationship generates a certain income that we call relationship revenue. Relationship revenue is the share of the total volume that the customer spends in the particular industry – the *total industry volume* (TIV). For example, in a retail banking context the customer may have deposits in several banks, or may have other means of saving, such as retirement insurance or investments in bonds and shares. The total industry volume, in turn, is a segment of the total amount of money that the customer has at his or her disposal, the *customer's total volume* (CTV). Customers have a certain amount of money at their disposal, and they divide this money among many different sectors of their life, including saving, housing, food, clothes, hospitality services, etc. Money in one sector is, of course, not available in another. The above logic is depicted in Figure 8.5.

As shown by Storbacka it would – in a relationship marketing approach – seem interesting to measure the provider's share of the total industry volume, TIV (or CTV, customer's total volume). We will call the RR/TIV ratio *patronage concentration* as it measures the actual patronage behaviour of the customer. The bigger the quota the stronger the provider's position is and the stronger the relationship can be argued to be. It is important to note that when RR<TIV, the customer has relationships with other providers in the same industry; the customer is

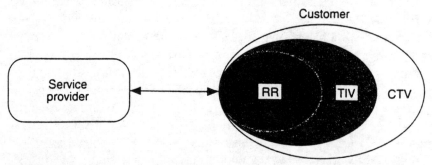

RR = Relationship revenue; TIV = Total industry volume; CTV = Customer's total volume
Source: Storbacka and Luukinen (1994)

Figure 8.5 Relationship revenue as a portion of the customer's total volume

only a partial customer. Partial customers obviously constitute a key potential when trying to increase relationship volume and thus relationship revenue.

Based on the above logic there are basically two ways to increase relationship revenue: to raise prices or to increase the patronage concentration of the customer under consideration, ie to increase RR/TIV. Usually the customers use several providers in the same industry – they are partial customers. Getting customers to concentrate their businesses on one provider increases the relationship revenue provided that the volume is acquired at a reasonable price. Additionally, the provider may want to increase the RR/CTV ratio, ie also try to cross-sell products outside its industry to the customer.

The key question is, however, how does a provider influence its customers to concentrate their patronage? Increasing relationship strength is obviously one dimension but certainly there are others to consider, relationship pricing being one of the more important ones.

The difficulty in calculating customer relationship profitability stems from the problems in allocating costs to specific relationships. Analysing relationship costs brings forth the need to identify cost drivers in relationships. Storbacka (1994b) argues that the best cost drivers are the episodes in a relationship. All relationships have a number of different types of episode that differ as to content, frequency, duration, etc. A long-term relationship with one provider can thus be described as a string of episodes. This is especially valid for services that are of a continuous

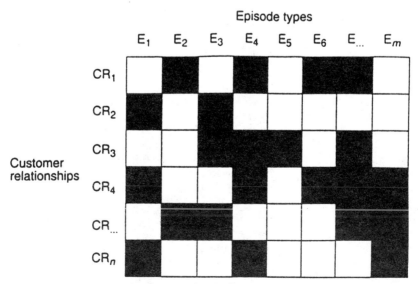

Figure 8.6 Episode configuration matrix

nature and that contain many different types of episode, such as retail banking. In order to analyse relationship costs we have to understand the relationship's configuration of episodes. Different customers generate different types of episode, they use different variations of each episode type, and they use different amounts of them. Each and every relationship is thus configured differently. Provided that we can create a typology of possible episodes and episode variants we can depict relationships with an *episode configuration matrix*, as shown in Figure 8.6 (inspired by Gummesson's (1993) notion of contextual matrices).

The horizontal axis describes the customer relationship and shows what kinds of episode the provider has had with the customer (not the number of episodes). The matrix can be analysed from the provider's perspective and from the customer's perspective. From the provider's point of view, we need to add the number of episodes. The total number of episodes is the sum of the demand of all customers who have chosen the specific type and variation of a discrete episode.

The intensity of episodes will be different for all customer relationships, independent of their relationship volume. This may relate to the fact that their main relationship rests with another provider. Customers who generate the same relationship revenue may, however, have different episode configurations. Thus the relationship costs and the profitability of the relationships will be different.

We can, based on the above way of arguing, conclude that long-term

| | **Customer relationship profitability** | |
	Low/negative	High
Short	Expected outcome	High revenues based on pricing and patronage concentration OR low relationship based on the episode configuration
Relationship longevity		
Long	High relationship costs due to unfavourable episode configuration OR low relationship revenue due to poor pricing or low patronage concentration	Expected outcome

Figure 8.7 The link between relationship longevity and customer relationship profitability

relationships are not a sufficient prerequisite for customer relationship profitability. We have to understand two other dimensions of the relationship: relationship revenue and relationship costs (see Figure 8.7). An important aspect of relationship revenue is the customer's patronage concentration. Another aspect which has received far too little attention (also in this chapter) is pricing. In contexts where continuous customer relationships dominate, the episode configuration of different customer relationships is a key explanatory factor that drives relationship costs and thus affects customer relationship profitability.

What is needed is a systematic analysis of relationship configurations: the services used by the customer, the episode configuration, and the delivery channels used by the customer (Storbacka, 1994b). Based on this information the providers can start a process of relationship enhancement, the key objective being to find ways to improve the profitability of customer relationships. One of the ways of doing this may be quality improvements but there are evidently many other issues to consider.

CONCLUSIONS AND FURTHER RESEARCH

In order to enable a firm to capitalize on available customer relationship economics opportunities and manage its customer relationships at a profit, the dynamic nature of such relationships has to be understood. The more or less static conceptual and measurement models of service quality of today have to be geared to this long-term perspective and towards a relationship quality notion. In this chapter we have pursued such a dynamic relationship quality perspective by linking together the concepts of service quality, customer satisfaction, relationship strength, relationship longevity and relationship profitability as well as related constructs.

The model developed in this chapter is thus a step towards a theory of relationship quality and profitability. From a theoretical point of view, this serves at least two important purposes. First, it adds the dynamic perspective to service quality which has been called for by service quality and customer satisfaction researchers for some time now (eg Grönroos, 1993). Second, it ties service management and its notion of perceived service quality to relationship marketing. This is an important step, because as successful relationship marketing to a large extent depends on the capability of firms to add value, through various types of service, to the core solutions offered to customers and clients, a relationship marketing strategy cannot be implemented without a thorough understanding of service management (eg Grönroos, 1994). Without an understanding of how to manage the quality of services in customer relationships on a long-term dynamic basis the firm will not be able to make full use of the competitive advantage opportunities offered by a relationship marketing strategy.

There is obviously a need for research on all the links suggested in the model. We would, however, like to emphasize two important areas. The first relates to pricing of services, both as a part of the sacrifice and as a major determinant of relationship revenue. Pricing is particularly important in services as it is a key communicator of value, and as it is used in many industries to regulate the demand for different types of episode over time. We also feel that there is very little written about pricing in the services marketing literature, especially from the perspective of pricing mechanisms and procedures.

The second area in which research is needed is relationship strength. As the strength of the relationship is of the utmost importance when designing action programmes for customer relationship enhancement, we feel that what is needed first is a good understanding of what constitutes relationship strength and how it can be affected. The ideal situation is of course that a customer relationship with a high level of customer relationship profitability would have a high level of relationship strength. If these customer relationships have a low level of relationship strength the organization under consideration is obviously very vulnerable and exposed to competitive action. If customers with negative profitability have a high level of relationship strength, the strength can be used to influence the customers' behaviour. As the relationship is strong it may also be possible to use more persuasive means of influence without endangering relationship longevity.

References

Albrecht, K and Zemke, R (1985) *Service America*, Dow Jones-Irwin, Homewood IL.

Anderson, E W and Fornell, C (1994) 'A customer satisfaction research prospectus', in Rust, R T and Oliver, R L (eds), *Service Quality: New Directions in Theory and Practice*, Sage, Thousand Oaks, CA, pp 241–268.

Berry, L M (1983) 'Relationship marketing', in Berry, L L, Shostack, G L and Upah, G (eds), *Emerging Perspectives on Services Marketing*, American Marketing Association, Chicago, Proceedings Series, pp 25–28.

Bitner, M J and Hubbert, A R (1994) 'Encounter satisfaction versus overall satisfaction versus quality: the customer's voice', in Rust, R T and Oliver, R L (eds), *Service Quality: New Directions in Theory and Practice*, Sage, London, pp 79–94.

Bitner, M J, Booms, B H and Tetreault, M S (1990) 'The service encounter: diagnosing favorable and unfavorable incidents', *Journal of Marketing*, Vol 54, January, pp 71–84.

Bolton, R N and Drew, J H (1994) 'Linking customer satisfaction to service operations and outcomes', in Rust, R T and Oliver, R L (eds), *Service Quality: New Directions in Theory and Practice*, Sage, London, pp 173–200.

Campbell, N C G. and Cunningham, M T (1983) 'Customer analysis for strategy development in industrial markets', *Strategic Management Journal*, Vol 4, pp 124–136.

Dabholkar, P A (1993) *Customer Satisfaction and Service Quality: Two Constructs or One?*, paper presented at the 1993 Conference on Consumer Satisfaction, Dissatisfaction and Complaining Behaviour, 2–5 June, Knoxville, TN.

Dwyer, R F, Schurr, P H and Oh, S (1987) 'Developing buyer–seller relationships,' *Journal of Marketing*, Vol 51 April, pp 11–27.

Easton, G and Araujo, L (1989) 'The network approach', in Hallen, L and Johanson, J (eds), *Networks of Relationships in International Industrial Marketing, Advances in International Marketing*, Vol 3, JAI Press, London, pp 97–119.

Ford, D (1980) 'The development of buyer–seller relationships in industrial markets', *European Journal of Marketing*, Vol 14, Nos 5/6 pp 339–354.

Fornell, C (1992) 'A national customer satisfaction barometer: the Swedish experience', *Journal of Marketing*, Vol 56, January, pp 6–21.

Fornell, C and Wernerfelt, B (1987) 'Defensive marketing strategy by customer complaint management: a theoretical analysis', *Journal of Marketing Research*, November, pp 337–346.

Gronhaug, K and Gilly, M C (1991) 'A transaction cost approach to consumer dissatisfaction and complaint actions', *Journal of Economic Psychology*, Vol 12, pp 165–183.

Grönroos, C (1990) *Service Management and Marketing*, Lexington Books, Toronto, Ontario.

Grönroos, C (1993) 'Toward a third phase in service quality research: challenges and future directions', in Swartz A T, Bowen, D E and Brown, S W (eds), *Advances in Services Marketing Management*, Vol II, JAI Press, Greenwich, CT, pp 49–64.

Grönroos, C (1994) 'From marketing mix to relationship marketing: towards a paradigm shift in marketing', *Management Decision*, Vol 32, No 2, pp 4–32.

Gummesson, E (1993), *Quality Management in Service Organizations – An Interpretation of the Service Quality Phenomenon and a Synthesis of International Research*, International Service Quality Association, New York.

Hakansson, H (1982) *International Marketing and Purchasing of Industrial Goods*, John Wiley & Sons, Chichester, pp 10–27.

Hart, C W L, Heskett, J L and Sasser, W E Jr (1990) 'The profitable art of service recovery', *Harvard Business Review*, Vol 68, July–August, pp 148–156.

Johnston, R (1994) 'Service recovery: an empirical study', in *Proceedings of the*

3rd International Research Seminar in Service Management, Institute d'Administration des Enterprises, Aix-en-Provence.

Kennedy, J R and Thirkell, P C (1988) 'An extended perspective on the antecedents of satisfaction', *Journal of Consumer Satisfaction, Dissatisfaction and Complaining Behaviour*, Vol 1, pp 2–9.

Liljander, V and Strandvik, T (1993a) 'Estimating zones of tolerance in perceived service quality', *International Journal of Service Industry Management*, Vol 4, No 2, pp 6–28.

Liljander, V and Strandvik, T (1993b) 'Different comparison standards as determinants of service quality', *Journal of Consumer Satisfaction, Dissatisfaction and Complaining Behaviour*, Vol 6, pp 118–132.

Liljander, V and Strandvik, T (1994) 'The relation between service quality, satisfaction and intentions', in Kunst, P and Lemmink, J (eds), *Quality Management in Services II*, Van Gorcum, Assen/Maastricht, The Netherlands.

Liljander, V and Strandvik, T (1995) 'The nature of customer relationships in services', in Swartz, T A, Bowen, D E and Brown, S W (eds), *Advances in Services Marketing and Management*, Vol 4, JAI Press, London, forthcoming.

Muller, K and Wilson, D T (1988) *Interaction Perspective in Business Marketing: An Exploratory Contingency Framework*, Institute for the Study of Business Markets, Report 11:1988, Pennsylvania State University, University Park, PA.

Oliver, R L (1989) 'Processing of the satisfaction response in consumption: a suggested framework and research propositions', *Journal of Consumer Satisfaction, Dissatisfaction and Complaining Behaviour*, Vol 2, pp 1–16.

Oliver, R L (1993) 'A conceptual model of service quality and service satisfaction: compatible goals, different concepts', in Swartz, A T, Bowen, D E and Brown, S W (eds), *Advances in Services Marketing Management*, Vol II, JAI Press, Greenwich, CT, pp 65–85.

Parasuraman, A, Zeithaml, V A and Berry, L L (1994) 'Reassessment of expectations as a comparison standard in measuring service quality: implications for further research', *Journal of Marketing*, Vol 58, January, pp 111–124.

Reichheld, F (1993) 'Loyalty-based management', *Harvard Business Review*, March–April, pp 64–73.

Rust, R T and Oliver, R L (1994) 'Service quality. Insights and managerial implications from the frontier', in Rust, R T and Oliver, R L (eds), *Service Quality. New Directions in Theory and Practice*, Sage, London, pp 1–20.

Rust, R T and Zahorik, A J (1993) 'Customer satisfaction, customer retention, and market share', *Journal of Retailing*, Vol 69, No 2, Summer, pp 193–215.

Rust, R T, Zahorik, A J and Keiningham, T L (1994) *Return on Quality – Measuring the Financial Impact of Your Company's Quest for Quality*, Probus, Chicago.

Storbacka, K (1992) *Developing Service Business Processes*, Working Paper No 250:1992, Swedish School of Economics and Business Administration, Helsinki, Finland.

Storbacka, K (1993) *Customer Relationship Profitability in Retail Banking,*

Research Report No 29, Swedish School of Economics and Business Administration, Helsinki, Finland.

Storbacka, K (1994a) *Analyzing the Profitability Distribution of Customer Bases in Retail Banks – The Stobachoff Index*, unpublished manuscript.

Storbacka, K (1994b), *The Nature of Customer Relationship Profitability. Analysis of Relationships and Customer Bases in Retail Banking*, Swedish School of Economics and Business Administration, No. 55, Helsingfors.

Storbacka, K and Luukinen, A (1994) 'Managing customer relationship profitability – case Swedbank', in the proceedings from *Banking and Insurance: From Recession to Recovery*, ESOMAR, Amsterdam.

Strandvik, T and Liljander, V (1994) 'Relationship strength in bank services', unpublished paper presented at 1994 Research Conference on Relationship Marketing, 11–13 June 1994, Atlanta, GA.

Strandvik, T and Liljander, V (1995) 'A comparison of episode performance and relationship performance for a discrete service', in Kleinaltenkamp, M (ed.), *Dienstleistungsmarketing – Konzeptionen und Anwendungen* Gabler Varlag, Deutscher Universitäts-Verlag, Wiesbaden.

Wilson, D T and Mummalaneni, V (1986) 'Bonding and commitment in buyer–seller relationships: a preliminary conceptualisation,' *Industrial Marketing and Purchasing*, Vol 1, No 3, pp 44–58.

Woodruff, R B, Cadotte, E R and Jenkins, R L (1983) 'Modeling consumer satisfaction processes using experience-based norms', *Journal of Marketing Research*, Vol 20, August, pp 296–304.

Zeithaml, V, Berry, L and Parasuraman, A (1993) 'The nature and determinants of customer expectations of service', *Journal of the Academy of Marketing Science*, Vol 21, No 1, Winter, pp 1–11.

9

MANAGING SERVICE RECOVERY*

Colin G Armistead, Graham Clark and Paula Stanley

INTRODUCTION

In service organisations the link has been made between customer retention over a period of time and profitability based on the assumption that the costs of maintaining customers are lower than the costs of recruiting new customers, and that there are further opportunities to sell additional services to the retained customer base and gain from their word of mouth advertising (Heskett, Sasser and Hart, 1990). Heskett (1992) has developed a proposition from the findings of customer retention that customer retention links to customer satisfaction. This assertion is supported by the work of Technical Assistance Research Programme Inc. (TARP) (Lash, 1989) who have demonstrated for a range of service organisations that the propensity to repurchase (ie to be retained) is linked to customer satisfaction.

The question arises as to what leads to customer satisfaction. The commonsense supposition that a positive outcome of service is linked to the matching of expectation and experience of the service provision has been demonstrated quantitatively in the use of the SERVQUAL approach of Parasuraman, Ziethaml and Berry (1988). However, the expression of satisfaction is linked not only to the provision of fault free service, but also to what happens when things go wrong. Hart, Heskett and Sasser (1990), Zemke (1991) and Zemke and Bell (1990) argue that service recovery (ie the ability to put things right for the customer in a meaningful way when they go wrong) is an important element in customer satisfaction. Again the work of TARP would lend support to the argument; they demonstrate that customer satisfaction and willingness of customers to stay with the

---

* This chapter was first published in Kunst, P and Lemmick, J (eds) (1995) *Managing Service Quality*, Paul Chapman Publishing Ltd and Jacques G M Hendrikx Innovation Trading B V, pp 93–106, and is reproduced with the permission of Innovation Trading BV.

service provider are strongly associated with the way in which complaints are dealt with. Poor resolution of complaints or a perception on the part of the customer of being mollified leads to greater ill feeling towards the service provider than if no complaint had been made.

In the literature there is no consideration of differences which might arise in business-to-business and business-to-consumer service provision, in both the need for service recovery and the way in which service recovery is triggered and carried out.

Another strand to the argument of what makes for customer satisfaction comes from a consideration of service guarantees and services pledges. Hart (1988) and Hart, Schlesinger and Maher (1992) argue the case for unconditional guarantees as a powerful way of gaining customer satisfaction by in effect saying 'we will meet all of your expectations'. It is acknowledged by these authors that while the benefits to customers of unconditional guarantees which are meaningful may be self evident, there are clearly risks associated with the cost of delivering on the promise.

THE SERVICE PROFIT CHAIN

The picture emerges of a chain of activities which are linked. Heskett (1992) refers to this as the chain of profitability. Customer retention results from customer satisfaction which is itself a consequence of unconditional guarantees (if offered) and the ability to recover when things go wrong. It is perhaps a reasonable proposition that if a service organisation is able to offer meaningful service guarantees without 'giving away the shop' it should be capable of delivering consistent service for 80–90 per cent of service encounters and only have to put things right either through recovery or delivering the guarantee in the remaining 10 per cent. It has been argued elsewhere (Armistead and Clark, 1992) that the ability to recover is linked in part to the adoption of 'coping' strategies in managing capacity. Consistency of service delivery will arise from designing delivery systems with capable structures, processes, people and systems, and having effective operational control in the areas of quality management, capacity management, and resource productivity management. The resulting chain to customer retention is shown in Figure 9.1.

THE ROLE OF EMPOWERMENT

The writers (Hart *el al.*, 1990) on service recovery suggest that the empowerment of front line staff is an important element in the ability to recover. The case for empowerment has been discussed by Bowen and Lawler (1992). These authors consider employees are empowered 'if they:

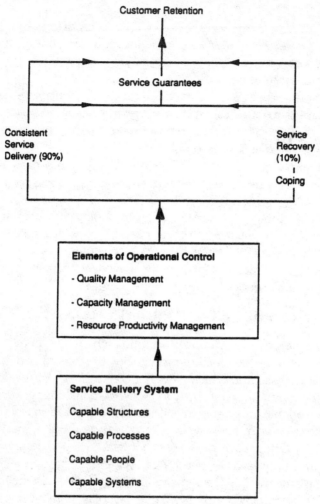

Figure 9.1 The chain to customer retention

- get information about organisational performance
- are rewarded for contributing to organisational performance
- have the knowledge and skills to understand and contribute to organisational performance
- have the power to make decisions that influence organisational direction and performance.'

Other authors (Thomas and Velthouse, 1990) have discussed in detail the relationship of empowerment to what they describe as the 'intrinsic task motivation' linking empowerment with motivation to successfully complete a task. The task for service providers is associated with four elements:

- *impact,* ie the degree to which what the individual does is seen as making a difference;
- *competence,* ie the extent to which an individual can perform a task with confidence that the result will be satisfactory;
- *meaningfulness,* ie the extent to which the task of the individual leads to commitment and involvement rather than apathy and feelings of detachment;
- *choice,* ie the extent to which the individual can determine what is done and when it is done.

In the context of service delivery and service recovery the task is managing the service encounter and effecting service recovery.

Alpander (1991) has suggested empowerment is concerned with meeting the needs of individuals in five areas that are relevant to the work situation. These are economic security, a sense of belonging, recognition, control and self-worth. Alpander's research indicated that *need to control* was the highest need.

These expressions of empowerment around the task of the individual suggest the importance of the individual's perception of empowerment rather than any intent on the part of an organisation to be an empowered organisation. A recognition of this potential inconsistency between the organisation's intent and the individual's needs and motivation has led us to propose the following model for considering the implications of changes caused either by the organisation's movement along a scale between being driven by procedures and systems, ie an *imposed* organisation and a freer *empowered* organisation. Against this there is the individual's need and motivation to have discretion over the task in terms of what is done, how it is done, and when it is done; this discretion can be expressed on a scale of low to high. Bringing the two scales together produces the matrix in Figure 9.2 with the following four characteristics:

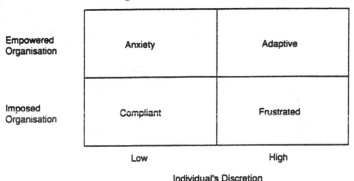

Figure 9.2 Empowerment matrix

- *Case 1 : Compliant (Low Discretion - Imposed System).* In this case the organisation runs on imposed systems and the level of discretion expected of the employee is low. It relates to routine services which are often cost sensitive or where quality consistency is important. Here the system drives service delivery although attempts should be made to humanise it through involvement and communication.
- *Case 2: Adaptive (High Discretion – Empowered Organisation).* In this case the organisation's employees are given a high degree of discretion in their roles. It relates to professional services where there is considerable freedom to shape the service delivery to the needs of clients and customers.

In cases 1 and 2 there is a match between the type of organisation and the expectation of the degree of discretion expected of the employees by managers and by the employees of themselves. Both cases are acceptable alternatives. However in some circumstances an organisation may wish to move from one state to another and here the problems arise because it is very improbable that a move can be made instantaneously between the *compliant* and the *adaptive* states. Instead any movement tends to be into the other two boxes in the matrix, ie the *anxiety* state or the *frustration* state.

- *Case 3: Anxiety (Low Discretion – Empowered Organisation).* In this case the organisation may be seeking to empower employees but the perception either real or imagined on the part of employees is that they have a low level of discretion. This leads to people feeling anxious about their role. If the movement has been from the *compliant* state people are uneasy with the lack of a strong guiding system. If the movement is from the *adaptive* state people are confused by the loss of discretion.
- *Case 4: Frustration (High Discretion – Imposed Systems).* In this case employees are frustrated by the constraints imposed by the systems when there is the expectation of a high degree of discretion. This is especially true when there is movement from the *adaptive* box into the *frustration* box or when employees are told and trained to have greater discretion but find that formal systems still constrain and dictate what happens.

A proposition is that any movement from either *empowered* to *imposed* by an organisation will lead to *frustration* or *anxiety* in some or all of its employees.

The model has implications for service recovery performed by front line service staff and would lead to the propositions that:

- *Proposition 1:* In the *compliant* state service recovery could only be delivered successfully within clear guidelines on what employees could do and when.
- *Proposition 2:* In the *adaptive* state service recovery relies on individuals responding to the needs of customers with the assurance that the organisation will support their actions.
- *Proposition 3:* In the *anxiety* or *frustration* states it is unlikely that service recovery could be successfully achieved.

RESEARCH QUESTIONS AND METHODOLOGY

The present study investigated service recovery across a range of organisations in the service sector. The aims of the study were to find out:

- the perception of managers of the importance of service recovery to maintaining customer satisfaction;
- the actions being taken to build recovery into the service delivery system;
- how recovery is triggered, either by formal measurement systems or by informal means.

Research Propositions

In association with the research questions a number of propositions were established on the basis of the literature and anecdotal dealings with service organisations.

1. Service managers perceive a link between service recovery and customer retention.
2. Few organisations measure customer loss rates.
3. Most recovery is initiated by customer complaint.
4. Front line staff can act to recover when the problem is seen as minor.
5. Service recovery is more likely to involve refunds and replacement where this is possible (ie when a product is involved).
6. There are differences in recovery behaviour for service encounters which are business-to-business relationships compared to business-to-consumer.

The research was based on a postal survey which was sent to 2000 service managers across the services sector. In the preface to the survey, service recovery was defined as follows:

It is said that one of the marks of a good service organisation is the ability to recover effectively from problems and mistakes.

We define 'recovery' as specific actions required to ensure that the customer receives a reasonable level of service after problems have occurred to disrupt 'normal' service. These problems may be as a direct result of problems or errors in the service organisation itself, or may be to some extent outside its control. These may be customer induced or the result of the actions of other associated organisations. The three groups of situations requiring recovery are illustrated below, using the example of an airline:

Service Provider Error: The airline fails to have aircraft ready on time or loses luggage in transit.

Customer Error: A customer forgets his or her passport or fails to meet the check-in time.

Associated Organisation Error: Immigration is overloaded, or air traffic controllers are on strike.

Many service organisations are able to tell stories about specific occasions when employees have worked exceptionally hard, beyond the call of duty to keep customers happy. The problem is that these examples of exceptional service may not be the norm, customers experiencing on average rather more indifferent service.

We are interested in your organisation's experience of the following:
a) Avoiding the need for recovery by 'doing it right first time'.
b) Developing techniques and procedures for dealing with problems.
c) Changing attitudes throughout the organisation to increase the degree of responsiveness of employees to customer needs.
d) Establishing the importance of recovery to the customers' perception of the service you provide.

The survey instrument contained a mix of open-ended and specific questions.

RESULTS

Replies were received from 157 managers with a distribution across the service sector as shown in Table 9.1. The category Customer Service includes service activities associated with manufacturing organisations. One of the reasons for a relatively low response rate might be that some manufacturing organisations do not recognise the service aspects of their task.

Table 9.1 Spread of respondents

Sector	%
	17.5
Professional Services	9.5
Banking and Finance	8.0
Retail and Hotels	48.9
Customer Service	9.5
Distribution	6.6
Public Sector	

Respondents were asked to indicate the importance of service recovery to their business on a scale of not important (1) to vital (5). The weighted result of 4.5 indicates the strength of the perceived importance.

Respondents were asked the extent to which they linked service recovery and customer retention. The responses were not quantified but fell into the following categories:

- 'We perceive a strong link.'
- 'It is difficult to prove the link.'
- 'We are trying to measure the link.'
- 'There is no link!'

An attempt was made to explore the extent to which the respondents measured either the cost of a lost customer or the level of customer retention. The cost of a lost customer was claimed to be measured by 40 per cent of respondents. However the way in which measurement occurs was in most cases on the basis of the perception of lost business rather than detailed measurement. There was only one respondent who has a system for tracking customer satisfaction.

Table 9.2 Frequency of the need for recovery in a typical operating unit

Timing	% of sample
Continuously	25.6
Daily	19.5
Weekly	13.4
Fortnightly	7.3
Monthly	6.1
Quarterly	6.1
Every two years	1.2
Not known	20.7

Only 43 per cent of respondents measure customer retention with repeat business or renewal of service contracts or market research information being the indicators of retention. There was no clear evidence of service organisations tracking the retention of specific customers over a period of years.

Respondents were asked to identify the need for recovery in a typical operating unit and the replies are shown in Table 9.2.

Respondents were asked to state the factor which caused the need for service recovery on a scale between 'it never occurs' (1) and 'very frequently' (5). The results are shown in Table 9.3.

Table 9.3 Most common causes of problems

Cause	Weighting 1–5
Customers	3.2
Other service organisations	3.0
Front-line staff	3.3
Information system faults	3.0
Equipment faults	2.9
Back-room support	3.0
Communication	3.5

The means by which a judgement of the causes was made was either on the basis of the perception of managers (64 per cent of replies) or measurement (44 per cent of replies). There was no attempt to reconcile which factors were assessed by measurement and which by perception.

Respondents were asked the extent to which service recovery was initiated by staff or management monitoring, formal measuring systems, customer complaints or on the initiative of front-line staff. The extent of the responses was on a scale of 'it never occurs' (1) to 'very frequently' (5). The results are shown in Table 9.4. Perhaps not surprisingly, customer complaint was the most frequent trigger for recovery.

Table 9.4 How service recovery is triggered

Action	Weighting 1–5
Staff/management monitoring	3.5
Formal measurement systems	3.0
Customer complaint	4.1
Front-line initiative	3.5

Respondents were asked how quickly they needed to initiate service recovery. The results were within minutes for 30 per cent of respondents, within hours for 46 per cent of respondents, and within days for 24 per cent of respondents. Associated with time to initiate recovery is the time to complete service recovery. Respondents reported times within minutes (13 per cent of replies), within hours (35 per cent of replies), within days (44 per cent of replies). Only 47 per cent of respondents reported having escalation procedures for service recovery (for when front-line staff need assistance).

Respondents were asked the extent to which front-line staff take extraordinary action to resolve problems when there is a minor problem, a major problem, and when the problem is clearly caused by the customer on a scale between never (1) and always (5). The results are shown in Table 9.5. There is a greater tendency for front-line staff to deal with minor problems and to seek additional advice or support for major problems.

Table 9.5 The extent to which front-line staff take action to solve problems

Problem type	Weighting
When there is a minor problem	4.4
When there is a major problem	3.5
When the customer has caused the problem	3.9

Respondents were asked to identify if they were empowering staff; 75 per cent claimed to be doing so. Critical factors in the process of empowerment included: training, support, communication and information availability, delegation and partnership.

As recovery is often associated with a spend on resources the authority given to front-line staff to spend up to a given amount may be important. Respondents were asked the extent of this authority given to front-line staff and the results are shown in Table 9.6.

Table 9.6 Extent of authority of front-line staff

Extent	% of sample
Nil	27.4
Less than £50	12.4
Less than £100	6.2
Over £100	49.6
No Limit	4.4

The value of the spend allowed to front-line staff as a percentage of the average customer spend is shown in Table 9.7.

Table 9.7 Value of average customer spend front-line staff can use for recovery

Value	% of sample
Less than 25%	61
25% to 50%	6
50% to 75%	4
More than 75%	29

The actions taken to recover can be grouped in the categories of replacement (particularly if a product is involved), financial reparation or other gifts, refunds, or reparation and refunds. It was not possible from the survey data to establish the extent to which each was viewed as the most important. However there are some indications that replacement was the more likely mode of recovery when a product is part of the service package; if not, some reparation and partial refund was preferred. Full refunds or financial reparation are the less likely actions.

When recovery is clearly initiated by customer complaints the following comments summarise the statements given by respondents:

- there is little evidence of statements which indicate finding out exactly what customers want;
- there were few statements of offering apologies to customers;
- there is a recognition of the need to respond honestly and with a personal contact which may involve more senior staff if the problem is perceived to be major;
- refunds and doing work free of charge where appropriate are common approaches;
- relating to recovery more generally, some respondents made the point of the need to balance recompense and resolution of problems.

Finally, respondents were asked to reflect on the future importance of service recovery. Some saw it becoming more important especially with respect to increasing the speed of response. Others talked of quality programmes removing the need for service recovery through a right-first-time approach.

DISCUSSION AND ANALYSIS

The results from the survey go some way to providing answers to the questions raised earlier. Service managers do perceive that service recovery is important to their business and many feel there is a link with customer retention. However others would hold that there is no link or that it is difficult to measure. The issue of measurement corresponds with the lack of evidence of many service organisations having formal methods of measuring customer retention, and no stated cases from the sample of measuring customer perceptions of service recovery as an indicator of customer retention.

The need to recover can be caused by many different factors associated with service delivery by front-line staff and no one factor emerged as significantly more prone to cause things to go wrong. The ability of managers to give a view of causes on the basis of measurement rather than perception was encouragingly high, suggesting that many have formal measurement of when things go wrong. This is substantiated by the responses to the question on their need to recover; 80 per cent of the respondents were able to identify the frequency. The 20 per cent who claimed not to know how often recovery occurs may be delivering highly consistent service or, more likely, may be in a constant state of recovery.

The ways in which service recovery is initiated tends to be as a result of customers complaining rather than by the action of staff and management. If service firms were to be more proactive in anticipating when recovery is necessary, future surveys of this type would perhaps see a greater emphasis on front-line initiative or formal measuring systems.

What happens when service recovery occurs depends on whether it is perceived by the front-line staff to be a minor or a major problem. This is not surprising, although it would be interesting to know more about how front-line staff make a decision to deal with the matter themselves or to call for assistance. What would have been expected would be that in all cases front-line staff start the process of recovery, if only by acknowledging the fact either to colleagues or supervisors or customers. The fact that only 30 per cent of respondents said that recovery is started within minutes is disturbing, if it is a true reflection of what happens.

The extent of the authority given to front-line staff to make reparation, give refunds or replacements, or financial gifts, and the value related to the cost of the service show two zones. Over 50 per cent of the sample reported that front-line staff have the authority to spend over £100 and about 30 per cent say that this amounts to more than 75 per cent of the value of the service. This suggests that for 30 per cent front-line staff are providing a straight replacement or refund for a product and or service as the means of recovery.

Some of the responses appear to blame front-line staff for lack of responsiveness. It would be interesting to repeat this research from the perspective of the employee rather than that of the manager.

For the 25 per cent of respondents who give no authority to front-line staff to spend to recover, it suggests either that they must refer all cases to managers or other groups, or that the respondents were only considering the authority to spend money rather than to consume resources in the service recovery process.

Business-to-Business versus Business-to-Consumer

The business-to-business relationship is likely to be different to the business-to-consumer. In business-to-business relationships the buyer and user are often different individuals or groups and the overall value of services bought are greater. The consequence is that the expectations of service delivery and the need for recovery may be different.

The sample was split into two categories, business-to-business and business-to-consumer, using data on the nature of their business. Separate analyses for each group were undertaken.

The results showed significant differences in some areas for the sample. The business-to-consumer firms are more likely to be part of a network rather than single site and consequently employ more staff. They are more likely to need to recover continuously or daily or not know how frequently. In consequence, they are more likely to initiate service recovery within minutes rather than the hours for business-to-business service firms. Also business-to-consumer firms are more likely to authorise front-line staff to spend more than 50 per cent of the value of the average customer spend on service recovery. In other respects there are no significant differences.

These results correspond with the business-to-consumer service organisation which has a high number of service encounters; hence the need to recover continuously. The service package is more likely to be fairly standard; hence the authority given to staff to spend a high proportion of the average customer spend on service recovery, as the costs of what is being given are known and the risks of giving away too much can be assessed.

Implications for Empowerment

The present study was focused on service recovery and not empowerment of service workers. However 75 per cent of the respondents claimed to be empowering staff through training, delegation with authority, involvement in procedures, communication of policy. There was also considerable mention of formal measurement systems including the quality standard BS5750.

These findings would suggest that the service organisations represented in the sample perceive themselves to be moving upwards on the imposed empowered scale of the empowerment matrix. What is not known is the perceptions of staff of these changes. Talk of formal procedures would suggest that in reality the *modus operandi* is more *imposed*. Hence it is likely that staff are often frustrated unless the extent of the empowerment for service recovery is clearly defined.

There are indications of a realisation of the dangers of moving staff into the *anxiety* quadrant of the matrix as instanced by one comment:

> Empowerment must mean something to the staff themselves. I believe front-line staff do not necessarily want to be empowered at all times. It needs to be handled with care and gradually implemented so it becomes part of the culture of the organisation.

CONCLUSIONS

Service managers perceive service recovery to be important to their business and likely to increase in the future with the need to meet service pledges associated with service charters. They also generally perceive a link between service recovery and customer retention.

Less than half the service organisations currently measure the cost of a lost or dissatisfied customer and customer retention.

Service recovery is still most likely to be triggered by customer complaint and if it is a business-to-consumer service, it will be initiated within minutes and be resolved by front-line staff having the authority to use over 50 per cent of the average customer spend to put things right, mainly by replacement or refund. Business-to-business services take longer to activate service recovery (hours or longer) and the front-line staff have less authority to use a high proportion of the average spend, although there may be no difference in the actual amounts involved between the classes of services.

Overall the service organisations in the sample are taking steps to bring about service recovery. However the indications are that it could be improved by better measurement and triggering and by a consideration of the most appropriate strategies for recovery (for instance, a wider use of escalation procedures). Whether a true reflection or not, the impression given by respondents is of a lack of checking with the customers of what is needed.

Over 75 per cent of the service organisations claim to be empowering service staff. However doubts remain as to the overall effectiveness of the changes. In some cases the front-line staff do not wish for the change or are not adequately prepared and consequently fail to fulfil their new expected roles. In other cases the intention to empower is blocked by inappropriate systems and frustrated staff.

References

Alpander, G G (1991) 'Developing managers' ability to empower employees', *Journal of Management*, Vol 10, No 3, pp 13–24.

Armistead, C G, Clark, G (1993), 'The "coping" capacity management: strategy in service and the influence on quality performance', *International Journal of Service Industry Management*, Vol 4, No 4.

Bowen, D E, Lawler, E E (1992) 'The empowerment of service workers: what, why, how, and when', *Sloan Management Review*, Spring , pp 31–39.

Hart, C W L (1988) 'The power of unconditional guarantees', *Harvard Business Review*, July–August, pp54–62

Hart, C W L, Heskett, J L and Sasser, W E Jr (1990) 'The profitable art of service recovery', *Harvard Business Review*, Vol 68, No 4, pp 148–156.

Hart, C W L, Schlesinger, L A and Maher, D (1992) 'Guarantees come to professional service firms', *Sloan Management Review*, Spring, pp 19–29.

Heskett, J L (1992) 'A service sector paradigm for management: the service profit chain', in Armistead, C G (ed.), *Service Sector Seminar proceedings at Cranfield*.

Heskett, J L, Sasser, W E Jr and Hart, C W L (1990) *Service Breakthroughs: Changing the Rules of the Game*, Free Press, New York.

Lash, L M (1989) *The Complete Guide to Customer Service*, John Wiley, Chichester.

Parasuraman, A, Zeithaml, V A and Berry, L L (1988) 'SERVQUAL: a multiple item scale for measuring consumer perceptions of service quality', *Journal of Retailing*, Vol 64, Spring, pp 12–40.

Thomas, K W and Velthouse, B A (1990) 'Cognitive elements of empowerment: an interpretive model of intrinsic task motivation', *Academy of Management Review*, Vol 15, No 4, pp 666–681.

Zemke, R (1991) 'Service recovery: a key to customer retention', *Franchising World*, Vol 23, No 3, May June, pp 32–34.

Zemke, R and Bell, C (1990) 'Service recovery: doing it right the second time', *Training*, Vol 27, No 6, pp 42–48.

PART FOUR

SERVICE QUALITY THEMES IN RELATIONSHIP MARKETING

10

IMPROVING THE QUALITY OF SERVICES MARKETING: SERVICE (RE)DESIGN IS THE CRITICAL LINK*

David Ballantyne, Martin Christopher

and Adrian Payne

INTRODUCTION

The issue of service is one of vital interest to marketers. Research supports the view that customer-focused quality is a critical strategic dimension. The PIMS (Profit Impact of Market Strategies) research undertaken by the Strategic Planning Institute shows relative customer-perceived quality as a critical variable in profitability. Their study (Buzzell and Gale, 1987) concluded 'In the long run, the single most important factor affecting a business unit's performance is the quality of its products and services, relative to those of competitors.' More recent PIMS-based services research, which focused on 50 high performers in service industries, confirms this relationship. The research showed that high-quality service providers earned an average return on investment of 8 percentage points above low-quality service providers (Allio and Patten, 1991)

The services quality movement is gaining momentum from its slow start in the early 1980s. Many scholars are now working in this area, reflecting the place of services in a firm's total 'offer' as well as the strategic importance of quality in service performance. It is this second aspect that specifically relates quality to services marketing. Since the start of the 1990s service quality has moved to be the central agenda point for services marketing as evidenced by a specialised professional journal *(Managing Service Quality,* launched in 1990); dedicated issues of academic journals on service quality (eg *The International Journal of*

* This chapter is based on an article published in the *Journal of Marketing Management*, Vol II, No 1, 1995, pp 7–24, and is reproduced with permission ©1995, The Dryden Press, Harcourt Brace and Company Ltd.

Service Industry Management special issue in 1993 on 'Advances in Research on Service Quality'); workshops on the theme of quality management in services such as those run annually, since 1991, by the European Institute for Advanced Studies in Management (EIASM); the biennial International Quality in Services Symposium (QUIS) co-launched in 1988 by the University of Karlstad in Sweden and Arizona State University and most recently held at St John's University, New York in 1994; and the formation of combined academic and professional groups, such as the International Service Quality Association in New York in 1991. Also a multidisciplinary range of books on service quality has emerged (Boomsma and van Borrendam, 1987, Berry, Bennett and Brown, 1989; Rosander, 1989; Zeithaml, Parasuraman and Berry, 1990; Townsend, 1990; Brown *et al* ., 1991; Kunst and Lemmink, 1991; Berry and Parasuraman, 1991; Gummesson, 1993).

The aim of this chapter is to examine the linkages between services marketing and quality management and to propose a practical approach to improving and monitoring service quality. It commences with the idea of the 'quality gap' (Parasuraman *et al.,* 1985) derived from services marketing concepts of quality (especially Grönroos, 1984). The concept of quality and process management is then examined and the role of internal customers and suppliers outlined. The chapter argues that the variability of service processes and outcomes demands fundamentally new approaches to diagnostic problem-solving in order to 'design in' quality improvements continuously. The chapter identifies four specific diagnostic levels for service system (re)design which require the commitment and collaboration of the services marketer. A practical six–point approach to monitoring service quality is then described and illustrated with reference to service activity in a network retail branch. Finally, we outline some of the challenges facing marketing and quality management in service organisations, the customer of such organisations and academic researchers.

SERVICES MARKETING CONCEPTS OF QUALITY

One of the most remarkable features of Total Quality Management (TQM) is the way in which it has drawn practising managers from many parts of an organisation to work together across traditional functional boundaries to improve quality and productivity (Crosby, 1979; Deming, 1982; Imai, 1986; Juran, 1989; Oakland, 1989; Dale and Cooper, 1992). This highlights a rather simple yet dramatic link that has not yet been widely brought to attention. It is this: *quality has become an integrating concept between production-orientation and marketing-orientation* (Gummesson, 1988). This is especially the case in the service sector where production, delivery and consumption can occur simultaneously.

The concept of quality referred to here is the match between what customers expect and what they experience. This is perceived quality (Grönroos, 1984). Any mismatch between these two is a 'quality gap'. As perceived quality is always a judgement by the customer, whatever the customer thinks is reality, is reality. Thus, quality is whatever the customer says it is. The service quality management goal is to narrow the quality gap. This not only facilitates getting customers, but *keeping* them. As quality goes up, non-value added activities and time-related costs come down (Leonard and Sasser, 1982). Furthermore, when staff participate in the quality improvement process the beneficiaries are the staff, shareholders and customers because stakeholder expectations are less often in tension with each other.

The quality gap between customers' service expectations and service experience is seductive territory for research. However, relatively few researchers, with the notable exception of a body of work initiated by Parasuraman, Zeithaml and Berry, have attempted to model the generic determinants of service quality and the kinds of quality gaps that lead to quality shortfalls (see Parasuraman *et al.,* 1985, 1988, 1991; Carman, 1990; Cronin and Taylor, 1992; Oliver, 1993; and Zeithaml *et al.,* 1993).

The difficulty is that customers are continually experiencing and evaluating service performances in particular settings. They are continually 'adjusting' their perceptions of customer service. Once something is 'fixed' or 'improved' other important service issues will naturally emerge. And when one among many critical service issues is resolved the priority levels naturally change places.

One starting point is that service quality is perceived in a personal way by every single customer (Grönroos, 1984; Parasuraman *et al.,* 1985). The experience of service (following Grönroos) is influenced in turn by:

- what the customer gets as a result of the interaction between buyer and seller – 'technical quality';
- how the buyer and seller interact in each and every service encounter – 'functional quality'.

In effect 'technical quality' is about outcomes of service encounters and 'functional quality' is about the interactive process of achieving those outcomes. The dichotomy between 'technical' and 'functional' qualities in services is useful in exploring and coming to terms with the intangibility of service quality. In particular, it gives emphasis to the key role of front-line staff in the service marketing process and shows how emphasis on the service relationship might in itself become a competitive strategy.

However, the 'functional' and 'technical' qualities are clearly inter-dependent. At this point, some conceptual difficulties arise. The technical dimension is not just a prerequisite for total service quality. In the eyes of the customer, technical quality is often experienced as though it were functional quality. For example, staff may be blamed for 'service' problems if the internal data processing 'back-up' is not supportive. Quality must be built into the total service system or variation will be experienced as poor or inconsistent service.

QUALITY AND PROCESS MANAGEMENT IN SERVICES

In Total Quality Management (TQM) we find structures for planning and introducing the kinds of integrating and coordinating changes that need to be made to meet quality goals but these are often only tenuously linked to *customer expectations* and strategies for building a loyal customer base. Clarifying customer expectations from a market-based point of view is helped by the concept of *customer value chain* .

The customer value chain is a series (or linkage) of things a customer does with a product or service that produce value for that customer. A firm's offering is the input into the customer value chain (Porter, 1985). The activity patterns of a customer are represented by the links in the chain. These control or modify the way in which a firm's output is actually used. For example, a banking account may be input into a customer value chain as a bill paying device, an investment for a 'rainy day' or a day-to-day savings account, according to how the customer goes about managing money and the priorities which are given value. The appropri-ate marketing aim is to identify what a customer is *trying to do* with the firm's service offering before reaching any conclusions about how this can be facilitated.

The value a firm creates for a customer is a function of the alignment it can achieve between the *firm's* value chain and the *customer's* value chain. Marketing management must share some of the responsibility for this. The continuing task is about adjusting the way a firm manages its service intangibles. How can we come to grips with this?

Consider first a sole trader or self-employed professional. The activities he or she performs on behalf of a customer are sequenced and integrated along the value chain without the need for any command structure of functional differentiation within the 'organisation'. The whole design, production, delivery and personal service is integrated within one head.

However, if the business grows in staff numbers, new coordinating work activities arise which require functional specialisation and some kind of hierarchical command and control.

However, the vertical controls are usually strengthened to the detriment of the integration of working relationships *between* people and *across* departments. Coordination and collaboration usually receive scant attention until quality falters.

Organisational quality problems are found *between* divisions rather than *within* divisions. To the extent that one department's output is mismatched with another department's required input needs, there is a quality gap. Failure to manage work flow and processes laterally across the firm's value chain has a way of multiplying costs and quality failures all along one value chain to the next, through to the end customer. The

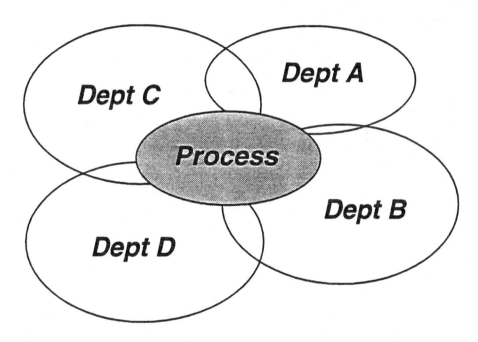

Who owns the process?
Who recognizes the opportunity for quality improvement?

Figure 10.1 Process management

cost of quality is swollen by the sum total of all these mismatched activities, which invoke delays and higher level 'firefighting' decisions. One key task of service quality management is to identify and examine the most critical cross-functional organisational linkages and remove any blockages, thereby reducing the cost of achieving quality, as shown in Figure 10.1.

Internal customers and internal suppliers each supply the other, and are invisibly connected in terms of the input–output links in the value chain. Diagnosing these cross-functional links *within* the organisation from their starting point with the external customer and back *upstream* to the external supplier represents quality and process improvement opportunities with dividends for both customer and service supplier.

Quality is also at the mercy of variability built into work processes. This has to be managed as it will not correct itself. Every work process generates outputs which in some way fall short of perfection and uniformity. All processes contain sources of variability and these differences may be large, or small beyond measurement. This is because in service quality management the customer is also part of the process and, indeed, a *special cause* of variability. Waste in all kinds of business activity can be brought under control by minimising process variability. Process variation is generated and passed along the whole chain of customers and suppliers to the end customer. Indeed, the eminent Japanese statistician, Taguchi, says that there is an incremental economic 'loss' for each deviation from customer 'target requirements', which has a flow-on effect to society as a whole (Taguchi and Clausing, 1990).

Coming to grips with service intangibles challenges the traditional approaches to quality assurance developed in manufacturing industries. At first glance marketers may tend to attribute the quality of front-line service to the strengths or weaknesses of service staff. This is a natural enough perception but it is nonetheless a partial observation. What constitutes service 'performance' is the *sum* of the performance processes for which staff are the agents and customers the participants. Certainly front-line service staff must perform well and need training in customer service skills. This is an important marketing function. However, efforts to improve front-line service performance by improving staff customer service training typically add cost, not value, unless the design and redesign of work activities, the environment in which service is delivered, and the work processes involved are also targeted for quality improvement, and are part of a continuous service system review.

The challenge for managers is to allocate time and resources for diagnostic problem-solving and service redesign, placing the efforts where it counts most. How should this task be approached?

DIAGNOSTIC LEVELS FOR SERVICE SYSTEM (RE)DESIGN

We have conceptualised four diagnostic levels in the service quality and delivery process which help focus the options to be considered in service system design and redesign.

All service elements need to be seen as part of a total system where any action or development in one area is likely to influence action or development in another. This *systemic structure* is what we see as the multisided face of service quality management. It permits us to consider customer service solutions from different points of view so that the most cost-effective ones are adopted. It allows us to consider these 'problems' as symptoms of problems for which root causes and solutions may be found elsewhere in the total system.

The diagnostic model shown in Figure 10.2 is built on this systemic structure and it reveals how some organisations are approaching service (re)design. Customer service research drives each of the four diagnostic levels in this figure – the environmental setting, processes, job design and people.

These levels of analysis, discussed below, potentially contain a range of solutions to any given service quality problem. Again each level is part of a total system where all parts are interrelated. They should not be seen as mutually exclusive but as revealing many threads which may be woven in different ways into the total design fabric.

LEVEL 1: *Environmental Setting*

The environments in which the customer 'faces' the service provider are critical to the perceived quality of service. The 'situational' variables are often overlooked. The physical aspect is obviously a major component of environmental design but there are emotional and psychological features as well (Bitner, 1990; Schneider and Bowen, 1985).

In other words, the environment affects behaviour by influencing the meaning a customer draws from a particular setting (Fox and Bender, 1986). This includes issues of orientation, learning where we are, where we are going, how things work and what behaviour is expected from us as a customer or as a service provider (Wener, 1985).

Every visit by a customer to a bank, a shop or a service centre, every telephone call and every order exists in a specific context defined by

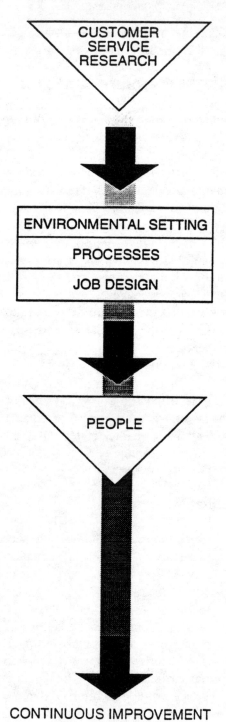

Figure 10.2 The diagnostic levels in service system design and redesign

people, time and place. Each and every service encounter may therefore be said to prescribe and to be prescribed in a 'service interaction zone' (Ballantyne, 1987). Consider, for example, the transaction (tellers) and the lending (managerial) zones in a bank. People visiting the bank and depositing money see the bank in a different context and have a different set of service expectations to those waiting to see the manager for a loan. In any service organisation there will be multiple service interaction zones, or service 'channels', through which service is seen differently by the customers. Defining these key access zones can provide a 'grounded' framework for any market research analysis of customers' service quality expectations and experiences which can, in turn, lead to 'breakthrough' redesign of these zones.

Some service companies have not paid much attention to the good fit of place, times and service function. As a result, by default, the customer experiences disorientation effects. The ideal environment setting will prepare the customer by giving visual, procedural and psychological clues, which both support and define service quality expectations.

LEVEL 2: Processes

Processes are the backbone of a service firm's marketing performance and service quality (Booms and Bitner, 1981; Shostack, 1987; Payne, 1993). Service support processes directly influence the quality of customer service experienced at the front counter and information desks, ie they help to destroy, or support, the face-to-face service experience.

Service (re)design, therefore, is about changing the way a firm sequences its external (interactive) processes and manages its internal processes. Deming has frequently stated that workers are never to blame for flaws in the design of a process. Ineffective process design is management's responsibility. Poor process design prevents workers from giving their best and increases the time required to complete a service process cycle.

The development of 'user friendly' data processing systems over the last decade is a case in point. This development was not so much the outcome of a new focus on customers' needs as it was on technological breakthroughs. Given that there has been further technological break-throughs in terms of capacity, enquiry languages, interconnectivity and relational databases, the next step is towards 'customer friendly' systems, ie narrowing the gap between customer effective systems and operation-ally efficient systems.

What at first seems impossible to change is often found to be possible when the assumptions being made about the nature and purpose of the underlying process are made visible. An increase in routinisation, productivity and customer service is not an impossible goal (Todd, 1985). A major contributor to service design has been the use of flow charting techniques, sometimes called blueprinting (Shostack, 1987) or service mapping (Kingman-Brundage, 1992). There is still more development work required in this area and indeed a change of mind-set among managers to exploit and develop these techniques (Gummesson, 1994).

LEVEL 3: Job Design

A service company earns its reputation for good service by consistently delivering what customers expect of it. Over time, jobs often develop haphazardly with little focus on customer concerns. In the extreme cases jobs can become arbitrary groupings of activities that machines cannot do, with role conflict or ambiguity being the likely outcome. Also, badly designed jobs unwittingly tend to conceal the environment and process design defects.

There is a natural tendency to think that the design of a job is a 'given' dictated by the technology and that poor performance on the job must be the fault of the worker (see, for example, Campion and Thayer, 1987).

Job design does not imply rigid and excessively prescribed job description. Considerable latitude is necessary for service performance in professional contexts. For example, one approach to improving job design is to draw on the classical Tavistock socio-technical job design approaches which focus on motivational outcomes (Hackman and Oldham, 1980) and then analyse and modify the structural design (see, for example, Shostack, 1987). This means changing the actual structure of the jobs people perform, not just changing the processes of which people are part.

LEVEL 4: People

With services there is a difference in the sequence of events to that in product marketing – the 'sale' of a service must be made before production and consumption take place. Unlike manufacturing systems, the operations processes cannot be sealed off from customers and staff, ie both customers and staff may contribute to the service performance. Through the interactions of customers and staff, the service production and delivery system is transformed from a static to a dynamic system. This provides some new problems for markets but also some opportunities.

First, when we think of service as an 'ongoing sale', both customers and front-line staff become part of the service (process) cycle. The well known service concept of the 'moment of truth' was popularised at SAS Airlines to show staff how this service cycle is a series of critical encounters with the customer (Carlzon and Hubendinck, 1984; Carlzon, 1987).

Second, staff tend to find that service quality itself is motivating when the goal is seen to be about improvements that customers value, an opportunity to test one's personal limits and in so doing, contribute to the customer relationship and the organisation's success. This goal diverted activity can contribute greatly to the success of an organisation's marketing activities.

Some organisations are tempted to place strong emphasis on training in their plan for improving service quality. Training is vital but *education* is better. Sometimes the first has to be prevented from interfering with the second. An internal marketing approach is helpful because it gives training a strategic customer focus (see, for example, Grönroos, 1982, 1985; George, 1990; Piercy and Morgan, 1991; Christopher, Payne and Ballantyne, 1991; Collins and Payne, 1991). Some key elements are:

- staff selection processes and induction;
- training design and the measurement of competency;
- staff 'climate' monitors;
- internal (staff) communications;
- support for company-wide service quality improvement.

Our definition of internal marketing is that it is *any* form of marketing within an organisation which focuses staff attention on the internal activities that need to be changed in order to enhance external market-place performance.

Our own work in this area suggests that there is a recursive relationship between the environmental setting for service, the design of jobs, the people (who are involved in the operational processes) and the processes (which involve people). Each diagnostic level is the key to learning about the other. Each is the key to the effectiveness of the other.

Service system (re)design involves collaboration across departmental borders and a shift towards inviting the support and participation of people to work on improving the way services are designed and organised. A body of literature is now pointing to how to both improve systems *and* 'empower' service workers, as aspects of the one strategy (Bowen and Lawler, 1992a,b).

PRACTICAL APPROACHES TO MONITORING SERVICE QUALITY

The promise of Quality Management is an improvement in both quality and productivity. However, many of the attempts made in the service sector to implement TQM procedures have viewed service processes narrowly through manufacturing eyes, often without the active involvement of marketing managers or disciplined customer service research (Witcher, 1990). This is both surprising and disappointing as both disciplines share the identical goal of meeting customer requirements. The special challenge is that the production and delivery of service occurs invariably at the same time and place. This gives rise to the moment of truth referred to earlier, when the parties in the service relationship come together.

The external starting point for service quality improvement, therefore, is measuring and monitoring customer requirements and perceived service performance on an ongoing basis. This is clearly a marketing responsibility. The challenge for services marketing is that service quality measurement must stay close to the customer, and yet the customer's requirements are a moving target, with the customer entering and leaving the service interaction zone(s) at will. The research approach taken in practice will depend on the specific service context being examined. To set some context for discussion in this chapter a retail bank branch with a regional structure is used to illustrate the potential for a triangulation of methods.

As shown in Figure 10.3, a multi-method and monitoring approach to service quality is proposed. The sequence moves logically from customer service research and a staff attitude survey (or climate monitor) to setting up a range of 'risk point' feedback systems. Last of all comes the progressive introduction (and review) of internal TQM statistical performance standards.

The six market monitors of service quality are as follows.

1. Customer Service Quality 'Benchmark'

First, a two-step qualitative/quantitative research study, which benchmarks the strength of particular customer satisfactions and dissatisfactions in specified service contexts, is used for the supplier company and its main competitors.

Qualitative customer service research provides managers with information on the service quality issues that require attention. Quantitative

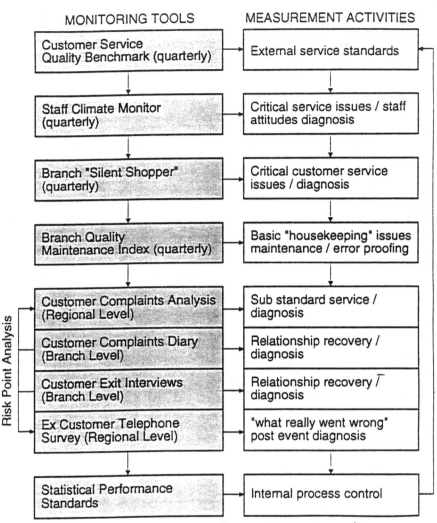

Figure 10.3 Monitoring and measuring service quality

research gives managers the customer priority order for action. Further quantitive testing as to which service issues are critical from the point of view of staff (as well as customers) permits more powerful diagnosis of overall results (described later in this section).

Paradoxically, no one person or department can uniquely implement the findings from these studies. The customer service solution is always a mix of changes that cross departmental boundaries. What is required is a diagnostic review of the critical service issues using interdepartmental teams for review of the major (chronic) quality problems, thus achieving significant interdepartmental commitment to 'breakthrough' improvement.

The diagnostic process can involve a review of both service centre and 'head office' related issues. Critical action in head office policy and/or systems areas is often overlooked unless a formal review process is established.

2. Staff Climate Monitor

This survey is an empirical measure of branch/district/head office staff opinion about the quality of customer service, and also the quality of work life. These two elements impact on the quality of service experienced by the customer (see, for example, Greenway and Southgate, 1985). A comparative analysis between customer perceptions (see above) and staff perceptions is a powerful additional step (Parasuraman *et al* 1985, 1991).

3. Silent Shopper

The 'silent shopper' is a survey measurement system based on the real shopping experience of customers. The measurement is done by skilled market researchers who are also genuine customers. This ensures that the shopping experience is as genuine as possible. This is now being recognised as a legitimate and important area of research (Hurst, 1993). The purpose of this measure is not evaluative but purely diagnostic. Staff should be encouraged to challenge the information received. That is, how might the work processes be improved?

4. Quality Maintenance Index

This maintenance audit incorporates basic 'housekeeping criteria' (specimen items for a retail bank are illustrated in Figure 10.4) and can be administered by service centre staff or by district level audit, or both. It is intended as part of an overall service centre performance assessment.

5. Risk Point Analysis

There are a range of research options appropriate to risk point analysis. All of them are intended to locate negative customer experiences including those leading to loss of customers. Four examples – customer complaints analysis, customer complaints diary, account closure interviews and ex-customer telephone surveys – are shown in Figure 10.3. The fact that the data are not fully representative of the customer base as a whole is not the point. Any negative customer experience is a variance

In your assessment are the following service
issues up to satisfactory customer standard?

Please tick appropriate box in
response to Question.

If not applicable leave blank.

	Yes	No, but action is being taken	No
OUTSIDE THE BRANCH			
● Pathways and/or gardens, branch front neat and tidy	☐	☐	☐
● Windows and Door glass clear and clean	☐	☐	☐
● Door handles and closers working and easy to open	☐	☐	☐
● Door step easy to use and accessible	☐	☐	☐
● Exterior lighting working and adequate	☐	☐	☐
● Car parking available to customers (not occupied by staff)	☐	☐	☐
● Visibility of signs (various views)	☐	☐	☐
AUTOMATIC TELLING MACHINE CASH DISPENSER, NIGHT SAFE			
● Lighting adequate	☐	☐	☐
● Cleanliness of facia and screens (and lobby)	☐	☐	☐
● No damaged parts (keyboards, security panel)	☐	☐	☐
● Points of reference decal and advertising up to date	☐	☐	☐
● Litter bin tidy	☐	☐	☐
● Deposit envelopes available	☐	☐	☐
● Keypad volume audible	☐	☐	☐
"IN HOUSE" ATM / LOBBY			
● Air conditioning working	☐	☐	☐
● Automatic doors working	☐	☐	☐
● Customer entry / exit easy and sign posted	☐	☐	☐

Progressive Totals [| | |]

Figure 10.4 Branch maintenance (housekeeping) criteria

within the system, and provides valid data for diagnosis and quality
improvement.

6. Statistical Performance Standards

Only the customer can 'set' service standards. Therefore, how these
external standards are signalled and interpreted within the company is
the central issue. It is characteristic of an authoritarian approach to quality
improvement to move quickly to *internal* standard setting (or statistical
process controls) as a prerequisite for improving service.

However, there are better ways. The first step is to identify which work processes (or service interaction zones) are connected with the customer service issues that are of critical concern to the customer (Ballantyne, 1990). What is needed is a clear picture of the key processes involved. This is usually achieved by flow charting. What is often revealed at this point is that the key processes have no clear ownership patterns. The question as to who does *own* the process is the next issue to be resolved. This may involve negotiation with other departments, perhaps using a Departmental Purpose Analysis technique (Oakland, 1989).

One design technique sometimes used in linking the 'vital few' critical service issues to key processes is Quality Function Deployment (Burn, 1990). Through a process of linking and matching, a target performance value might be generated after careful consideration of customers' needs (what needs to be done) and the ideal process design (how it needs to be done). This is the *standard* at which to aim, but it is by no means the standard by which performance of the process in its current state can be measured in the short term. Of course, intermediate goals can be set as standards in service businesses and these relate to particular periods of time and operating conditions (see, for example, Kacker, 1988). The internal quality goal is really the progressive elimination of variation against a target value.

In service industries, setting internal standards for front-line service staff and managing these standards absolutely can work only where there is very little technical process back-up needed for front-line service staff. It is more common to find that the *total process* is the service experienced by the customer, so it is the process capability that must be monitored.

CONCLUSIONS

In this chapter we have reviewed the links between services marketing and quality management. A number of concluding observations are now made.

Firstly, the linkages between profitability and service quality (Thompson *et al.*, 1985; Allio and Patten, 1991) and profitability and customer retention (Reichheld and Sasser, 1990; Reichheld, 1993; Clark and Payne, 1993) are increasingly being recognised. However, the linkages between services marketing and quality management are not uniformly understood. Our work in a number of British, North American and Australian banks suggests much needs to be done to introduce structural approaches to service system (re)design. The environmental setting, work processes, job design and the role of the people who bring it all together are seldom treated in a coordinated way. The approach outlined in this chapter has been tested with considerable success in one major financial service institution.

Second, it is often stated that 'what gets measured gets done'. This is a useful structural coordinate but it is the *quality* of the measurement systems and the internal *diagnostic* review process on which attention should be focused. What is needed is not feedback about performance but *feed forward* which effectively channels staff commitment and teamwork into problem-solving and the *internal* marketing function and is therefore, a marketing responsibility.

Third, improving the quality of services marketing means keeping customers as well as getting them in the first place. This has been expressed as a developmental approach to relationship marketing (Grönroos, 1980; Berry, 1983; Gummeson, 1987; Christopher, Payne and Ballantyne, 1991). That the service product is intangible means that service variability will be an ongoing management problem. This is a challenge for marketing management and quality management alike. Marketing needs quality management to reduce service process variability, just as surely as quality management needs marketing information inputs to make sense of customer needs and to review its process capability. If the dynamic links between these parts of the corporate whole are absent or broken, then neither can succeed.

This chapter has focused on how academic concepts and managerial advances in service quality can be brought together to improve marketing effectiveness. Whilst much progress has been made, a significant number of challenges remain. Such issues are of relevance to three audiences: managers in service organisations, customers of these service organisations and academic researchers.

For managers in service organisations the emergence of service quality as a key issue in their business is a vital concern. In particular, they are confronted with how to translate service quality into a tool for improved marketing results, increased customer retention and long-term profitability. They are also facing the challenge of conforming to prescribed service quality standards or award criteria laid down by third parties.

The need to conform to such service quality standards is certain to increase during the balance of this decade. This view is confirmed by the rapid adoption of standards and awards such as the BS 5750/ISO 9000 standard, the Malcolm Baldridge Award, the European Foundation for Quality Management Award and the British MQA qualification. In certain countries, such as Sweden, service quality management has become a topic of major national interest with the government taking a leading role through initiatives such as the Swedish Customer Satisfaction Barometer.

For the customers of service organisations the issue of service quality has become one of urgency especially where institutional buyers of services are requiring service providers to conform to specific quality standards, frequently through some form of accreditation process. Many are moving from a position of having a fairly limited specification of their requirements to requiring their suppliers to adopt the standards of an independent quality audit such as those required by the BS 5750 and ISO 9000 standards. A more flexible development has been termed 'partnership contracting' whereby purchasers and providers use quality award criteria to agree on specific requirements that have to be met by the supplier organisations, including joint quality monitoring arrangements (Ovretveit, 1993). Thus, many suppliers are shifting from a position of having to conform to their own internal service audit (or none at all) to a position of being externally audited. For example, in many companies in the UK and elsewhere, customers are requiring their service provider to be certified under a quality standard by a certain date or they will be discontinued as a supplier.

A key issue customers need to address is: what are the most appropriate forms of auditing their suppliers and which particular audit standards, or award criteria, are appropriate to specific suppliers of services? For services, this is becoming increasingly confused, despite specific guidelines for quality systems in service organisations being introduced by the British Standards Institute in 1992. Criticisms are still directed at BS 5750/ISO 9000 service quality standards for bearing too close a resemblance to the quality standards used for manufactured goods. Additional criticism is that certain quality audits do not emphasise performance outcomes. Unlike the BS 5750/ISO 9000 standards, the Malcolm Baldridge National Quality Award and the European Foundation for Quality Management Award devote points to customer satisfaction as well as to conformance to standards. Overall, approximately half the points of the US Award are directed towards external issues and half internal issues. This seems a far more sensible balance than that used in other quality standards which fail to emphasise 'customer perceived' quality.

For academic researchers services quality research is entering its third phase (Grönroos, 1993). The first phase has been concerned with understanding what service quality is and the context in which quality perceptions are determined through what has been termed the 'confirmation/disconfirmation concept of perceived service quality'. The second phase has been concerned with the development of measurement approaches based on the static model of phase one. The third phase will be concerned with developing more refined measurement methodologies to enable the dynamics of perceived service quality to be addressed. As Grönroos (1993) points out, a more dynamic model is needed of how the quality of services is perceived by customers – one in which the service quality context helps us understand more fully the dynamics of expectations and experiences and of the quality formation process. Our view is that this will involve a more profound understanding of the role of service (re)design in achieving on-going customer relationships.

References

Allio, R J and Pattern, J M, (1991) 'The market share/excellence equation' *Planning Review,* September/October, p 15.

Ballantyne, D F (1987) 'Service concepts and the retail banking environment', *International Journal of Bank Marketing,* Vol 5, No 1, pp 31–32.

Ballantyne D F (1990) 'Coming to grips with service intangibles using quality management techniques', *Marketing Intelligence and Planning.* Vol 8, No 6, pp 4–10.

Berry, L L (1983) 'Relationship marketing', in Berry L L, Shostack, G L and Upah, G D (eds), *Emerging Perspectives on Services Marketing.* American Marketing Association, Chicago, pp 25–28.

Berry, L L and Parasuraman, A (1991) *Marketing Services: Competing Through Quality,* Free Press, New York.

Berry, L L, Bennett, D R and Brown, C W (1989) *Service Quality: A Profit Strategy for Financial Institutions,* Dow Jones-Irwin, Homewood, Ill.

Bitner, M J (1990) 'Evaluating service encounters: the effects of physical surroundings and employee responses', *Journal of Marketing.* Vol 54, pp 69–82.

Booms, B H and Bitner, M J (1981) 'Marketing strategies and organisation structures for service firms', in Donnelly, J H and George, W R (eds) *Marketing of Services,* American Marketing Association Proceedings Series, Chicago, pp 47–51.

Boomsma, S and van Borrendam, A (1987) *Kwaliteit in Diensten,* Klewer,

Bowen, D and Lawler, E (1992a) 'The empowerment of service workers: what, why, how and when', *Sloan Management Review,* Vol 33, pp 31–39.

Bowen, D and Lawler, E (1992b) 'Total quality-oriented human resources management', *Organizational Dynamics,* Vol 20, No 4, pp 29–41.

Brown, S W, Gummesson, E, Edvardson, B and Gustavsson, B O (eds) (1991), *Service Quality – Multidisciplinary and Multinational Perspectives,* Lexington.

Burn. G R (1990) *'Quality Function Development',* in Dale, B G and Plunkett, J J (eds), *Managing Quality,* Philip Allan/Simon & Schuster, Hemel Hempstead (For a more conceptual treatment, see Hauser and Clausing *op. cit.*

Buzzell, R D and Gale, B T (1987) *The PIMS Principles: Linking Strategy to Performance,* Free Press, New York.

Campion, M A and Thayer, P W (1987) 'Job design: approaches, outcomes and trade-offs', *Journal of Organisational Dynamics.* Vol 15, No 3, pp 66–79.

Carlzon, J (1987) *Moments of Truth,* Ballinger.

Carlzon, J and Hubendinck, U (1984) *The Cultural Revolution in SAS,* Scandinavian Airline System.

Carman, J M (1990) 'Consumer perceptions of service quality: an assessment of the SERVQUAL dimensions', *Journal of Retailing,* Vol 66, No 1, pp 33–35.

Christopher, M, Payne, A F T and Ballantyne, D (1991) *Relationship Marketing: Bringing Quality, Customer Service, and Marketing Together,* Butterworth-Heinemann, Oxford,

Clark, M and Payne, A F T (1993) 'Customer retention: does employee retention hold a key to success?', *1993 Annual Marketing Education Group Conference,* Loughborough.

Collins, B and Payne, A F T (1991) 'Internal marketing: a new perspective for HRM', *European Management Journal,* Vol 9, No 3, pp261–270.

Cronin, J J and Taylor, S A (1992) 'Measuring service quality: a reexamination and extension', *Journal of Marketing,* Vol 56, July, pp 55–68.

Crosby, P B (1979) *Quality is Free,* McGraw-Hill, New York.

Dale, B and Cooper, C (1992) *Total Quality and Human Resources: An Executive Guide,* Blackwell, Oxford.

Deming, W E (1982) *Out of the Crisis,* Massachusetts Institute of Technology.

Fox, K and Bender, S (1986–87) 'Diagnosing bank service environments as behaviour settings', *Journal of Retail Banking,* Vol 8, No 4, pp 49–55.

George, W R (1990) 'Internal marketing and organisational behaviour: a partnership in developing customer-conscious employees at every level', *Journal of Business Research,* Vol 20, pp 63–70.

Greenway, G S and Southgate, P W (1985) *Quality of Service in the Branch – The View from Either Side of the Counter,* ESOMAR/EFMA Seminar, Zurich, pp 123–137.

Grönroos, C (1980) 'Designing a long range marketing strategy for services' , *Long Range Planning,* Vol 13, April, pp 38–42.

Grönroos, C (1984) *Strategic Management and Marketing in the Service Sector,* Chartwell-Bratt, Bromley, Kent, pp 38–40.

Grönroos, C (1985) 'Internal marketing – theory and practice', in Block, T M, Upah G D and Zeithaml, V A (eds) *Service Marketing in a Changing Environment,* American Marketing Association, Chicago, pp 41–47.

Grönroos, C (1990) *Service Management and Marketing,* Lexington Books.

Grönroos, C (1993) 'Towards a third phase in service quality research', in *Advances in Services Marketing and Management,* Vol 2, JAI Press, Greenwich, Conn.

Gummesson, E (1987) 'The new marketing – developing long term interactive relationships', *Long Range Planning,* Vol 20, No 4, pp 10–20.

Gummesson, E (1988) 'Service quality and product quality combined', *Review of Business,* Vol 9, No 3, Winter, pp 14–19.

Gummesson, E (1993) *Quality Management in Service Organisations,* Internal Services Quality Association.

Gummesson, E (1994) 'Service management: an evaluation and the future', *International Journal of Service Industry Management,* Vol 5, No1, pp 77–96.

Hackman, J R and Oldham, G R (1980) *Work Redesign,* Addison-Wesley, Mass.

Hauser, J R and Clausing, D (1988) 'The house of quality', *Harvard Business Review,* May–June, pp 63–73.

Hurst, S (1993) 'Revealed at source', *Managing Service Quality,* January, pp 449–45.

Imai, M (1986) *Kaizen: The Key to Japan's Competitive Success,* Random House, London.

Juran, J M (1989) *Juran on Leadership for Quality,* Free Press, New York.

Kacker, R N (1988) 'Quality planning for service industries', *Quality Progress,* August, pp 39–42.

Kingham-Brundage, J (1992) 'Service mapping: gaining a concrete perspective on service system design', *The Third Quality in Services Symposium (QUIS 3),* University of Karlstad, Sweden, June.

Kunst, P and Lemmink, J (eds) (1991) *Quality Management in Services,* Van Gorcum Publishers.

Leonard, F S and Sasser, W E (1982) 'The incline of quality', *Harvard Business Review,* Vol 60, September–October, pp 163–171.

Oakland, J S (1989) *Total Quality Management,* Heinemann Professional Series, Oxford, pp 30–35.

Oliver, R L (1993) 'A conceptual model of service quality and service satisfaction: compatible goals, different concepts', in Swartz, T A, Bowen, D E and Brown, S W (eds) *Advances in Services Marketing and Management: Research and Practice,* Vol 2, JAI Press Greenwich, Conn.

Ovretveit, J A (1993) 'Auditing and awards for service quality', *International Journal of Service Industry Management,* Vol 4, No 2, pp 74–84.

Parasuraman, A, Zeithaml, V A and Berry, L L (1985) 'A conceptual model of service quality and its implementations for future research', *Journal of Marketing,* Vol 49, pp 41–50.

Parasuraman, A, Zeithaml, V A and Berry, L L (1988) 'SERVQUAL: a multiple-item scale for measuring consumer perceptions of service quality', *Journal of Retailing,* Vol 64, No 1, Spring, pp 12–40.

Parasuraman, Zeithaml, V A and Berry, L L (1991) 'Outstanding customer expectations of service', *Sloan Management Review,* Spring, pp 39–48.

Payne, A F T (1993) *The Essence of Services Marketing,* Prentice-Hall, New Jersey.

Piercy, N and Morgan, N (1991) 'Internal marketing – the missing half in the marketing programme', *Long Range Planning,* Vol 24, No 2, pp 82–93.

Porter, M E (1985) *Competitive Advantage: Creating and Sustaining Performance,* Free Press, New York, p 130.

Reichheld, F F (1993) 'Loyalty-based management', *Harvard Business Review,* March–April, pp 64–73.

Reichheld, F and Sasser, W E (1990) 'Zero defections: quality comes to services', *Harvard Business Review*, September–October, pp 105–216.

Rosander, A C (1989) *The Quest for Quality in Services*, Quality Press.

Schneider, B and Bowen, D E (1985) 'Employee and customer perceptions of service in banks: replication and extension', *Journal of Applied Psychology*, Vol 70, pp 423–433.

Shostack, G L (1987) 'Service positioning through structural change', *Journal of Marketing*, Vol 51, January, pp 34–43.

Taguchi, G and Clausing, D (1990) 'Robust quality', *Harvard Business Review*, January–February, pp 65–75.

Thompson, P, DeSouza, G and Gale, B T (1985) *The Strategic Management of Service Quality*, The Strategic Planning Institute, Mass.

Todd, P P (1985) *Automation and the Quality of Services: Conflicting or Complementary*, ESOMAR/EFMA Seminar, Zurich, p 76.

Townsend, T L (1990) *Commit to Quality*, Wiley, Chichester.

Wener, R E (1985) 'The environmental psychology of service encounters', in Czepiel, J A, Solomon, M R and Surprenant, C F (eds), *The Service Encounter*, Institute of Retail Management, Lexington, Mass, pp 103–104.

Wither, B (1990) 'Total marketing: total quality of the marketing concept', *Quarterly Review of Marketing*, Vol 15, No 2, pp 1–6.

Zeithaml, V A, Parasuraman, A and Berry, L L (1990) *Delivering Quality Service*, Free Press, New York.

Zeithaml, V A, Berry L L and Parasuraman, A (1993) 'The nature and determinants of customer expectations of service', *Journal of the Academy of Marketing Science*, Vol 21, pp 1–12.

11

A PATHOLOGY OF COMPANY-WIDE QUALITY INITIATIVES: SEVEN PRESCRIPTIONS FOR FAILURE[*]

David Ballantyne, Martin Christopher

and Adrian Payne

INTRODUCTION

The meaning of quality, as well as customer service, is undergoing review. The traditional production concept of 'conformance to specifications' is giving way to a customer orientation of quality, ie perceived quality. The new view of customer service is set in a broader context, as a cross-functional coordination issue, which impacts on *relationships* with specific target groups across a broad range of a company's activities. Also the idea of *total quality* across all functions focuses the scope of quality management on the total relationship between the firm and its customers, suppliers and other key markets, on an ongoing basis.

Many of the techniques of Total Quality Management and its organisational values – based approach are now being introduced in the services sector and in customer service divisions of manufacturing companies.

Of concern is the widespread failure of quality initiatives, whether production or service based, in meeting customer requirements on the one hand and management expectations on the other. We recognise also the outstanding success of some quality initiatives and herein lies the problem: success breeds orthodoxy and orthodoxy breeds a logic of conformity to the exclusion of situational variables. Whether conformance to these emergent 'prescriptions' hinders thinking and action towards organisational change is the interesting question. Our evidence

* A version of this chapter was presented at the fifth Annual Conference of the British Academy of Management, September 1993.

is drawn from our action research and informal discussions with senior company executives in a cross-section of European, North American and Australian companies which we present in this chapter as the 'pathology' of company-wide quality initiatives. In so doing, we have defined *seven prescriptions* for the failure of initiatives in quality improvement, and offer suggestions and an antidote.

To begin, we describe the new relationship emerging between quality, customer service and marketing. Unless management bring these activities together with new forms of collaboration and cross-functional coordination, there can in our view be no *market-orientated* quality improvement and therefore no sustainable competitive advantage.

We then discuss quality strategies. Unless we come to grips with the *intangibility* of the quality goal, and indeed the change processes, there can be no company-wide understanding of the problem, or the 'continuous improvement' required for its solution.

Lastly, we describe what goes wrong in company-wide quality initiatives and why some apparently positive logics of action turn out to be prescriptions for failure.

The Role of Customer Service

The meaning of customer service varies considerably from one company to another (La Londe and Zinszer, 1976). These perspectives range from the marketing logistics required to accept, process, deliver and build customer orders through to the 'friendliness' of staff in the service encounter.

Our view is that it is an exchange process influencing long-term *relationships* of mutual advantage. Customer service can be seen as a process which provides time, place and form utilities for the customer and which involves pre-sale, sale and post-sale transactions (Christopher, Schary and Skjott-Larsen, 1979).

Customer service decisions fit within the context of a marketing strategy and in our view form a key interface within this activity. However, the 'demarcation' between production, distribution and marketing functions is never absolute and so an overlap in responsibility can occur between quality management and marketing, often to the detriment of the perceived quality and service received by the customer.

The Role of Quality

The typical approach to quality is moving from one of final inspection to one of assessing whether critical processes are in control and giving guidance to others in the techniques involved. This change of focus from inspecting production *outputs* to monitoring the variation in process *during the process* has special significance in distribution and service industries, where production and consumption can occur simultaneously and traditional quality inspection techniques are impossible or ineffective.

This change in the role of quality has been a long time coming. Dr Walter Shewhart of the Bell Laboratories (USA) first made the distinction between 'controlled' and 'uncontrolled' variation in work processes in the 1920s. He used statistical control charts to monitor the performance quality of a process. According to the type of process, this measurement might be temperature, units, dimensions, or error rate, etc. W Edwards Deming and J M Juran are widely regarded as the men who taught the Japanese to achieve high quality at low cost. Deming had worked with Shewhart in America before the Second World War and his methods were used extensively during that war. Afterwards, markets for American goods sought volume, and quality was put to one side. Meanwhile, the Japanese faced a 'do or die' economic situation, and they listened to Deming, Juran and others.

As quality management in the 1980s expanded from the factory floor to the purchasing department on the one hand, and distribution on the other, some mistakes have been made, techniques have become articles of faith, and expectations have been raised to dizzy heights, for customers, staff and shareholders alike. Many if not most customer service and quality improvement initiatives in the 1980s have turned out to be prescriptions for failure because they have not been correctly aligned with marketing.

The Role of Marketing

In the 1950s marketing interest was primarily focused on consumer goods. In the 1960s increased attention also started to be directed towards industrial markets. In the 1970s considerable academic effort was placed on the area of non-profit or societal marketing. In the 1980s attention started to be directed at the services sector, an area of marketing that had received remarkably little attention in view of its importance in the overall economy.

Historically much of marketing theory has evolved from a study of consumer markets. However, the study of service and industrial markets has suggested that new perspectives are needed. For example, Gummesson (1987) points out how industrial firms' international operations are not so much primarily concerned with the manipulation of the 'Four Ps', as used in consumer goods marketing, rather they are concerned with reaching a critical mass in terms of the *relations* with customers, distributors, suppliers, public institutions, individuals, etc. The new theory of industrial marketing, 'network-interaction marketing' embraces 'all activities by the firm to build, maintain and develop customer relations' (Gummesson, 1987).

Whilst a *relationship marketing* focus has been present in some firms' marketing activities for many years, it is by no means a common philosophy throughout industrial and service firms today. The 1990s will, in our view, see a much increased acceptance of the relationship concept.

The purpose of relationship marketing strategy is to shape the market to your favour (to *create* the market if necessary). Relationship marketing and its association with *quality* and *customer service* seeks always to create enough value in the sale to bring customers back for more.

QUALITY AS A COMPETITIVE STRATEGY

One point we would emphasise here is that while relationship marketing requires a look sideways to the competition; it also means looking straight ahead to the customer, and systematically building a relationship with them. This seems obvious enough but in practice we all know it is the exception, not the rule. If you do not have the right cost levels you can't achieve the right price levels. If you don't have a clear vision of where you want to go, you won't get to the right place. However, if you don't work on quality improvement and innovation, you may *sell* today but you are less likely to sell to the same person or company again, or to any of their friends and associates.

In fractured deregulated markets, companies will not survive without quality. Quality is the means by which the firm *sustains* its position among competing offers over time. Quality is how the offer *gains* uniqueness and value in the eyes of the customer. Quality is both the act of making the offer different and its evaluation by customers.

Research by Parasuraman, Zeithaml and Berry (1985), conceptualises a number of quality gaps or potential breaks in the relationship linkages which lead to quality shortfalls. Because quality has been difficult to control it has been 'left to operations' by too many marketing managers, and perhaps, we should add, left to chance by too many marketing academics. The fact that this research specifically focused on *service quality* by no means discounts its broader relevance. Gap *Type 1* occurs when managers do not know what customers expect. *Type 2* is an absence (for whatever reason) of managerial commitment to correcting what customers expect. *Type 3* is variability in the performance of what customers expect, (this research study focused on contact personnel). And *Type 4* occurs when external communications about the offering increase customer expectations and, in consequence, decrease perceived quality. These four gaps lead to a fifth gap which is in fact an aggregate of them all, ie the gap between quality expected and quality perceived to have been received.

Of course, the general characteristics of quality solutions and service support vary from industry to industry – and, indeed, person to person because we are talking about the customer's perceptual world. In medical care, for example, quality solutions tend to involve both the efficacy of individual drugs to produce intended effects, and the correct selection of the right drug and information as to correct dosage. These are highly sensitive core competencies sought by customers. Service support in this case involves issues of availability, home service or surgery extended hours, emergency services, the reassurance of personal well-being and the right balance of professionalism and empathy.

The problem is that quality solutions and service support dimensions have no connections to departmental divisions which would suggest some neat internal allocation of responsibility for quality. This is particularly the case in service industries, where production, delivery and consumption can occur at the same time. Making connections between the activities of departmental divisions and customer perceived quality is the job of quality management, whose task is to create change processes which produce quality improvement.

SEVEN FAILURE-PRONE PRESCRIPTIONS

In managing the change processes for quality improvement, most of what needs to be done inside the organisation is invisible from the outside, and as with disorders of the body, the signs and symptoms of change can be misread. If the part that is critical is hidden from sight, the part that is clearly visible can be wrongly interpreted as the whole of the action. A wrong diagnosis is a prescription for failure. In discussions with company executives and in our research we have found seven flawed 'common-sense' prescriptions which invite failure.

Prescription One: 'We will cascade our commitment down to the troops. That should do it.'

Internal marketing messages are going to be rejected by many staff unless the communications have a coherent logic which fits the evidence of their past experience. Just as with advertising, internal marketing communications work best when they are designed to 'preach to the converted'. Message making is a difficult job when it attempts to get people to change their minds. Messages work best when they reinforce how people already feel and think.

People do not so much resist change, they resist being changed, especially when the implications of the change are beyond their grasp. When internal marketing communications attempt to change people's minds, these messages can work as signals of strategic intent. People are often willing to suspend 'disbelief' while they wait for some demonstrable action which confirms the truth of the message. Their attitude is 'you've told me, now show me ...' This is particularly so at middle management level. They need to know that 'commitment' has substance before they can effectively cascade the message down. Middle management will be asking themselves what effect the change programme will have on their own roles and responsibilities. Unless commitment is *demonstrated* from the top, middle management may well go through the motions and then make sure that nothing happens.

As a safe planning dictum, expect staff (sometimes a majority of staff) to hear 'mixed messages' in all major communications from the top. In other words, 'they are saying this, but ...'

Organisational defensive routines can cause a serious block in communications because they are effectively 'undiscussable'. (For a discussion of the logic embedded in mixed messages and how to avoid the pitfalls see Argyris (1986).) The quality trap really opens up if the CEO fails to realise the potentially ambiguous effects that apparently direct and clear communications can have in terms of established decision-making processes and the alignment of organisational power. Communication without action as supporting evidence (both real and symbolic) is empty rhetoric.

Prescription Two: 'We must invest in more training.'

The most common mistake is to jump directly into intensive training. In marketing terms the questions that should be asked (and often are not) are:

- Who are my target audience?
- What are their expectations?
- What knowledge do they need now?
- What skills do they need now?

- How can we monitor the learning process?

The investment in training is wasted if too much training is provided for too many people too soon. These issues concern *scale*. On the other hand, training in skills is necessary so that *individuals* can adjust to changing work contexts. This kind of learning has been called 'single loop learning', especially where the intention is that organisational performance remains stable within organisational norms. The strategic issue however, concerns *scope*. The pathway to continuous quality improvement challenges the patterns of operations and the very organisational norms which have previously defined effective performance. This second kind of learning is called 'double loop learning'. (The subject of organisational learning is an evolving one. For an introduction see Garratt (1987); for 'single loop learning' see Bateson (1972), and for 'double loop learning' see Argyris and Schon (1978).)

If this must be called 'training', then what is needed is a new process in training for line managers and specialists which allows them access across functional borders for information, and works to integrate solutions to problems which transcend the usual departmental blocks. The ability to codify what is learned over time and retain the knowledge through the organisation is what is intended. This is a cyclical process, and one special representation of it is the 'quality wheel' presented in Figure 11.1. If the

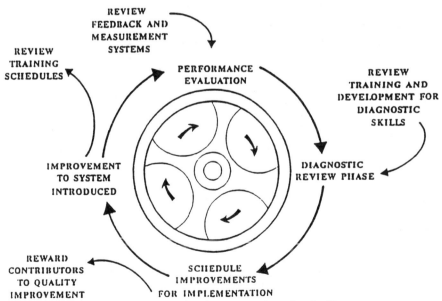

Figure 11.1 The 'quality wheel': turning the wheel of improvement – continuously

organisation cannot teach itself to learn, which is the intention of 'double loop learning', then investment in training is a never-ending story. A cost-effective business proposal would be to invest in learning how people learn, then develop the training.

Prescription Three: 'We intend to build a strong culture as a priority.'

Just as the culture of a nation is shaped and sustained by deeply held values and beliefs, so too is the world of business. Changing the 'culture' of a particular company is a task of great subtlety. It is possible, for example, to change surface appearances without changing the culture at all by changing the marketing artifacts such as logo, signage, mission statements, 'corporate wardrobe' and the design of the stationery. Giving a company a superficial change of identity, in itself, will have no significant or lasting cultural impact.

Yet corporate cultures do change. It is a question of intention and action. It starts with a vision of what the company might be, or its *strategic intent*. Having said that, you cannot take direct action to change cultures. Soft goals need hard plans. What is necessary is a series of coherent actions which confirm the strategic intention. It comes down to doing things in new ways, communicating the effects, and using some events symbolically to shine light on the meaning of those new ways.

The leaders of organisations have a major impact on corporate culture because they alter the way companies initiate and respond to opportunities and threats. Just as brand values must be congruent with brand image, so must corporate values be congruent with corporate aspirations. What kind of culture is desirable? One that suits the purpose, competencies and market opportunities of the company. There is a lot of nonsense written about corporate culture and we certainly do not want to suggest detailed prescriptive rules for engineering its change. We recommend Schein (1985) as a guide through the maze.

Prescription Four: 'We want to get everybody involved.'

Getting everybody involved sounds fine. It is a question of timescale. Many companies give the impression of wanting to get it over and done with. People in organisations are so focused on the daily problems to be sorted out and on the downside risk of not doing so they end up shutting out messages which signal opportunities and possibilities all around them. There is often virtue in starting small. In that way commitment can be built and confirmed by action programmes and the results broadcast across the organisation. This provides a signal to others that the commitment has integrity. More and more people become involved in each recurring cycle of activity. The movement through the involvement phases of *vanguard, ferment, followers* and *stabilisers* is described in Figure 11.2.

It is an exercise in futility to attempt to get people actively involved if they cannot be supported within a quality network of committed people and by training resources. Our view is that involvement should be *task* focused but *process* led. By that we mean people volunteer or are selected to work on the 'vital few' work processes which will create maximum impact (under the Pareto principle – see, for example, Juran 1989:150). Certainly, detailed planning must precede any communications to staff. (Ways and means to overcome barriers to creative involvement are discussed in Pace and McMullen (1988).) It is here that internal marketing

4. REWRITING CULTURAL 'SCRIPTS':
- Quality is reinforced by its own positive consequences

1. SELECTING AND SUPPORTING KEY CATALYSTS:
- Change Agents
- True Believers

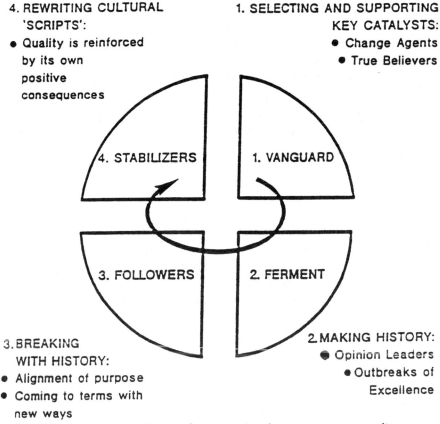

3. BREAKING WITH HISTORY:
- Alignment of purpose
- Coming to terms with new ways

2. MAKING HISTORY:
- Opinion Leaders
- Outbreaks of Excellence

Figure 11.2 Four phases of organisational commitment to quality

can function as a communications arm for quality mangement. There is a convergence of interests between marketing management and quality management at this point which is not often recognised or exploited.

Prescription Five: 'We will introduce Quality Circles and see what happens.'

A Quality Circle is a volunteer group of workforce members who have undergone training for the purpose of solving work-related problems (Juran, 1989:360). The Circle concept evolved in Japan in the early 1960s as a support for the quality management techniques which had been introduced there by Demming and Juran in 1950 and 1954 respectively.

Historically, Quality Circles are an adjunct to a more broadly based quality management approach. Quality Circles differ from other participative groups such as quality improvement teams or diagnostic review groups in that they are always volunteer based and usually select their own problems for diagnosis. It would be fair to say that their great advantage is in dealing with assignable (special) causes of variation. In other words, when the participants are close to the problem area, they are able to contribute valuable solutions to the 10,000 little issues that in aggregate make a difference. Because the main focus of such groups is assignable/special causes, they are able to effectively 'drain the swamp' so that the real characteristics of a process are revealed for statistical control or monitoring in other ways.

So far so good. Difficulties arise when groups are unsupported by management and they do not have access to valid customer data which guides the choice of problems for diagnosis. A closely related problem is that if Quality Circle networks are not connected to the organisation's hierarchy through a quality planning group or steering committee, they tend to 'float off' the organisational chart.

There are probably good reasons for introducing Quality Circles in some companies as a pilot venture towards a more broad-based quality improvement process. Without a champion, however, they will surely die. When Quality Circles demonstrate a better way of managing, and lead to a more substainable quality commitment, they serve as a catalyst. However, it is unwise to launch a Quality Circle programme to 'see what happens'. It will only make the launch of a full-scale initiative at some future time more difficult.

Prescription Six: 'We can't improve service unless we set standards.'

Only the customer can 'set' service standards. Therefore, how the customers' standards are signalled and interpreted by the company is the central issue. It is no good setting operational standards which have no meaning to the customer. It is characteristic of an authoritarian approach to quality improvement to move quickly to standard setting as a prerequisite for improving service. There are better ways.

The first step is to identify which work processes are connected with the 'vital few' customer service characteristics that are of critical concern to the customer. One 'sifting and sorting' design technique sometimes used is Quality Function Deployment (Burn, 1990; Hauser and Clausing, 1988). What is needed next is a clear picture of the key processes, usually achieved by flow charting (Ballantyne, 1990a). What is usually revealed at this point is that the critical processes have no clear ownership patterns. In other words, nobody is in charge! Who *owns* the process? This is next to be resolved. This involves negotiation with key departments. Linking the 'vital few' critical service issues to key processes is a matter of judgement and wisdom.

Through such a procedure of linking and matching, a *target value* might finally be generated after careful consideration as presenting the ideal state of a particular process characteristic. This is the *standard* at which to aim, but it is by no means the standard by which performance of the process in its current state can be measured. Its function is in giving *direction* to the process of continuous improvement. Of course, intermediate goals can be set as 'standards' and these relate to periods of time and certain operating conditions (see Kacker, 1988).

Prescription Seven: 'The bottom line tells us when we are succeeding.'

There is no one solitary way of monitoring progress and what is useful is a range of external and internal feedback mechanisms which enable a 'fix' on quality. A generic list of strategic audits and surveys is shown in Figure 11.3.

The final score is of course traditionally profit or surplus, expressed in numbers and set in a historical cost accounting framework. This is an important convention, but it is still only one dimension. (For an account of how Japanese management accounting systems have played a major role in integrating new business strategies see Morgan and Weerakon (1989).)

PRIMARY		SECONDARY	
1	Strategic intent	1.1	Mission statement
		1.2	Philosphy statement
2	Strategic audits and surveys	2.1	Staff markets (internal climate monitor)
		2.2	Customer markets analysis (critical service issues)
		2.3	Potential markets analysis (non-users)
		2.4	Competitors (benchmarking)
		2.5	Non-competitors (benchmarking)
		2.6	Suppliers (co-partnership opportunities)
		2.7	New product markets (product development)
3	Strategy formulation/ realignment	3.1	Strategic direction
		3.2	Market selection
		3.3	Revisit mission statement in 1.1
		3.4	Revisit philosophy statement in 1.2

Figure 11.3 Strategic scanning process for quality leadership

There is no doubt that many quality improvements can actually *reduce* the cost of quality. It is a question of eliminating waste in resources and time without reducing value to the customer (see Figure 11.4). Time is a powerful dimension of success in cost-effective quality improvement. This has been the Japanese experience. The strategic imperative is not to set up projects at great speed, rather it is to set the sights on the quality leadership goal, take small steps, check the outcomes and effects as you go, then take more decisive action according to the evidence from internal and external sources of feedback.

Turning the quality improvement wheel is slow at first but produces results, which have all the appearance of 'fast and flexible' action when viewed from your competitor's watch-tower.

With a few minds at work, the sum total of inputs starts to organise itself into an outcome. In a sense, the solution becomes 'obvious'. This is not

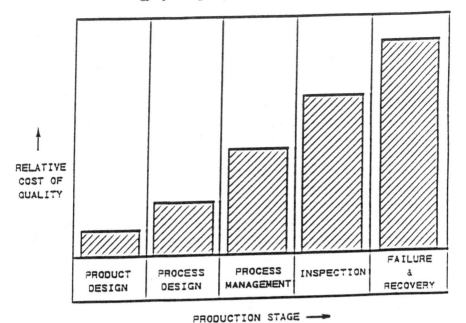

Figure 11.4 How to eliminate quality costs

our 'natural' way of thinking things through because our traditional Aristotelian logic is based on judgement and analysis.

Company-wide, we need to *design* our way out of quality problems. We are not naturally good at this because we have not in business life developed the constructive and creative habits of thinking that are required for design. This is why management must empower staff and create the changes that enable the new ideas and problem-solving approaches to come forward.

GETTING THE PRESCRIPTIONS RIGHT

How can we possibly 'break-out' of our 'culture-bound' prescriptions for failure?

What is needed is a framework for the diagnostic review of work processes, within a strategy for 'continuous improvement'. There are a number of alternative approaches. They all involve 'turning the wheel' of continuous improvement. This means continuously reassessing the historic role of managers in the planning, organising and controlling of work. It also means diffusing responsibility for *knowledge generation* so that staff at all levels can contribute to the process of continuous improvement by knowledge sharing. The decision authority of managers rests on *knowledge application* and need not be affected. In this way, there is more knowledge for managers to work with and a better informed workforce. Knowledge is the antidote to failure in our pathology of company-wide quality initiatives.

At issue here are two incompatible views of what management can reasonably expect of workers and the kind of partnership they can share with them. One is based on imposing *control* to achieve compliance. The other is based on eliciting *commitment*. The shift is not as radical as it may seem at first glance. A transitional approach is suggested. The cornerstone of the transitional stage is the voluntary participation of employees in cross-functional problem-solving groups.

If a real commitment to quality involves organisational change, then management must change. A common error, especially in mature organisations, is to make only token changes and rely on internal and external 'communications' to achieve effects. Alternatively, or in conjunction with 'communications', management tries a succession of technique-oriented changes to achieve quality effects. None of this is wrong. It is just not sufficient. This is particularly evident in service industries, where the realisation comes early that an improvement in customer service involves actually changing the way work is organised and the way managers must 'manage' the activities of the business.

Where quality change programmes are well intentioned, and not merely 'this year's marketing promotion', a third approach has emerged. This approach works in the domain of both people *and* processes with continuous improvement as the long-term goal. This involves a transitional step for managers to make about what managers do. It is a strategic step because it has a profound effect on the quality of internal marketing communications and managerial styles, and challenges the corporate culture. Such an approach is an antidote to slavishly 'managing' the prescriptions for failure and will improve the chances of sustained quality improvement. It may be difficult but the options are looking worse.

References

Argyris, C (1986) 'Reinforcing organisational defensive routines: an unintended human resources activity', *Human Resource Management*, Vol 25, No 4, pp 541–555.

Argyris, C and Schon, D (1978) *Organizational Learning: A Theory of Action Perspective*, Addison-Wesley, Reading, Mass.

Ballantyne, D F (1990a) 'Coming to grips with service intangibles using quality management techniques', *Marketing Intelligence and Planning*, Vol 8, No 6.

Bateson, G (1972) *Steps to an Ecology of Mind*, Ballantine, New York.

Burn, G R (1990) 'Quality Function Deployment', in Dale, B G and Plunkett, J J (eds), *Managing Quality*, Phillip Allan/Simon & Schuster, Hemel Hempstead.

Christopher, M G, Schary, P P and Skjott-Larsen, T (1979) *Customer Service and Distribution Strategy*, Associated Business Press.

Deming, W E (1982) *Out of the Crisis*, Massachusetts Institute of Technology, Cambridge, Mass.

Disney, J and Bendell, A (1990) 'The potential for the application of Taguchi methods of quality control in British industry', in Dale, B J and Plunkett, J J (eds), *Managing Quality*, Phillip Allan/Simon & Schuster, Hemel Hempstead.

Garratt, B (1987) *The Learning Organisation*, Fontana, London.

Gronroos, C (1983) 'Innovative marketing strategies and organisation structure in service firms', in Berry, L L, Shostack, G L and Upah, G D (eds), *Emerging Perspectives on Services Marketing*, American Marketing Association, Chicago.

Gronroos, (1984) *Strategic Management and Marketing in the Service Sector*, Chartwell-Bratt, Bromley, Kent.

Gummesson, E (1987) 'The new marketing – developing long-term interactive relationships', *Long Range Planning*. Vol 20, No 4, pp 10–20.

Gummesson, E (1988) 'Service quality and product quality combined', *Review of Business*, Vol 9, No 3.

Hauser, J R and Clausing, D (1988) 'The house of quality', *Harvard Business Review*, May–June, pp 63–73.

Juran, J M (1989) *Juran on Leadership for Quality*, Free Press, New York.

Kacker, R N (1988) 'Quality planning for service industries', *Quality Progress*, August, pp 39–42.

La Londe, B J and Zinszer, P H (1976) *Customer Service: Meaning and Measurement*, NCPDM, Chicago.

Morgan, M J and Weerakon, S H (1989) 'Japanese management accounting: its contribution to the Japanese economic miracle', *Management Accounting*, June, pp 40–43.

Oakland, J S (1989) *Total Quality Management*, Heinemann Professional Series, Oxford.

Pace, L and McMullen, T B (1988) 'What is true involvement?' *Journal for Quality and Participation*, Vol 11, No 3, pp 36–38.

Parasuraman, A, Zeithaml, V A and Berry, L L (1985) 'A conceptual model of service quality and its implications for future research', *Journal of Marketing*, Vol 49.

Schein, E H (1985) *Organisational Culture and Leadership*, Jossey-Bass, London.

PART FIVE

VALUE CREATION THROUGH RELATIONSHIP MARKETING

12

RELATIONSHIP MARKETING FROM A VALUE SYSTEM PERSPECTIVE*

Uta Jüttner and Hans Peter Wehrli

INTRODUCTION: RELATIONSHIP MARKETING – STATE OF THE ART

Relationship marketing has emerged in response to the new claims of the environment which include blurring boundaries between markets or industries, an increasing fragmentation of markets (Shani and Chalasani, 1992), shorter product lifecycles, rapid changing customer buying patterns and more knowledgeable and sophisticated customers (Shapiro 1991; Webster, 1993). In this higher market and competitive turbulence in general (Joshi, 1993) long-term relationships with customers are seen as a prerequisite for competitive advantages of a company (Webster, 1992).

The new strategic focus on customer relationships by its proponents is seen at the same time as the foundation for the development of relationship marketing as a new marketing concept (Ellis *et al.*, 1993; Webster, 1993). The core idea of the new concept can be expressed as a shift from the 'tell us what colour you want' school to a 'let's figure out together whether and how colour matters to your larger goal' marketing philosophy (McKenna, 1991). The idea of customer satisfaction is hence complemented by the comprehensive integration of the customer into an interactive value-generating process, based on interdependence and reciprocity.

Major research has been carried out in this area in industrial marketing (Anderson and Narus, 1991; Arndt, 1979; Ford, 1980; Frazier *et al.*, 1988; Hallen, *et al.*, 1991; Heide and John, 1990; Spekman, 1988; Jackson, 1985; Shapiro, 1991), service marketing (Crosby *et al.*, 1990; Czepiel, 1990; Grönroos, 1990), marketing channels (Anderson and Narus, 1990) and in

---

* This chapter was first published in the *International Journal of Service Industry Management,* Vol 5, no 5, 1994, pp 54–73, and is reproduced with permission.

retailing (Berry and Gresham, 1986). Recently – mainly with the help of new information and communication technologies – the concept has been applied to consumer marketing as well (Blattberg and Deighton, 1991; Copulsky and Wolf 1990; McKenna, 1988; Shani and Chalasani, 1992; Vavra, 1993a). Besides these 'business marketing-oriented fields' there are also attempts to transfer relationship marketing to non-profit or social marketing problems (McCort, 1993).

The overall objective of relationship marketing, the facilitation and maintenance of long-term customer relationships, leads to changed focal points and modifications of the marketing management process. The common superior objectives of all strategies are enduring unique relationships with customers ('relationship customisation') (Berry and Gresham, 1986) which cannot be imitated by competitors and therefore provide sustainable competitive advantages. A precondition is the provision of tools that help to assess the potential of the individual customer over time. Those 'customer lifecycles' are proposed on the basis of phase sequences until now not commonly defined (Dwyer *et al.*, 1987; Ford 1980).

Concerning market segmentation, 'bottom-up' as opposed to 'top-down' approaches gain importance (Day, 1980). Those are superior when dealing with highly fragmented markets, because the starting point is the needs of a single or a few customers. These needs can gradually be built up to larger customer bases while still addressing each customer as a niche ('segment-of-one marketing': Pine, 1993). From this perspective, every customer in the sense of a 'micromajority' (McKenna, 1988) can invent a new market for the company.

The assessment of the 'segment potential' of the customer not only follows on the basis of individualised customer characteristics, but also includes factors about the existent or potential relationship. Hence, tools are necessary that secure the identification of those 'relational characteristics' (Shapiro, 1991). In the same way the positioning should reflect not only customers' perceptions of products and services, but also the perception and evaluation of the relationship from the customers' point of view (McCort, 1993).

New aspects concerning the design of the *marketing mix* result from emphasising activities that start 'after the sale is over' (Levitt, 1983), aimed at reaching a balance between marketing efforts for gaining new customers and those for keeping the existing customer base (Vavra, 1993b). These include:

- The core idea of products and *product policy* is that the value of a product or service is determined by the interactions between buyer and seller ('relationship specific offering', Anderson and Narus, 1991). The complexity of this relationship hence leads to a higher density of values ('offer augmentation') (Berry and Gresham, 1986; Levitt, 1983) and the integration of multiple service aspects – even in manufacturing goods (McKenna, 1991).

- The fact that every single relationship should be treated as an investment for the company shows 'customer lifetime value' (Blattberg and Deighton, 1991) as the guiding criterion for *pricing policies*. This customer lifetime value reflects the value of the individual customer over time.

- Within the *communication mix,* the prime objective is to learn from the customer (Shapiro, 1991). As a consequence, communication messages do not primarily deal with the features of the products,[1] but address directly individual customer characteristics and preferences. The additional customer information gained in each new contact (transaction) is collected and saved in a 'customer information file' (Vavra, 1993b). The increasing importance of new information and communication technologies for the implementation of relationship marketing can therefore be explained by its ability to enable the handling of large amounts of data. This in turn embodies programmability and permits the provision of information bases for individualised dialogues even in large market segments.

- A *distribution system* not only provides the delivery of an end product, but also influences the way and manner in which the important customer contact takes place – the 'moment of truth' (Normann, 1984). Distribution is a critical variable and has to be assessed for its value-generating potential. Exploiting this potential can result in either a reduction of barriers for relationship maintenance (eg time, knowledge) (Smith and Johnson, 1993) or an enhancement of future customer contacts (eg by gaining additional customer information, 'blueprinting customer contact points') (Vavra, 1993b). The superior idea for designing distribution systems is the individualised delivery – 'customising distribution' (Fincke and Goffard, 1993).

These principles of objectives, strategies and the marketing mix design of relationship marketing can be implemented effectively only when the basic philosophy of customer commitment is supported by and rooted within the whole company (Levitt, 1983; Shapiro, 1991). The ability to create and develop long-term relationships is strongly connected with personal skills and the individual motivation of the personnel (Ulrich, 1989). For this reason, organisational culture (Webster, 1992) and internal marketing (Grönroos, 1990; Gummesson, 1987) are treated as important aspects influencing the implementation of the concept. Concerning aspects of organisational culture, a focus on elements (norms and personal values) which enhance an appreciation for relationships can be observed (Ellis *et al.*, 1993). The emphasis on internal marketing on the other hand is based on the idea that relationship-oriented companies can improve by turning their strategic vision inward (Grönroos, 1990). Internal marketing is hence considered a prerequisite for successful external marketing.

The economic benefit resulting from the introduction and implementation of relationship marketing can be related to the following causes:

- The marketing or transaction costs for every customer can be reduced within long-term relationships (Grönroos, 1990).
- The sales volume per customer can be increased in relationships for example by 'cross-selling' products (Shani and Chalasani, 1992).
- Having a 'core group' of customers provides the company with a market for testing and introducing new products with reduced risk and lower costs.
- Market research can be conducted more efficiently because resource-intensive isolated projects are replaced by continuous customer contact data collection and processing.
- Relationship marketing provides a basis for the facilitation of individualised exchange processes on mass markets 'mass customisation' (Pine, 1993; Pine *et al.*, 1993) and hence has the potential to combine advantages of large volume and differentiation (Glazer, 1991).

The main issues of the new marketing philosophy, as well as the suggestions derived from them for the marketing management process, illustrate the variety in the different contributions and the main thrust of research. Parallel to reaching a well defined conceptual framework a precise understanding of the theoretical scope must be developed. This discussion will adhere to the context of the marketing exchange paradigm, as the relationship marketing concept strives for a redefinition of transactions as the core of marketing (Alderson, 1957).

RELATIONSHIP MARKETING WITHIN THE EXCHANGE PARADIGM

In outlining the conceptual framework the shift from transactions to relationships as the centre of marketing exchange processes is one central

Table 12.1 Marketing exchange understanding

	Transaction	**Relationship**
Objective	To make a sale (sale is end result and measure of success) Customer needs satisfaction (customer buys values)	To create a customer (sale is beginning of relationship) Customer integration (interactive value generation)
Customer understanding	Anonymous customer Independent buyer and seller	Well-known customer Interdependent buyer and seller
Marketers' task and performance criteria	Assessment on the basis of products and prices Focus on gaining new customers	Assessment on the basis of problem-solving competence Focus on value enhancing of existing customers
Core aspects of exchange	Focus on products Sale as a conquest Discreet event Monologue to aggregated broad customer segments	Focus on service Sale as an agreement Continuing process Individualized dialogue

proposition. Numerous publications compare the old and new exchange understanding (transactional versus relational exchange) (Dwyer *et al.*, 1987; Frazier *et al.*, 1988; Gundlach and Murphy, 1993; Joshi, 1993; Shapiro, 1991; Webster, 1993). The main distinctive differences are summarized in Table 12.1.

A comprehensive discussion about the criteria that mark and distinguish marketing exchange processes can be traced in the literature in the mid-1970s and 1980s. One framework that originated out of this discussion is the 'conceptual exchange framework' (Bagozzi, 1975), which facilitates the identification and conceptualization of marketing behaviour. The relationships underlying the new concept can be positioned within this framework.

Bagozzi differentiates two core dimensions in his exchange framework: exchange 'types' (restricted, generalised and complex) and exchange 'meanings' (utilitarian, symbolic and mixed) (see Figure 12.1). Types refer to the number of actors involved and the direction(s) of the exchange. 'Meaning' concerns the reasons for the occurring exchange. By relating meanings to the three different types, the whole framework can be presented as a matrix as shown in Figure 12.1.

Exchange Types

Restricted exchanges refer to exchange dyads, ie the structure is restricted

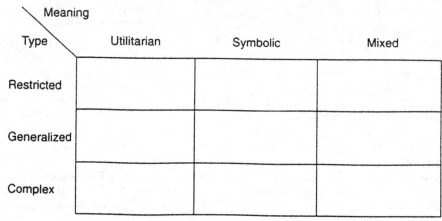

Figure 12.1 Conceptual exchange framework

to two actors (eg buyer/seller). Both persons directly give and receive a valued offering and hence the exchange situation reflects the attempt to maintain a quid pro quo (something of value in exchange for something of value).

The *generalised* exchange types involve at least three parties. The actors do not directly benefit from each other, but receive a transferred value from a third person. This indirect reciprocity constitutes marketing exchanges with common interests (Carman, 1980) and the actors form a social system.

Complex exchange types further enlarge the system perspective. The integration of direct (restricted) and indirect (generalised) sequences of exchanges generate an open or closed system of interdependent partners. The interdependence of the whole system can be analysed only if, apart from dyadic sequences, their effects on the total web of exchanges and relations are also considered.

Exchange Meanings

In exchanges with *utilitarian* meanings goods are given in return for money or other goods. The explanation of the occurrence is strongly related to the objects exchanged. The objects are evaluated by actors maximising self-interest and are purchased on the basis of physical attributes, availability and price.

Symbolic meanings explain the occurrence of exchanges by transfer of psychological, social or other intangible values. Compared with utilitarian meanings there is a changed focus from the value of the object to the symbolic meaning of the process.

Exchange processes with *mixed* meanings integrate utilitarian (object-related) and symbolic (process-related) values. The generated value can therefore reflect tangible or intangible attributes of the products and/or intangible aspects of the process. This perspective leads to a differentiation of three potential value dimensions: an outcome-related (received products/objects), an experience-related (psychological states associated with the process) and an action-related dimension (actions performed by the actors eg cooperation) (Bagozzi, 1979; Houston and Gassenheimer, 1987). Whereas the first dimension is restricted to the object exchanged, all three value dimensions can be exploited only in exchange processes with mixed (object- and process-related) meanings, as illustrated in Figure 12.2.

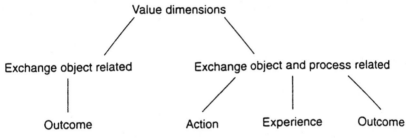

Figure 12.2 Exchange value dimensions

Positioning the conclusions that have emerged from the debate about relationship marketing, until now, shows two interesting focal points regarding content and structure: a limitation of the perspective to dyadic situations, ie restricted exchange types; and the focusing of symbolic and intangible, process-related meanings. Compared with the restricted types

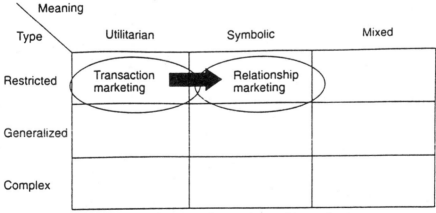

Figure 12.3 Exchange focus relationship marketing

with mainly utilitarian meanings characteristic for transaction marketing[2] now the exchange focus within the matrix shifts, as shown in Figure 12.3.

Relationship marketing proposes interactive approaches, integrating the seller and buyer perspective in isolation (Anderson and Narus, 1991) as well as the perspective common to both actors (Ellis *et al.*, 1993; Martin and Sohi, 1993). Even though proponents agree that relationships develop in social systems, the system is considered only as a constellation of situational contingencies that determine the exchange (Anderson and Narus, 1991; Jackson, 1985: Joshi, 1993; Shapiro, 1991). It is thus a constellation of exogenous variables affecting the behaviour of the relationship partner in dyads (individual actors or organisations within the value chain). This system perspective in the sense of 'dyadic exchanges within superior social systems' is consistent with Bagozzi's formal theory of transactions (Bagozzi, 1978, 1979). It has been criticised for its limitation by Ferrell and Perrachione (1980).

The shift of focus from object (utilitarian) to process-related meanings (symbolic) can not only be deduced from the proposed terminology (relationships), but also is expressed in suggestions for implementation. Focal points for facilitating and maintaining relationships are psychological and social factors of the individual actors and their interacting, eg the generation of trust (Moorman *et al.*, 1992; Moorman *et al.*, 1993; Schurr and Ozanne, 1985; Swan and Nolan, 1985; Swan *et al.*, 1985), the quality of communication (Dwyer, *et al.*, 1987) and the emergence of relational norms (Dwyer *et al.*, 1987; Gundlach and Murphy, 1993; Heide and John, 1992). The almost exclusive emphasis on symbolic meanings leads to the neglect of substantial elements (resources and competencies) that determine the quality of products (eg technological or process-related know-how) and represent the outcome value dimension. Instead, the authors stress the capability of the boundary-spanning personnel as well as the combination of their capabilities with information processing capacity (Berry and Gresham, 1986). Individual product-related competences are not valued as a success-determining factor: 'The interactive marketer is constrained less by its current production and technical expertise than by the affinity group it serves. The company must make affinity the first consideration and treat its ability to produce the service or product as secondary' (Blattberg and Deighton, 1991). Summarising the cooperative actions and their psychological effects are seen as the main reasons for the enhancement of the overall value (including all three value dimensions).

This discussion of the main contributions to relationship marketing, thus far, suggests an area of potential development that has been

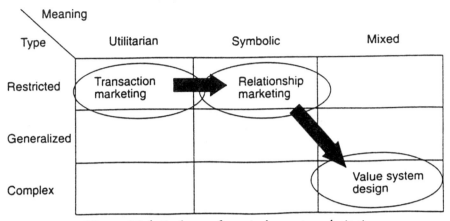

Figure 12.4 Exchange focus 'value system design'

neglected: the consideration of relationships in systems (complex exchange). Complex systems are, in our view, at the same time networks. Both have a structure of independent relationships that has emerged unconsciously or was consciously designed. In order to describe, explain or influence the system or network the independent influence *between* the relationships, as well as the interdependence of object-related competences and process-related intangible elements (mixed meaning) *within* each isolated relationship, have to be considered. In Figure 12.4 we use the term 'value system design' for the conscious design of these complex exchange types with mixed meanings.

Value system design requires a change from relationships in systems to 'systemic relationships'. This perspective refers to first steps within the relationship marketing literature that outline the potential enlargement to 'system relationship marketing'. Furthermore it corresponds to the proposed differentiated relation between transactions and relationships. Both references underline that value system design should be seen as supplementary to relationship marketing.

The first steps of an intensified system or network view were taken in industrial marketing, when it was recognised that an increasing complexity of values (value constellations) made strategic partnerships a necessity for their implementation (Arndt, 1979; Shapiro, 1991). This is the central reflection of 'symbiotic marketing', which transfers to marketing the idea of various organisms living together for mutual advantage (Alder, 1966; Varadarajan and Rajaratnam, 1986). However, the idea of an organisation, which is embedded in a sequence of isolated dyadic exchange relations with its customers, retailers, suppliers and strategic partners of the same value-generating activity, remains. A stronger reference to the idea of value system design can be found in Kotler (1991) and Webster (1992). Kotler (1991) differentiates between 'transaction marketing', 'relationship marketing' and 'network marketing', the latter of which is classified as the 'ultimate outcome of relationship marketing'. Webster (1992) views network marketing as a future challenge that leads to a new determination of the role of marketing and needs an enlarged conceptual framework in order to catch the phenomena involved.[3] The strongest correspondence with the value system design is represented by the network approach proposed by Mattsson (1985). His approach takes into consideration the 'whole set of dyadic relationships' (p 268), 'the causal relationships between the sequences' and the complementary, heterogeneous and long-term character of the processes.[4] All points are important for the value system design as well. This perspective should not be mixed up with the macro marketing approaches (eg commodity approach) through which the marketing discipline was born. Instead it is an intermediate prospective that supplements the 'micro marketing management approach' with the analysis of the marketing manager's tasks in value systems.

Transactions in our understanding and consistency with Shapiro (1991: 436), Dwyer *et al.*, (1987), Jackson (1985) and Joshi (1993) are not contrary concepts, but phases of a potentially evolutionary process. Relationships arise from a multiplication of transactions with a higher interdependence between the single events shown in Figure 12.5. However, not every transaction has the potential to contribute to a

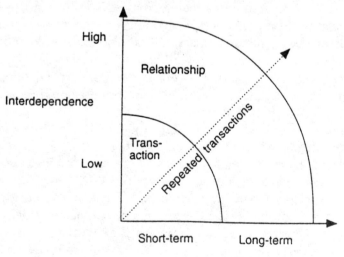

Figure 12.5 Transactions and relationships

relationship. This is why a thorough cost–benefit analysis is required before a decision to invest in the development of a relationship is taken.

This integrating perspective does not originate from the contributions to relationship marketing. Rather, relationships have been part of the discussion about marketing relevant exchange processes (Carman, 1980; Bagozzi, 1974a, 1974b, 1975; Hunt, 1983). In addition, the consequences for the design of marketing activities depending on the isolated or continuous character of transactions or relationships, respectively, and the corresponding larger or smaller social distance have already been introduced (Houston and Gassenheimer, 1987).

VALUE SYSTEM DESIGN

The phenomenon of value system design is based on the conviction that marketing transactions and relationships increasingly take place in groups of actors (organisations) that change over time. A value system is defined as a system of interdependent actors who raise the total value of the system by interactive value-generating processes and compete with other value systems in the 'competition system' of which they are parts. Accordingly, the competition system is the system of actors competing and cooperating in isolation or in value systems which determine the rules and structures of the competition taking place. A value system at the same time is a marketing system, because it is formed, stabilised and transformed by a network of functionally interdependent marketing exchange processes (Lazer and Kelley, 1962).

The understanding of value generating inside the value system requires a departure from the value-chain orientation, where the company is embedded in a great variety of isolated, dyadic relationships (Norman and Ramirez, 1993). With the help of the value chain, however, it is still possible to show the extraction of singular activities or the entanglement

Table 12.2 Interactively generating system value

Understanding of values	Customer uses value as input into his own value-generating activities
	Value must be generated through interactive value-generating activities
	Product value as a prerequisite for new interactions
Understanding of value-generating activities	System of value generating activities
	Company designs the system through relationships
	Company has an agent who arranges value-generating activities

with customer value chains (Porter, 1985). However, in a sequential line-up of value-generating activities there is no way to represent complex networks, where relations between all links are possible and feedbacks between any single relation onto the whole system are likely. The central characteristics of interactively generated system value are shown in Table 12.2.

In the interactive generation of system value the offering (value offered), analogous to the perspective of relationship marketing, is viewed as an input into the value-generating activities (customer strategies). By the respective orientation to the value-generating activities the potential for value generating activities is increased. Simultaneously, because of the contribution to a variety of activities the value generated is characterised by a higher density. The product value is seen as a precondition and as a foundation for maintaining durable interactions that already exist (transformation of transactions into relationships) and for new interactions to be created (increase of the expandable transaction potential).

The interaction of value-generating activities takes place in a value system without clearly defined starting and finishing points. Thus all actors can be customers and suppliers of values simultaneously. The roles of actors can be affected, too, in such a way that any single company will try to influence the structure of the value system. The central goal of all actors is to improve the value system in order to increase the share of value per actor by co-productive interactions. Thus, the perspective on competition as such also changes: the competitivity of the value system and not that of a singular actor is important (Johnston and Lawrence, 1988:95).

The release mechanism for the creation of a value system is a value constellation (complex problem solution), which becomes the central value system function. This central idea or value constellation is a unique interpretation of customer needs (eg home shopping). The value constellation is at the same time a result and expression of company-specific competences: their creation as well as realisation depend on product-overlapping competences.[5] In the form of market values the constellation normally is composed of several partial, sometimes even industry-crossing products (or performances) and forms a product-service hybrid (eg personal computers as a combination of consumer electronics, information and communication services). The implementation of the value constellation starts with transactions between various actors that evolve over time into relationships and by linking and/or structuring, finally lead to a stabilisation of the value system. Since out of

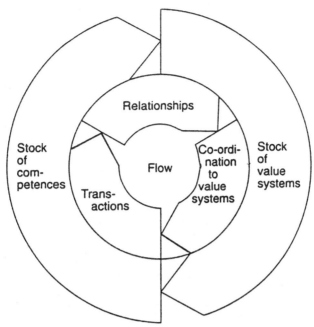

Figure 12.6 Model of value system generation and renewal

an existent value system new possibilities for transactions evolve (increase of the transaction potential), development, improvement and self-renewal (generation of substituting value constellations by the value system itself) proceed through an endless evolutionary process, where transactions turn into relationships and these into value systems.

The endless 'flow' of exchange processes should lead to an increase of the 'stock' of value object-related competences, which in turn increase the stock of self-renewing value systems. Figure 12.6 presents the reciprocal effect between the different exchange processes as process dimension 'flow' and 'stocks' of competences and value systems.

The objective of marketing is centred on securing the company's ability to act in existing and changing (new) value systems by guaranteeing the process function of 'flow'. For both levels (existing and new value systems) two central tasks can be differentiated: first, raising its proper contribution to value generation; and second, achieving control over all value-generating activities. As design tasks for the company, they are alternative, but at the same time complementary, eg a company in a given position can concentrate on raising its proper value contribution, reach for control over all value-generating activities while neglecting value object-related competences, or try to put into use its creative potential to develop new value constellations. To concentrate resources it is required to focus one design task in the sense of a strategic focus at a particular

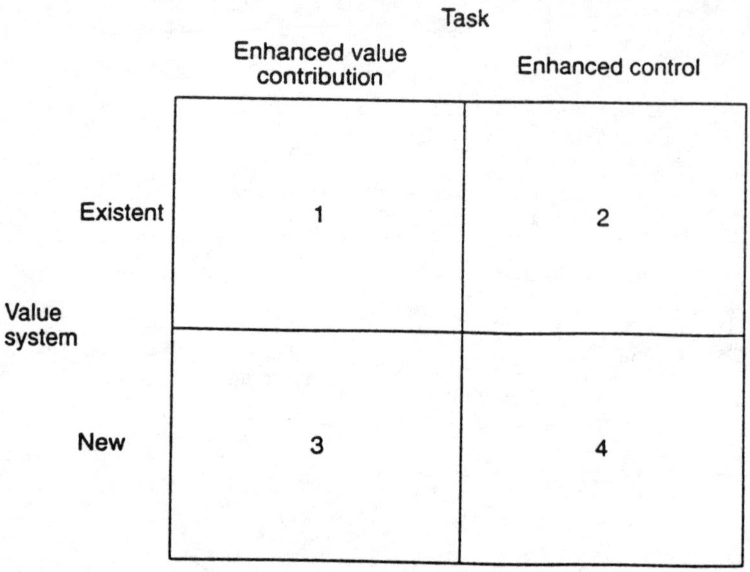

Task

	Enhanced value contribution	Enhanced control
Existent	1	2
New	3	4

Value system

Figure 12.7 Marketing in value systems

point of time. The alternative design tasks can be isolated from the model as singular parts presented in matrix form in Figure 12.7. The left half of the model corresponds with the first and third quadrant (raising its proper value contribution in existing and new value systems) and its right half with the second and fourth (increased control in existing and new value systems).

MARKETING IN EXISTING VALUE SYSTEMS

The precondition for *raising the own-value contribution in existing value systems (quadrant 1)* is the development or exploitation at maximum of idiosyncratic competences, that are indispensable for the implementation of the value constellation (eg Microsoft's competence in software development and innovation; Apple's clientele in its target market 'computer users' as a precondition for warehouses to distribute catalogues on CD-ROM). The relevance of competences can be explained by the fact that stability in a value system can be achieved only on the basis of the actors' mutual appreciation. This in turn only arises when the actors dispose of different idiosyncratic competences, which are complementary with regards to the value constellation being focused. Competences thus are the basis for strategic interdependences in the value system.[6]

As can be seen from the model competences are built from and exploited through transactions and relationships. Transactions and relationships are the basis for transforming repeated and continuous dialogues with the market-environment (customers, suppliers, retailers) into internal competences. They adopt a 'monitor function' in the process of building and exploiting, eg when the value object-related 'key buying factors' of various products emerge, becoming a long-term competence (eg product-overspanning process capability). Compared with transactions the special function of relationships results from the closer contact with the customer and a higher information content guaranteeing that the competence leads to a differentiation from a customer point of view (higher customer proximity). The exploitation of competences by transforming them into customer values (marketable products) and their integration into value systems is related to transactions and relationships as well (Wehrli and Juttner, 1994).

Improvements to a value system, achieved by improving the proper value contribution, because of the reciprocal effect shown always proceed through transactions/relationships *and* competences independent of the point of departure. Prerequisite for raising the value contribution by improving the process of developing and exploiting competences are analyses of the 'proper transaction and relationship profile', respectively (see the example given in Wehrli and Juttner, 1994). They show the critical transactions and relationships for the build-up and exploitation of competences and at the same time reveal the potential points for improvements. The objective for improvements can be new customers (broadening of target markets) as well as new products (product modifications). However, all of these still correspond to the original interpretation of the customer need (spin-offs of the original value constellation). To be able to exploit these possibilities for development to the maximum any transaction/relationship inside the value system must be viewed as a customer relation. Exploiting the potential of the value constellation to a higher degree through new customers and product modifications simultaneously leads from a 'single-centred' (final customer-oriented) to a 'polycentric' (multiple-customer) value system. The primary role of marketing is the improvement of those transactions and relationships that are critical for the build-up, the exploitation and the integration of idiosyncratic competences.

The precondition for increasing the control over all value-generating activities in existing value systems (second quadrant) is the design of the relationships inside the value system. By influencing the relationships, and especially by coordinating them, the company becomes a mediator for value generation and attempts to redesign the value generating processes to its proper advantage.[7] A way to gain control in a value system is the pooling of information. Here the company tries to extract information from all transactions and relationships taking place between the actors of the value system and to save it. Then this information can be processed into new bundles and be used for initiating new transactions and relationships (eg mediating or selling, respectively, of retailer-related information to suppliers of raw materials). By mediating the information further on, the company's position in the value system can be reinforced. Especially in information-intensive value systems, eg in value systems with high parts of immaterial values (value systems in the service industries) the information pooling and its management can become an indispensable value in itself.[8] As can be derived from the model the stabilisation of a value system needs long-term relationships. Further, they support the information pooling as a control function, since the feedback data about singular transactions in long-term relationships are increasing when time elapses, while costs for gaining additional pieces of information decrease.

In order to be able to influence relationships, and through this the structure of the value system as a whole, the company has to get insight into the framework of relationships with the help of 'relationship profiles of the value system'. These enable it to:

- anticipate the effects of dyadic relationships on other relationships in the value system;
- estimate different effects of direct (restricted) and indirect (generalised) sequential relationships in the system;
- identify the system borders. These are reached when the inter-dependencies of the relationships do not contribute more value increases for the whole value system. The identification of the system borders of the value system at the same time is the precondition for modifying them.

The primary criterion for restructuring value systems, ie increasing proper control, is the value potential of relationships supplemented by the orientation towards costs of transactions and relationships (Zajac and Olsen, 1993). The primary role of marketing lies in the coordination of relationships in order to maximise control of the company over the critical, value-generating processes.

MARKETING IN CHANGING VALUE SYSTEMS

When transforming a value system, a substitution of the old value constellation from the given value system occurs. The change corresponds to a new interpretation of customer needs (eg from 'eating' to 'enjoying') and is connected with a detachment of the old value system. The new central idea for satisfying the needs in general presumes new competences, new relationships and the exchange of some of the actors (organisations) of the old value system. New value constellations possess a creative design potential since their implementation at the same time can change existing markets or industries.[9]

In new value systems and during the transformation process, respectively, the company has to *safeguard its proper value contribution as an indispensable part of the new value constellation,* ie it has to adapt it accordingly (quadrant 3). Here, the process of developing new competences through transactions and relationships run through inside existing value systems obtains enlarged functions. The product-overspanning character of competences holds a creative potential, allowing the company to develop new value constellations.[10] Thus the proper value contribution in itself immediately becomes the impulse for value system transformation. As a result, the orientation towards competences instead of products overcomes the thinking oriented towards existing product-market segments. Instead, it utilises competences as a basis for new, innovative value constellations. Besides that, the product-overspanning character of competences also ensures the proper value contribution for new value systems, which are not initiated by the company itself, but by partners from the same value system. The company also generates experiences through continuous repetitions of competence building and exploiting of transactions and relationships, which over time affect it, not only regarding specific competences, but also in a way that overreaches its competences;[11] ie by multiplying transactions and relationships it obtains the ability to build up new competences faster and more efficiently. With the help of this competence overreaching capability, the company is provided with the precondition to adapt to the changing requirements of competences in new value constellations. The primary role of marketing is to design the transactions and relationships for the exploitation of the creative potential of competences and to develop the competences' overreaching capability.

The design and coordination of relationships in new value systems also fulfils a function of control (quadrant 4). When initiating the new constellation itself, the company's control over relationships safeguards quick implementation and through this its return on investment. However, when a partner from the value system initiates the new constellation, by using its controlling and coordinating function its proper attraction increases as well as the chances for a successful integration of the company in the new value system. As a result, the primary role of marketing is the design of relationships in order to maintain control, even when a new value constellation is implemented.

Finally, on the transformation level of existing value systems the differentiated role of long-term relationships attracts attention. These necessary processes of change can block each other and thus turn the value system rigid. In this case, there is a risk that substituting value constellations from competing value systems out of the higher level competition system will be developed. The claim that long-term relationships in relationship marketing are always right has to be questioned. Relationships with selected customer groups in the sense of a mutual obligation are necessary in order to maintain constancy until new value constellations can be implemented and exploited.

IMPLICATIONS FOR FUTURE RESEARCH

The main challenge of marketing in the 1990s is the higher market turbulence that generates complex problems, whose solutions bring single organisations to their limits. Marketing has to facilitate and maintain value-creating exchange processes that respond to individualised and fast-changing customer needs and wants, while simultaneously keeping in touch with the increasing cost pressures resulting from the increasing intensity of competition.

Relationship marketing sees long-term relationships with customers as a stabilising element that supports the mastering of this challenge: the intensified information exchange within customer relationships provides a basis for personalised offerings and the long-term character contributes to the reduction of marketing costs per customer. By concentrating especially on overcoming psychological barriers of relationships (eg mistrust, communicative, ethical or personalised barriers) relationship marketing is in close dialogue with 'mass customisation', which focuses the individualisation of exchange objects.

This chapter suggests an enriched perspective, transferring the idea of stabilising relationships to the creation and design of value systems, while emphasising linkages and interactions of the value-generating processes. Within a value system the role of marketing management is the coordination of all interactive value-generating activities as a means of enhancing flexibility and responsiveness towards the turbulence of markets and at the same time supporting their own influence (creating or changing market structures). Supported by our model, we show the differentiated roles of marketing, when securing the own-value contribution or enhancing control over all value-generating activities within existing (stabilised) and transforming value systems. The explanation of the basic principles has at the same time pointed at the main variables that have to be operationalised for its practicability. Our proposition represents in this sense a foundation for future research efforts. We would propose and encourage first the integration of existing knowledge gained within the relationship marketing debate to the model (eg application of the findings about trust and relational norm-building processes to value system creation and stabilisation) and second the isolation of different parts of the model (eg competence building and exploiting by transactions and relationships), which supports the application and empirical evaluation in practice.

Notes

1. In the following we use the term product in its broader sense, including services (any market value offering).
2. See as an expression of this understanding the 'law of exchange' developed by Alderson (1965).
3. The network approach is very similar to the combination of the exchange and system approaches suggested by Carman (1980); See also the more detailed evaluation of the 'system' and 'exchange school of thought' in isolation in Sheth *et al.* (1988)
4. Mattsson is one of the proponents of a network approach in industrial marketing that has been developed by the Industrial Marketing and Purchasing Group (IMP). For one of the latest publications see Cavusgil and Sharma (1993).
5. The importance of competences within strategic management has recently been stressed by Prahalad and Hamel (1990). For first contributions that examine the role of marketing within the competence-based perspective see Bharadwaj *et al.* (1991), Day and Wensley (1988), Wehrli and Juttner (1994).
6. The integration of competences (capabilities) as factors effecting transactions or relationships, respectively, has been recognised already by Bagozzi (1974a). In his 'exchange system' he assigns 'capabilities' to the endogenous variables 'acting as a causal determinant'.
7. See also Handy (1992), who because of the interdependence of relationships and the federal structure resulting from them, pledges for replacing the term 'control by 'coordination'. In our understanding the measure consists in 'coordination of relationships'. The objective, however, retards the strengthening of the proper position, which is inseparably linked with control. Regarding the differentiation of strategies with the objective of changing and

maintaining of positions inside networks more comprehensively see Mattsson (1985).

8. See Quinn (1992), Quinn *et al.* (1990); also Glazer (1991) who refers to information-intensive networks as 'transaction- based information systems', where the function of steering the information determines the efficiency and effectiveness of the whole value system.

9. An exemplifying differentiation of various 'lifecycle phases of value systems' can be found in Moore (1993), who uses the term 'business ecosystems' (p 76).

10. See the comprehensive outline of market-oriented, creative potential of competences of Hamel and Prahalad (1991) using the term 'expeditionary marketing'.

11. See the terms 'organisational capability' (Collis, 1991), 'metaskills' (Klein *et al.*, 1991) and 'metacompetence' (Normann and Ramirez, 1993), all of which are referring to the higher-level capability of repeated developments of different competences.

References and Further Reading

Adler, L (1966) 'Symbiotic-marketing', *Harvard Business Review,* Vol 44, November–December, pp 59–74.

Alderson, W (1957) *Marketing Behavior and Executive Action,* Irwin, Homewood, Ill.

Alderson, W (1965) *Dynamic Marketing Behavior,* Irwin, Homewood, Ill.

Anderson, J and Narus J (1990) 'A model of distributor firm and manufacturer firm working partnerships', *Journal of Marketing,* Vol 54, January, pp 42–58.

Anderson, J and Narus, J (1991) 'Partnering as a focused market strategy', *California Management Review,* Vol 33, Spring, pp 95–113.

Arndt, J (1979) 'Toward a concept of domesticated markets', *Journal of Marketing,* Vol 43, Autumn, pp 69–75.

Bagozzi, R (1974a) 'Marketing as an organized behavioral system of exchange', *Journal of Marketing,* Vol 38, October, pp 77–81.

Bagozzi, R (1974b) 'What is a marketing relationship?', *Der Markt,* Vol 51, pp 64–69.

Bagozzi, R (1975) 'Marketing as exchange', *Journal of Marketing,* Vol 39, October, pp 32–39.

Bagozzi, R (1978) 'Marketing as exchange: a theory of transactions in the marketplace', *American Behavioral Scientist,* Vol 21, No 4, pp 535–556.

Bagozzi, R (1979) 'Toward a formal theory of marketing', in Brown, S and Lamb, C (eds), *Conceptual and Theoretical Development in Marketing,* American Marketing Association, Chicago, Ill pp 431–447.

Berry, L and Gresham, L (1986) 'Relationship retailing transforming customers into clients', *Business Horizons,* Vol 29, November–December, pp 43–47.

Bharadwaj, S, Varadarajan, R and Fahy, J (1991) 'Sustainable competitive advantage in service industries: a conceptual model and research propositions', *Journal of Marketing*, Vol 57, October, pp 83–99.

Blattberg, R and Deighton, J (1991) 'Interactive marketing: exploiting the age of addressability', *Sloan Management Review*, Vol 33, Autumn, pp 5–14.

Carman, J (1980) 'Paradigms for marketing theory', in Sheth, J N (ed.), *Research in Marketing*, JAI Press, Greenwich, Conn, pp 1–36.

Cavusgil, S and Sharma, D (eds) (1993) *Advances in International Marketing*, Vol 5, JAI Press, Greenwich, Conn.

Collis, D (1991) 'A resource-based analysis of global competition: the case of the bearings industry', *Strategic Management Journal*, Vol 12, Special Issue, Summer, pp 49–68.

Copulsky, J and Wolf, M (1990) 'Relationship marketing: positioning for the future', *Journal of Business Strategy*, Vol 11, July–August, pp 16–26.

Crosby, L, Evans, K and Cowles, D (1990) 'Relationship quality in services selling: an interpersonal influence perspective', *Journal of Marketing*, Vol 54, July, pp 68–81.

Czepiel, J (1990) 'Service encounters and service relationships: implications for research', *Journal of Business Research*, Vol 20, pp 13–21.

Day, G (1980) 'Strategic Market Analysis: Top-down and Bottom-up Approaches, Working Paper No 80-105, Marketing Science Institute, Cambridge, Mass.

Day, G and Wensley, R (1988) 'Assessing advantage: a framework for diagnosing competitive superiority', *Journal of Marketing*, Vol 52, April, pp 1–20.

Dwyer, R, Schurr, P and Oh, S (1987) 'Developing buyer–seller relationships', *Journal of Marketing*, Vol 51, April, pp 11–27.

Ellis K, Lee, J and Beatty, S (1993) 'Relationships in consumer marketing directions for future research', in AMA *Educators' Proceedings 1993*, Chicago, Ill, pp 225–232.

Ferrell, O and Perrachione, J (1980) 'An inquiry into Bagozzi's formal theory of marketing exchange', in Lamb, C and Dunne, P (eds), *Theoretical Developments in Marketing*, American Marketing Association, Chicago, Ill, pp 158–161.

Fincke, U and Goffard, E (1993) 'Customizing distribution', *The McKinsey Quarterly*, Vol 30, No 1, pp 115–131.

Ford, D (1980) 'The development of buyer–seller relationships in industrial markets', *European Journal of Marketing*, Vol 14, Nos 5–6, pp 339–353.

Frazier, G, Spekman, R and O'Neil, C (1988) 'Just-in-time exchange relationships in industrial markets', *Journal of Marketing*, Vol 52, October, pp 52–67.

Glazer, R (1981) 'Marketing in an information-intensive environment: strategic implications of knowledge as an asset', *Journal of Marketing*, Vol 55, October, pp 1–19.

Grönroos, C (1990) 'Relationship approach to marketing in service contexts: the marketing and organizational behavior interface', *Journal of Business Research*, Vol 29, pp 3–11.

Gummesson, E (1987) 'The new marketing – developing long-term interactive relationships', *Long Range Planning*, Vol 20, No 4, pp 10–20.

Gundlach, G and Murphy, P (1993) 'Ethical and legal foundations of relational marketing exchanges', *Journal of Marketing,* Vol 57, October, pp 35–46.

Hallen, L, Johanson, J and Seyed-Mohamed, N (1991) 'Interfirm adaptation in business relationships', *Journal of Marketing,* Vol 55, April, pp 29–37.

Hamel, G and Prahalad, C (1991) 'Corporate imagination and expeditionary marketing', *Harvard Business Review,* Vol 6, July–August, pp 81–92.

Handy, C (1992) 'Balancing corporate power: a new federalist paper', *Harvard Business Review,* Vol 70, November–December, pp 59–72.

Heide, J and John, G (1990) 'Alliances in industrial purchasing: the determinants of joint action in buyer–supplier relationships', *Journal of Marketing Research,* Vol 27, February, pp 24–36.

Heide, J and John, G (1992) 'Do norms matter in marketing relationships?', *Journal of Marketing,* Vol 56, April, pp 32–44.

Houston, F and Gassenheimer, J (1987) 'Marketing and exchange', *Journal of Marketing,* Vol 51, October, pp 3–18.

Hunt, S (1983) 'General theories and the fundamental explananda of marketing', *Journal of Marketing,* Vol 47, Fall, pp 9–17.

Jackson, B (1985) 'Build relationships that last', *Harvard Business Review,* Vol 63, November–December, pp 120–128.

Johnston, R and Lawrence, P (1988) 'Beyond vertical integration – the rise of value-adding partnership', *Harvard Business Review,* Vol 66, July–August, pp 94–101.

Joshi, A (1993) 'Long-term relationships, strategic partnerships and networks: a contingency theory of relationship marketing', in AMA *Educators' Proceedings 1993,* Chicago, Ill, pp 138–139.

Klein, J, Edge, G and Kass, T (1991) 'Skill-based competition', *Journal of General Management,* Vol 16, Summer, pp 1–15.

Kotler, P (1991) *Marketing Management,* 7th edn, Prentice-Hall, Englewood Cliffs, NJ.

Lazer, W and Kelley, E (1962) 'The systems approach to marketing', in Lazer, W and Kelley, E (eds), *Managerial Marketing: Perspectives and Viewpoints,* Irwin, Homewood, Ill.

Levitt, T (1983) 'After the sale is over...', *Harvard Business Review,* Vol 61, September–October, pp 87–93.

Martin, M and Sohi, R (1993) 'Maintaining relationships with customers: some critical factors, in AMA *Educators' Proceedings 1993,* Chicago, Ill, pp 21–27.

Mattsson, L-G (1985) 'An application of a network approach to marketing: defending and changing market positions', in Dholakia, N and Arndt, J (eds), *Changing the Course of Marketing: Alternative Paradigms for Widening Marketing Theory,* JAI, Greenwich, Conn, pp 263–288.

McCort, J (1993) 'A framework for evaluating the relational extent of a relationship marketing strategy in nonprofit organizations', in AMA *Educators' Proceedings 1993,* Chicago, Ill, pp 409–416.

McKenna, R (1988) 'Marketing in an age of diversity', *Harvard Business Review,* Vol 66, September–October, pp 88–95.

McKenna, R (1991) 'Marketing is everything,' *Harvard Business Review*, Vol 69, January–February, pp 65–79.

Moore, J (1993) 'Predators and prey', *Harvard Business Review*, Vol 71, May–June, pp 75–86.

Moorman, C, Deshpande, R and Zaltman, G (1993) 'Factors affecting trust in market research relationships', *Journal of Marketing*, Vol 57, January, pp 81–101.

Moorman, C, Zaltman, G and Deshpande, R (1992) 'Relationships between providers and users of market research: the dynamics of trust within and between organizations', *Journal of Marketing Research*, Vol 29, August, pp 314–328.

Normann, R (1984), *Service Management: Strategy and Leadership in Service Businesses*, Wiley, Chichester.

Normann, R and Ramirez, R (1993) 'From value chain to value constellation: designing interactive strategy', *Harvard Business Review*, Vol 71, July–August, pp 65–77.

Pine, J (1993) 'Mass customizing products and services', *Planning Review*, Vol 22, July–August, pp 7–55.

Pine, J, Victor, B and Boynton, A (1993) 'Making mass customization work'. *Harvard Business Review*, Vol 71, September–October, pp 108–119.

Porter, M (1985) *Competitive Advantage: Creating and Sustaining Superior Performance*, Free Press, New York.

Prahalad, C and Hamel, G. (1990) 'The Core Competence of the Corporation', *Harvard Business Review*, Vol 68, May–June, pp 79–91.

Quinn, J (1992) *Intelligent Enterprise: A Knowledge and Service-based Paradigm for Industry*, Free Press, New York.

Quinn, J, Doorley, T and Paquette, P (1990) 'Beyond products: services-based strategy', *Harvard Business Review*, Vol 68, March–April, pp 58–67.

Schurr, P and Ozanne, L (1985) 'Influences on exchange processes: buyer's preconditions of a sellers' trustworthiness and bargaining toughness', *Journal of Consumer Research*, Vol 11, March, pp 939–953.

Shani, D and Chalasani, S (1992) 'Exploiting niches using relationship marketing', *Journal of Consumer Marketing*, Vol 9, No 3, pp 33–42.

Shapiro, B (1991) 'Close encounters of the four kinds: managing customers in a rapidly changing environment', in Dolan, R (ed.) *Strategic Marketing Management*, Harvard University Press, Boston, Mass, pp 429–452.

Sheth, J, Gardner, D and Garrett, D (1988) *Marketing Theory: Evolution and Evaluation*, Wiley, New York.

Smith, T and Johnson, R (1993) 'Facilitating the practice of relationship marketing', in AMA *Educators' Proceedings 1993*, Chicago, Ill, pp 232–233.

Spekman, R (1988) 'Strategic supplier selection: understanding long-term buyer relationships', *Business Horizons*, Vol 31, July–August, pp 75–81.

Swan, J and Nolan, J (1985) 'Gaining customer trust: a conceptual guide for the salesperson', *Journal of Personal Selling and Sales Management*, Vol 5, November, pp 39–48.

Swan, J, Trawick, F and Silva, D (1985) 'How industrial salespeople gain customer trust', *Industrial Marketing Management,* Vol 14, August, pp 203–211.

Ulrich, D (1989) 'Tie the corporate knot: gaining complete customer commitment', *Sloan Management Review,* Vol 30, Summer, pp 19–27.

Varadarajan, P and Rajaratnam, D (1966) 'Symbiotic marketing revisited', *Journal of Marketing,* Vol 50, January, pp 7–17.

Vavra, T (1993a) 'The database marketing imperative', *Marketing Management,* Vol 2, No 1, pp 47–57.

Vavra, T (1993b) 'Rethinking the marketing mix to maximize customer retention: an aftermarketing perspective', in AMA *Educators' Proceedings 1993,* Chicago, Ill, pp 263–268.

Webster, F (1992) 'The changing role of marketing in the corporation', *Journal of Marketing,* Vol 56, October, pp 1–17.

Webster, F (1993) 'Toward a new marketing concept', unpublished presentation given at AMA Educators' Conference, Boston, Mass.

Wehrli, H P and Juttner, U (1994) 'Competitive advantage by competence-based marketing management', in Park, C and Smith, D (eds), *Marketing Theory and Applications,* American Marketing Association, Chicago, Ill, pp 223–231.

Zajac, E and Olsen, C (1993) 'From transaction cost to transactional value analysis: implications for the study of inter-organizational strategies', *Journal of Management Studies,* Vol 30, January, pp 131–145.

13

RE-ENGINEERING BRAND MANAGEMENT PRACTICES WITHIN AN INTEGRATED ENVIRONMENT*

Simon Knox

INTRODUCTION: THE CASE FOR RE-ENGINEERING CORE BUSINESS PROCEDURES

In their book, *Re-engineering the Corporation*, Mike Hammer and Jim Champy set out an agenda for corporate change that has been described as the compass and maps for the twenty-first century business world. Their deceptively simple advice to corporations, whether market leaders or failing enterprises, is fundamentally to reassess key procedures and processes of business development and exchange (Hammer and Champy, 1993). Any such redesign that achieves dramatic improvements in the measures of performance, such as cost, service and speed, they refer to as process re-engineering. By adopting this if-we-were-to-start-again policy, a number of major corporations have been able to shake off conventional orthodoxies to rediscover the benefits of customer satisfaction through timeliness and responsiveness. To date, two core business processes have received most management attention in their re-engineering endeavours. The first is order fulfilment, the task of converting a customer's order into cash after it has been delivered (Earl and Khan, 1994). For example, an American life assurance company, Mutual Benefit Life, has reduced turnaround time of individual insurance applications to two or three days from, typically, over twenty under the previous protocol. The company can now handle more than twice the volume of new applications with a significantly reduced management

* This paper was first published in the *Journal of Marketing Practice*, Vol 1, No 2, 1995, pp 26–38, and is reproduced with permission.

team. Christopher (1993) cites other examples of this 'end-to-end' order fulfilment process and argues that this new approach to customer service is becoming a necessary condition for continuing competitiveness and customer retention.

The time-to-market for new products has also become a necessary condition for sustaining competitiveness and is the second process that has been redefined through concurrent engineering (Edwards and Braganza, 1994). The launch of Land Rover Discovery, from concept to market presence, was achieved in under three years by the management team (Peck, 1991). The team chose to redefine the traditional sequential process by paralleling key activities and multifunctional tasking, enabling them to compress the conventional launch timetable by three or four years. Likewise, Kodak's old product development process, partly sequential and partly parallel but entirely slow, was revolutionised using CAD/CAM and concurrency across functional management. The time to move the 35 mm, single-use camera from concept to production was halved to well under a year as competitive pressure intensified.

Whilst both these process re-engineering initiatives have yielded substantial and recurring benefits to management, they should only be regarded as signposts on the journey to redefining how the entire company offering or brand portfolio should be managed. In essence, through shifts in competitive pressure and collapsing response times (Handy, 1991), the ascendency of powerful intermediaries and single sourcing (Booz, Allen and Hamilton, 1991) combined with a post-modern customer and consumer disaggregation (King, 1994), corporations urgently need to redefine how they build and manage brand equity along the supply chain. In this context, brand equity refers to the perceptions of 'added values' which enhances the functional value proposition of the brand amongst customers and consumers (Aaker, 1991; Farquhar, 1989).

The objective of this chapter is to interpret how senior management are likely to redefine this process before their conventional power-base is eroded entirely. It is clear that in attempting to better integrate the management of brands with supply chain management, the organization needs an approach that entrusts the equity of brands to an integrated management team which is truly responsive to both customers and consumers alike. The key priorities of this team are identified in the second half of the chapter.

Before addressing this, however, it is necessary first to identify the inadequacies of the traditional brand management system which still relies upon 'Four Ps' marketing to build brand equity. These inadequacies are discussed in the next section as each of the traditional marketing mix components are critically examined.

THE TRADITIONAL APPROACH TO BUILDING BRANDS

Many of the classic brands, such as Mars, Lux Toilet Soap, Cup-a-Soup, Ariel, etc., have been built and sustained around consistent and ever-evolving functional and emotional value propositions (King, 1991). For instance, the value proposition for Mars bars during the 1950s press campaign, 'Mars are Marvellous ... Just chunks of sheer, delicious goodness made with chocolate to sustain, glucose to energise and milk to nourish', is, to all intents and purposes, identical to today's TV executions.

King argues, 'given adequate tender loving care, these classic brand leaders should prosper more or less indefinitely'. Their equity has been built over the years according to the doctrine of the Four Ps and a consumer that subscribes to the values of heritage, functional performance and ubiquity; nearly half the current top 50 brands in the UK were borne of this era and are still successfully managed on this basis (Brady and Davis, 1993). The approach is, however, largely anachronistic since it represents the activities of a functional marketing division that perpetuates an atomistic exchange process with its consumers and depends upon advertising 'pull' and repeat purchasing to build brand loyalty. The problems of managing brands on this basis are outlined below.

In the past, success at this process has enabled marketing management to price lead brands at a premium and to enjoy above-average earnings (Clifford and Cavanagh, 1985). During the early 1990s, however, these price premia have been largely eroded as very competitive own-label offerings have been re-evaluated by consumers (de Chernatony *et al.*, 1992). In fact, an analysis of the top ten brands across two leading UK grocery accounts shows that only three are able to sustain an acceptable price premium over the retailer's own-label and outsell it (Coopers & Lybrand, 1992).

With regard to promotion, advertising research from Millward Brown (Allan, 1992) shows that consumers are now dissociating the advertising style and content from the brand itself and evaluating the advertisement in parallel to the offer rather than as a component. With media costs significantly outpacing inflation during the 1980s (Bennett, 1993), the advertising budgets for most conventional brands which do depend on dedicated expenditure have become black holes and the advertisements themselves of questionable authority amongst their discerning target audiences.

Finally, the task of maintenance or achieving incremental gains in distribution through intermediaries, traditionally the domain of the sales team, is tackled with a level of management commitment broadly in proportion to the degree of channel concentration across the category (Diller, 1992). Increasingly, intermediaries within the channel are taking a proactive approach in the management of their downstream activities with brand suppliers to reduce system costs and build greater inter-dependencies (Buchanan and Gillies, 1990). In a later section of this chapter, it is argued that such relationship-building cannot be achieved whilst account management remains ringfenced by sales management.

It is evident that brand building through traditional, functional marketing is meeting with demand-side resistance in all but a few exceptional cases. Even here, amongst the most powerful consumer brand companies in the world, fundamental questions about brand equity are being asked by their senior management and new ways of delivering value in the supply chain are being tested.

THE SHIFT TOWARDS A RE-ENGINEERED BRAND MANAGEMENT PROCESS

Management in Procter & Gamble, the profitable US brands giant, are currently asking themselves 'if P&G did not exist today, how would we recreate it?' (Hammer, 1993). The company was also amongst the first of a number of major corporations to acknowledge that consumers are no longer willing to pay the premium for brands as a matter of routine (PaineWebber, 1992). Other multinational consumer goods companies are questioning the duality of sales and marketing by moving towards integration. For instance, Colgate-Palmolive in the UK have drastically rationalised their brand portfolio from over four hundred lines to under two hundred in order to focus on managing their major retail accounts as well as these retailers' customers. By improving their customer service levels and hence direct product profitability in major accounts, whilst at the same time increasing consumer advertising across their flagship brands, the corporation has moved back into profitability. In global business communications, AT&T: NCR have redefined functional responsibilities in support of the process of 'providing business solutions to meet customer needs'. This has also involved integrating sales and service to provide a customer-facing organisational structure.

Each of the re-engineered processes mentioned so far has involved company restructuring in recognition of the demise of stovepipe structures with command and control budgeting towards cross-functional management teams that introduce greater flexibility and coordination within organisations. It is these teams which define and refine the management of these core processes to build the organisation's competitive advantage.

Whilst the P&G study of their brands and perceived consumer value remains proprietary, there are enough straws in the wind to predict likely outcomes in the redesign of how their brands may be managed in the future. Indeed, some corporations have already set out on the journey of developing an integrated brand offering where the equity is managed across functional territories.

It seems very likely that the re-engineering of brand management practices will become commonplace during the 1990s and the process of integrated branding accepted as the core business activity, whilst order fulfilment and new product development are managed as synergistic support processes. It would seem less likely, therefore, that brand development can sit alongside these other processes, as Kaplan and Murdock (1991) suggest.

In the next section, we identify the main management activities which are likely to constitute the strategic building blocks of this integrated brand offering. These activities are presented as a value chain (Bower and Garda, 1986) which is divided into four zones, in recognition of the need for differing competencies (Figure 13.1). It is the successful *integration* of these management activities and competencies within the supply chain that will enable the *brands* to be managed as *the core business process.* In this paper, we refer to this process as integrated branding.

MANAGING THE INTEGRATED BRAND: PROCESS COMPETENCIES AND ACTIVITIES

What is really exciting about the integrated brand proposition is that it has wide applicability; it is within the grasp of management in business-to-business markets, just as much as it is for those in service or consumer goods industries. To be effective in any of these industry sectors, the process will require competencies drawn from each sector: the provision of a consumable product; an integrated service/corporate-values surround; and relationship management practices. The integrated brand value chain (Figure 13.1) identifies how these process

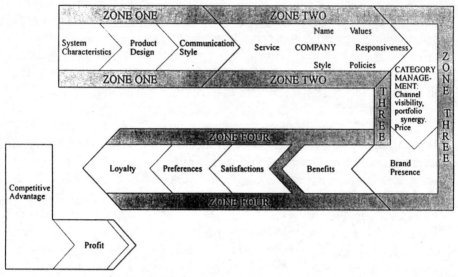

Figure 13.1 The integrated brand value chain

competencies can be translated into activities which build brand presence and reinforce loyalty. These management activities are described below.

Zones One and Two: The Company Brand

The emergence of an integrated approach towards the consumable product offering and its service and corporate surround (zones one and two in Figure 13.1), has been described in some detail by Stephen King in his articles referred to earlier. In these seminal papers, he recognises the limitations of conventional brand typologies and points towards the idea of a company brand.

The company brand, which is becoming increasingly evident in the market-place, offers values that extend beyond the identity and function of individual brands in the company portfolio. Companies such as Nestlé and United Biscuits are moving in this direction by redesigning their brand ranges to give a much stronger corporate identity and presence. In other words, company brands can come to reflect wider values by acting as the glass door of the company through schemes that lock in additional benefits – such as corporate quality guarantees, freephone advice lines and no-quibble replacement policies – in conjunction with a much higher level of visible corporate responsiveness. For instance, management responsiveness to environmental concerns and local community developments are *de rigueur* and have to be pursued with integrity, since consumers and other important constituents hold informed views against which company commitments are likely to be critically evaluated.

So, in addition to the consumable product, the company brand offers a corporate underpinning that Stephen King refers to as values, styles and behaviours which enrich the offering.

A good example of this component of the company brand comes from Schering Agriculture. In the trade press to the farming community, they claim 'to spend over fifty percent of our budget on product safety, to ensure our product's effectiveness is not achieved at the expense of the user, the environment or the consumer of the crop'. As a consequence, their brands, complete with the corporate identity, now compete at parity with their main competitors on functional product performance, but are perceived by the farming community to outperform these competitors in 'caring for the environment'. This perceived benefit is likely to give them a strong added advantage at point-of-sale.

The remaining component of the company brand that King describes is service, or the 'servitisation' of the consumable product, such as the home-delivery pizza or the rescheduling of credit and debt to stimulate purchase – consider the recent launch of General Motor's credit card scheme (Mitchell, 1993). Vandermerwe and Rada (1988) describe this 'servitisation' component as building new links in the buying system, such as the move by SAS from being in the airline business to being a businessperson's 'total travel package' with their own direct enquiries and hotel bookings, 'sleepclass' and 'workclass' tickets and a door-to-door limousine service.

It probably needs to be restated at this point, that without functional parity with competition, no amount of service or corporate gesturing can prop up an inferior product offering in the medium term. The emphasis must still be placed on continuous product improvement (and new product development as a synergistic company process) to ensure a consistent evolution of the consumable product.

Zone Three: Category Management

The third building block in the integrated branding process (zone three of Figure 13.1), is the explicit management of intermediaries to enable them to serve their customers more effectively. Marketers may have been quick to recognise the increasing power and influence of channel intermediaries in their planning, but they have been slow in practice to diffuse the build-up of adversarial trading conditions. Whilst the sales-related account management mentioned earlier helps build bridges in organisational relationships, it falls short of the multifunctional, multitiered approach advocated in this chapter. The account management style which currently comes closest to this is *category management*, as practised by some consumer goods companies in Europe and the USA. For instance, the French retailer Carrefour takes the view that, as an intermediary, it is in the business of providing scarce shelf-space for suppliers to sell to consumers. So, across certain product categories, they ask their suppliers to manage the space directly and to maximise shelf and pipeline profitability which the company then monitors on a weekly basis. Winners and losers emerge over time but, in either instance, relationship management skills are imperative. End-to-end order fulfilment must become an effective support process under these conditions, together with integrated sales and marketing, IT and manufacturing, if this account is to be served profitably and system costs contained.

The strategic importance of managing intermediaries is paralleled in service and industrial markets. During the 1980s, Saatchi & Saatchi were one of the first communications agencies to offer a 'boutique' of company services ranging from management consultancy and marketing research to advertising and direct selling, a portfolio approach that effectively allowed clients to outsource skills critical in building their own customer relationships and business. The success of the Saatchi venture was dependent upon their management team understanding their client's customers better than the clients themselves! Perhaps an over-ambitious mission for a company with a completely heterogeneous client base, it was, none the less, an early attempt to manage the offering in partnership with a customer.

Diversey Corporation, the Canadian industrial cleaning group, organise globally around key industry categories to provide their multinational customers with complete cleansing solutions on a country-by-country basis. In delivering this service to their customers, it is imperative that the very strict hygiene specifications are met, particularly in food processing and catering since these specifications are often determined and monitored by customers downstream in the food chain.

Each of these examples describe different stages of the intricate layering procedures involved in making the consumable product part of the final brand presence that is evaluated by the consumer. If purchased and deemed preferable to competition, repeat purchase and loyalty may then follow. Successful brands achieve higher levels of consumer loyalty (Doyle, 1989) and are more profitable directly as a result (Reichheld and

Sasser, 1990). Thus, managing consumer loyalty is the fourth and final zone of the integrated branding process.

Zone Four: Consumer Loyalty Management

In the past, marketing management have rather taken loyalty amongst existing purchasers as given and have focused on getting new or lapsed consumers 'to fill the leaking bucket'. It is most unusual to find a company that devotes a significant proportion of its marketing budget to 'consumer loyalty'. However, all this could soon very well change if Reichheld and Sasser's results are found to be of general application. Using Bain and Co data, they observed that a 5 percent increase in customer retention (loyalty without commitment) can boost profits anywhere between 25 to an astonishing 85 percent across service and manufacturing industries.

It is now time to view consumer retention and loyalty as a corporate responsibility and, thus, a component of the integrated branding process, since both aspects can be managed across flagship brands on a portfolio or category basis. Increasingly, corporations are recognising this and mounting loyalty programmes across their main brands, such as British Airway's Air Miles scheme, or as inter-company tie-ups between non-competing retailer, restaurant and hotel brands (Summers, 1993).

As with traditional brand management practices, sustaining consumer interest and preference involves maintaining the company's brands as routine and top-of-mind purchases within a product category. Customer retention implies that the derived satisfactions from usage of a particular brand enables the customer to simplify their decision-making process by reducing the purchasing risk and the need for a wide purchasing repertoire on subsequent occasions. Loyalty, on the other hand, implies a customer commitment that is explicit and which may lead to the referral of other customers through word-of-mouth to the organisation and a particular brand offering. Referral, which is the lowest cost and most powerful form of advertising, brings in new customers, increases category penetration and builds market share over time. Christopher *et al.*, (1991) term this referral mechanism as the 'ladder of loyalty' and regard it as a critically important outcome of the organisation's relationship with its customers and consumers.

Arguably, the auditing and development of loyalty schemes which present the total offering with a coherence that is of individualistic appeal to consumers, should be a functional marketing activity. Marketing should also retain other functional responsibilities drawn from each of the four zones, such as database marketing, brand positioning and portfolio synergy, price and value assessment, as well as marketing research. However, the development of relationship management practices amongst a wider constituency within the supply chain is, arguably, a multifunctional responsibility. These particular responsibilities of the integrated brand management team are discussed in the next section.

MANAGING RELATIONSHIPS IN THE SUPPLY CHAIN

The importance of explicitly managing the expectations of supply chain participants, such as intermediaries, suppliers and the company employees themselves, increases directly with the level of corporate exposure introduced by the integrated branding process. So, the case for improving retention amongst these specific interest groups is regarded as a matter of strategic significance, as, indeed, are the cost-benefits derived from achieving fewer defections. The benefits of managing these particular relationships are discussed briefly below.

Managing *intermediaries*, referred to as category management in this chapter (see p 254), implies building up their business in partnership so that they achieve category leadership amongst their primary* consumers who, in turn, then become primary to the organization marketing the brands. To facilitate this process of building brand preferences through availability and superior presence at point-of-sale requires selective targeting of primary and major accounts. As previously discussed, successful partnerships also aim to reduce systems costs by inter-organisational communications and collaboration, as well as through scale and experience effects.

Likewise, *suppliers* to the organisation should be rationalised and close relationships developed with remaining suppliers in areas that critically affect the quality of the consumable product. Japanese automobile manufacturers have done just this. They retain only one-tenth the number of suppliers that their American counterparts have. Each supplier, as a consequence, contributes 24 times more value per vehicle; they each enjoy much more business from the manufacturer and are very anxious to retain it through the cycle of contract renewal. Besides the commensurate cost reduction benefits that scale and experience effects can bring, these suppliers will be responsive to other initiatives that reduce systems costs, similar to the organisation's relationships with its upstream intermediaries.

---

* A primary purchaser, customer or account spends more on a particular organisation's brand or brands than any of its competitors in a period, ie the organisation enjoys the largest 'market share' of the primary purchaser's spend.

Within the organization, *employee* retention and loyalty should itself be an explicit goal of the integrated brand management team. Loyalty amongst employees not only lowers recruitment costs (Schlesinger and Heskett, 1991) but, more importantly, enables the culture of customer responsiveness to be inculcated through a learned sense of company values and participation in business processes. In fact, the efficacy of core and support processes is very dependent upon retaining experienced participants in the team to work comfortably in a system of iterative learning.

In summary, market penetration and leadership through this process of integrated branding leads to a number of very specific opportunities to reduce systems cost as relationship management practices and retention priorities are established. Also, amongst intermediaries and consumers, revenue and margins are very likely to grow through successful retention strategies as there is a tendency for their share of expenditure within each category to move in the organisation's favour (Edelman, Silverstein and Jones, 1993).

IMPLICATIONS FOR MANAGEMENT: DEVELOPING FUNCTIONAL AND MULTIFUNCTIONAL RESPONSIBILITIES

Most interest groups, particularly those involved with consumer goods organisations, wish to see the equity of brands survive and prosper. However, in today's tough trading conditions, brand virility is on the wane. Some sceptics claim their imminent demise, as intermediaries build their own-brands and consumers challenge traditional pricing conventions. To paraphrase the words of Mark Twain, these epitaphs could be greatly exaggerated, since new paths are emerging that can lead to brand renewal, strengthening and, for industrial marketers, the dawning of a new age.

With very few exceptions, business-to-business exchanges are not concluded with a feeling that the brand is building the loyalty bridge for future purchases. However, through business process redesign and acknowledgement by industrial management that brand equity does exist in their organisations, it is entirely possible to implement the integrated branding process in this sector. The same applies in services and consumer goods, where there is a more pressing urgency to blow away conventional orthodoxies, particularly amongst secondary and tertiary market performers.

The challenge for management is to take action by radically rethinking their customer-facing activities from first principles. It is almost certainly true that this would be the first time for marketing management and a fairly novel experience amongst other management functions!

How can it be achieved?

The starting point involves working together in teams and putting the fundamentals first: customer retention through preference for the organisational offering. This can really only be achieved through multifunctional teams which require effective integration both across the seam (vertical) and along the seam (horizontal) of the core process to be truly responsive and time-based. Hierarchies will become flatter as authority is delegated and brand equity managed as a cross-functional asset and an organisational priority. Although instruments for placing a net present value on this brand equity are inherently subjective (Barwise, 1990), do-it-yourself audits exist and are accessible for management purposes (Stobart, 1991). The purpose of such an audit would be to provide management with a metric to measure the impact of brand investment over time, both directly through cash and indirectly via the other corporate intangibles, such as building customer relationships and the management of organisational change. It emphasises the differing components and sources of brand power across functions and helps build management integration as a result.

Clearly, marketing management working in these multifunctional teams within the discrete zones of the integrated brand, will need to be restructured out of the traditional brand management dendogram and regrouped around suppliers and intermediaries. These teams should be led by marketing and consist of members drawn from appropriate disciplines. They can be broadly categorised into one of three types:

- The *product integrators*, through working with suppliers, are charged with improving the functionality of the consumable product through process and product improvements on a company-wide basis. Product redesign should also be part of their remit, in liaison with functional marketing management.
- *Customer integrators* are the category of management that have been described earlier in some detail. Their concern is to collaborate with major intermediaries to reduce excess costs in the forward supply chain and to improve profitability by increasing sales and gross margins for both concerned. In the grocery market, the potential benefits to be gained here have been estimated at 2.3 to 3.4 percentage points of sales turnover (GEA Consulenti Associati, 1994)
- Finally, *strategic integrators* have the internal marketing role of inculcating the corporation's values, styles and behaviours amongst employees and the external task of ensuring that the marketing of the

company brand, the wider company values that underpin individual brand offerings, is carried out with consistency and integrity. They should also carry the responsibility for dealing with other important constituents such as local communities, pressure groups and the media. Consequently, a looser organisational structure will be required for these 'strategic integrator' teams to remain flexible and responsive.

With regard to the functional activities of marketing management, pricing, like certain other tasks, such as customer value assessment and marketing research, should remain a functional responsibility.

One would predict that the future prospects for premium pricing, a central tenet of conventional brand management wisdom, are such that this may be earned as a bonus but cannot be taken as given. Category leaders will always remain price-makers and may occasionally create premium prices if their offer is perceived to be superior. Even at price parity, effective systems cost management may facilitate the release of additional investment to reinforce these values without margin hikes. At its most competitive, the integrated brand offering can be marketed at below price parity while producing the required returns, provided retention and cost goals are being achieved.

By re-engineering brand management practices now, customers in the next century will still be buying brands from intermediaries that still distribute them in partnership with the corporations that have been successful in adapting to an integrated environment.

FUTURE RESEARCH DIRECTIONS AND PROTOCOLS

Throughout the chapter we have stressed the integrative nature of business process redesign in general and the challenge of re-engineering brand management practices in particular. A number of aspects of this integrative process have been illustrated by examples drawn from management consultancy work rather than through scientific research. As a result, the integrated brand proposition developed here should only be seen as a broad framework and not a postulate for research. However, the need to develop a systematic approach to this research is now urgent as practice is running ahead of theory. Without a robust set of principles and techniques derived from empirical studies of successful transformations, theory cannot be forged nor grounded (Hewitt, 1994). As a consequence, management are currently proceeding on a trial-and-error basis. The research priorities that are signposted in this chapter fall into two categories. Firstly, research questions that focus on specific *intra-organisational brand management procedures*, such as:

- How best can an 'integrated environment' coexist with functional performance?
- How far should the brand portfolio planning be integrated with business planning to achieve supply chain objectives?
- As the degree of corporate risk increases with the development of the integrated brand, how should strategic decision-making procedures be distinguished from operational issues?

The second category of research questions arise from *inter-organisational and consumer marketing issues*. In a sense, the development of theory from best practices in building external relationships may prove pivotal in redesigning the integrated environment mentioned above. These research questions should include:

- To be effective, consumer loyalty management needs a new metric for segmenting and targeting appropriate consumers. How can loyalty segmentation be operationalised?
- How should category management teams be organised to interface variously with primary, major and secondary accounts and what are their information needs?
- In the event of a market-withdrawal crisis or a product or service announcement that alters the perception of the integrated brand offering, what are the main corporate communication channels and management procedures to ensure they are carried out effectively?

With regard to the proposed research protocol and methodology required to address the type of questions raised here, it would seem appropriate to adopt a case-based approach. Thus, qualitative research would be the preferred means of developing the necessary forward-looking insights, rather than quantitative techniques since the latter implies a greater degree of prior knowledge, the testing of deductive hypotheses and reflective explanation (Denison and McDonald, 1995). In order to get at the core of best-practices within organisations, one would first need to seek advice from practitioners, consultants and leading academics to identify which companies have successfully re-engineered their brand management practices. The sample should be drawn from both the services and consumer durable sectors, as well as fmcg companies, since the latter can no longer be regarded as having the monopoly on effective brand management. In fact, some non-fmcg companies, such as British Airways and Sharp Electronics who serve both consumer and business markets simultaneously, have been very adept at managing the equity of their brands on an inter- and intra-organisational basis.

Each of these case studies would be constructed around a series of iterative, semi-structured interviews and triangulated amongst key marketing, sales and supply chain management so that both the functional and multifunctional aspects of the integrated branding process can be captured. By comparing the organisational practices of 15–20 companies, initially with each other and then with the perspectives of leading consultants and academics who are likely to have a wider experience of current best-practices, it should be possible to develop deductive hypotheses for theory building purposes.

References

Aaker, D A (1991) *Managing Brand Equity*, New York, Macmillan, p 4.

Allan, G (1992) 'A brand as mental connections – developing the thinking', *Proceedings of the Millward Brown Seminar*, 'People, Brands and Advertising', London, pp 41–45.

Barwise, P (with Higson, C, Likierman, A and Marsh, P) (1990) 'Brands as "separable assets" ', *Business Strategy Review*, Summer, pp. 43–59.

Bennett, R (1993) *The Handbook of European Advertising*, Kogan Page, London, p 360.

Booz, Allen & Hamilton (1991) *Pan-European Pricing of Consumer Goods*, London.

Bower, M and Garda, R A (1986) 'The role of marketing in management', in Vuell, V P (ed.), *Handbook of Modern Marketing*, McGraw-Hill, New York.

Brady, J and Davis, I (1993) 'Marketing's mid-life crisis', *McKinsey Quarterly*, No 2, pp 17–28.

Buchanan, R W and Gillies C S (1990) 'Value managed relationships: the key to customer retention and profitability', *European Management Journal*, Vol 8, No 4, pp 523–525.

Christopher, M (1993) 'Logistics and competitive strategy', *European Management Journal*, Vol 11, No 2, pp 258–261.

Clifford, D K and Cavanagh, R E (1985) *'The Winning Performance: How America's High Growth Mid-size Companies Succeed'*, Sidgwick & Jackson, London.

Coopers & Lybrand (1992) *The Ascendency of Own-Labels*, Paper read by Gloover, J on 29 January at the 'Food and Drink Conference', Templeton College, Oxford.

de Chernatony, L, Knox, S D and Chedgey, M (1992) 'Brand pricing in a recession', *European Journal of Marketing*, Vol 26, No 2, pp 5–14.

Denison, T J and McDonald, M (1995) 'The role of marketing, past, present and future', *Journal of Marketing Practice*, Vol 1, No 1, pp 54–76.

Diller, H (1992) 'Euro-key-account management', *Marketing ZFP*, Vol 9, No 4, pp 239–245.

Doyle, P (1989) 'Building successful brands: the strategic options', *Journal of Marketing Management*, Vol 5, No 1, pp 77–95.

Earl, M and Khan, B (1994) 'How new is business process redesign?', *European Management Journal*, Vol 12, No 1, pp 20–30.

Edelman, D, Silverstein, M and Jones, B (1993) 'Discovering how to maximise customer share', *Marketing Business*, September, pp 12–16.

Edwards, C and Braganza, A (1994) *The Business Process Redesign Web: A Framework to Classify BPR initiatives and plan their implementation*, Paper read at the Second European Academic Conference on BPR, Cranfield, England.

Farquhar, P (1989) 'Managing brand equity', *Marketing Research*, September, pp 24–33.

GEA Consulenti Associati (1994) 'Supplier–retailer collaboration in supply chain management', on behalf of the Coca-Cola Retail Research Group, London.

Hammer, M (1993), Transcript from a radio interview, *In Business*, Radio 4, 27 October.

Hammer, M and Champy, J (1993) *Reengineering the Corporation*, Nicholas Brealey, London.

Handy, C (1991) *The Age of Unreason*, Business Books, London.

Hewitt, F (1994), *Intra-enterprise and Inter-enterprise Supply Chain Redesign*, Paper read at the Second European Academic Conference on BPR, Cranfield, England.

Kaplan, R S and Murdock, L (1991), 'Re-thinking the corporation: core process redesign', *McKinsey Quarterly*, No 2, pp 27–43.

King, S (1991) 'Brand-building in the 1990s', *Journal of Marketing Management*, Vol 7, pp 3–13.

King, S (1994) 'Brand-building and market research', in Jenkins, M and Knox, S D (eds), *Advances in Consumer Marketing*, Kogan Page, London.

Mitchell, A (1993) 'Vauxhall creates a flexible friend', *The Times*, 27 October, p 20.

PaineWebber Associates (1992) *'Everyday Low Pricing: An Idea Whose Time Has Come'*, New York.

Peck, H (1991) 'Land Rover Discovery A', Cranfield Case Clearing House, No 593-003-1.

Schlesinger, L A and Heskett, J L (1991) 'The service-driven service company', *Harvard Business Review*, September–October, pp 71–81.

Stobart, P (1991) 'Alternative methods of brand valuations', in Murphy J (ed.), *Brand Valuation*, Business Press, London.

Summers, D (1993) 'Rewards for the loyal shopper', *Financial Times*, 2 December, p 14.

Vandermerwe, S and Rada, J (1988) 'Servitisation of business: adding value by adding services', *European Management Journal*, Vol 6, No 4, pp 314–324.

14

RELATIONSHIP MARKETING: TOWARDS A NEW PARADIGM*

Moira Clark, Helen Peck, Adrian Payne
and Martin Christopher

INTRODUCTION

In recent years the traditional approach to marketing has been increasingly questioned. A new perspective is now emerging which recognises that marketing has two key concerns. The first concern is still the management of the classic marketing mix as a conventional, functional responsibility. The second concern is much broader and company-wide in its scope with a goal of developing a cross-functional, coordinated focus on customers – in other words, to reorient the entire business to face the market. It is probably true to say that most emphasis in the past has been placed upon the first concern with only limited attention being paid to the latter.

In this chapter we first examine some of the criticism that has been directed at the conventional approach to marketing. We then introduce the *relationship marketing* concept and develop the idea of a 'relationship management chain' as a framework for operationalising relationship marketing in a broader cross-functional context.

There is now a growing body of literature which casts doubt on the relevance of traditional marketing theory especially when applied to international, industrial, and services marketing (Gummesson, 1987; Grönroos, 1990a). A major concern is that the traditional paradigm – based on the marketing mix, and the concept of exchange (Borden, 1965; Bagozzi, 1975; Kotler, 1984) – was developed using assumptions derived from studies of the huge US market for consumer goods. Critics point out that its short-term transactional focus is inappropriate for industrial and services marketing, where establishing longer-term relationships with

---

* A version of this chapter was presented at the Rethinking Marketing Symposium, Warwick Business School, July 1993.

customers is critical to organisational success (Hakansson, 1982; Grönroos, 1990b). The concept has also been found wanting when applied to international marketing, as it makes no provision for the fact that trade barriers and politics may deny access to the market altogether (Gummesson, 1987). Other writers are more inclined to point to widespread difficulties with implementation as grounds for questioning the validity of the concept (Brownlie and Saren 1992).

THE RELATIONSHIP MARKETING PARADIGM

In response to the earlier criticisms of the marketing concept, Grönroos (1990c) formulated a relationship-focused definition of marketing: 'The purpose of marketing is to establish, maintain, enhance and commercialise customer relationships (often, but not necessarily always, long-term relationships) so that the objectives of the parties involved are met. This is done by the mutual exchange and fulfilment of promises.' The relationship marketing paradigm builds on the concept of relationship marketing as first introduced by Berry (1983) but discussed by many others (Levitt, 1983; Rosenberg and Czepiel, 1984; Jackson, 1985; Crosby and Stephens, 1987; Christopher, Payne and Ballantyne, 1991; McKenna, 1991; Gummesson, 1981; Grönroos, 1978) when describing a longer-term approach to marketing. Our own view of relationship marketing extends from the work of Christopher, Payne and Ballantyne (1991) who suggest a theory of relationship marketing based on a broader perspective than earlier contributions. The key elements of this view are:

- The nature of the relationship with customers is changing and the emphasis is shifting from a transaction to a relationship focus.
- The relationship marketing approach focuses on maximising the lifetime value of desirable customers and customer segments.
- Relationship marketing strategies are concerned with the development and enhancement of relationships with six key 'markets'. It is concerned with 'internal marketing', providing a framework for the management of internal staff relationships, as well as building substantial external relationships with customers, suppliers, referral sources, influence markets and recruitment markets.
- Quality, customer service and marketing are closely related. However, frequently they are managed separately. A relationship marketing approach brings these elements into a much closer coherence.

This chapter is concerned with developing this view of relationship marketing further. The relationship marketing concept suggests that, instead of the narrow, transactional, one-sale-at-a-time view of marketing, marketing should emphasise relationships more strongly. However, it is not just the transaction-orientation of the traditional marketing paradigm which hampers the development of customer relationships. In many instances the structure of an organisation can also limit its ability to satisfy its customers.

STRUCTURAL WEAKNESS IN ORGANISATIONS

Traditional vertical organisations which are hierarchically structured and functionally orientated often optimise individual functions at the expense of the whole business and the customer. The core problem is their lack of coordination across functions, departments and tasks. This functional approach often means that while problems manifest themselves in one part of the organisation, their root cause may remain unattended elsewhere. This results in low levels of corporate performance and even lower levels of customer satisfaction, as customers are passed from one functionally focused department to the next in the quest for a solution to their problems. Unfortunately performance measurement systems often exacerbate these problems and lead to even further functional emphasis as shown in Figure 14.1. Increasing competition and fast changing markets have meant that flexibility and coordination within organisations have become as important as functional performance. Companies need to achieve excellence in quality, service levels, cycle times and other performance measures. These challenges require managers to rethink the

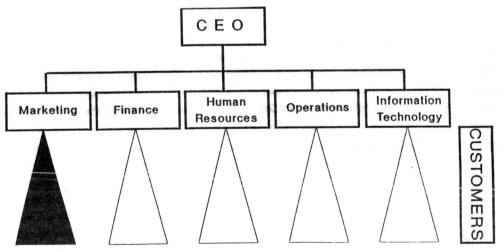

Figure 14.1 Marketing as a functional activity

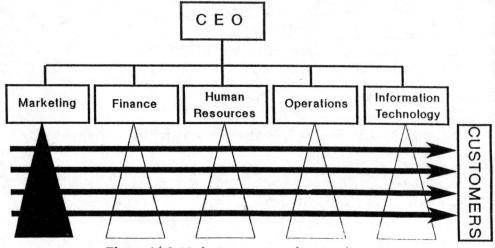

Figure 14.2 Marketing as a cross functional activity

way companies interact with their suppliers, channels and customers. Hence an approach that organises the flow of work around company-wide *processes,* as opposed to *functions,* that ultimately link with customer needs is necessary. In market-facing organisations key players are drawn together in multidisciplinary teams or groups that seek to marshal resources to achieve market-based objectives. The functions may still exist but they are now seen as 'pools of resources' from which the market-facing teams draw expertise. According to Ostroff and Smith (1992) 'there is real performance leverage in moving toward a flatter more horizontal mode of organisation, in which cross-functional, end-to-end work flows link internal processes with the needs and capabilities of both suppliers and customers'. This market-facing focus is illustrated in Figure 14.2.

INTRODUCING THE RELATIONSHIP CHAIN

Combining the relationship concept of marketing with the need for a cross-functional, coordinated focus on customers, leads us to the idea of the *relationship management chain* ('the relationship chain'). The relationship chain, shown in Figure 14.3, recognises that the new cross-functional paradigm of marketing is essentially process- rather than function-oriented.

The notion of the relationship chain draws on the idea of mapping the steps in the business process, such as suggested by Gluck (1980) (the business system) and Porter (1985) (the value chain). The relationship

Figure 14.3 The relationship management chain

chain differs from these, in that rather than describing a set of sequential steps that *may* add value to a business, its focus is on how value can be created through improved relationships. In the following pages we describe the key components of the relationship chain and identify the critical activities and linkages that must be managed if the relationship marketing concept is to be implemented.

First, though, we identify certain factors – relating to the management of internal as well as external markets – which impact on every stage of the relationship chain. An understanding of the significance of each is a prerequisite to the successful implementation of any relationship marketing strategy. The external marketing management issues are for the most part directional in nature. In contrast, the internal marketing inputs are essentially facilitators which, if managed correctly, create an environment that is conducive to cross-functional working and the effective delivery of customer satisfaction.

MANAGING EXTERNAL MARKETS

Much of the marketing emphasis in the past has rightly been directed at external customers. However, other 'markets' are also important. In this section the importance of developing marketing plans is highlighted.

These plans may embrace other 'non-customer' markets which can have a profound impact on how successfully we ultimately satisfy our customers. A further critical element of managing external markets is the need to place adequate emphasis on existing customers – a task which is neglected in many companies. Thus customer retention strategies should form a vital part of marketing activities.

The Marketing Planning Process

The marketing planning process (McDonald, 1989) is a key input into the Relationship Chain and is critical for managing external markets. Essentially the aim of the planning process is to determine where the company is now, where it wants to be and how to get there. It is a logical sequence and series of activities leading to the setting of marketing

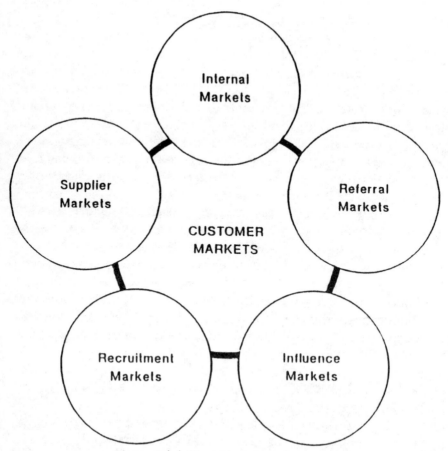

Figure 14.4 The 'six markets' framework

objectives and the formulation of plans for achieving them. Since relationship marketing is concerned with a much broader view of marketing, in order to provide the best value proposition – in terms of both the product and service – it is necessary to consider a wider range of markets than has traditionally been the case. Therefore, in addition to forthcoming marketing plans for existing and potential customers, a company should also consider developing marketing plans for supplier markets, referral markets, influence markets, recruitment markets and internal markets. The 'six markets' model, shown in Figure 14.4, illustrates this broadened view of marketing (Christopher, Payne and Ballantyne, 1991).

Customer Retention

A second input into the relationship chain is the management of customer retention. That is, ensuring that the company devotes a large part of its resources to retaining existing customers rather than simply attracting new ones. In practice most companies' marketing effort is focused on 'getting' customers with little attention paid to 'keeping' them. Research undertaken by the consulting firm Bain & Co (Reichheld and Sasser, 1990) suggests that there is a high degree of correction between customer retention and profitability. Established customers tend to buy more, are predictable and usually cost less to service that new customers. Furthermore, they tend to be less price sensitive and may provide free word-of-mouth advertising and referrals. Retaining customers also makes it difficult for competitors to enter a market or increase share in that market. Research has also shown that by increasing service quality, and consequently customer satisfaction, a higher percentage of customers are likely to be retained (Porter, 1985; McDonald, 1989; Reichheld and Sasser, 1990; Berry and Gresham, 1986; Heskett, 1987; Hart, Heskett and Sasser, 1990).

One study of the car market in the USA found that a satisfied customer is likely to stay with the same supplier for a further 12 years after the first satisfactory purchase. During that period he or she will buy a further four cars of the same make. It is estimated that, to a car manufacturer, this level of customer retention is worth $400 million in new car sales annually (*Business Week*, 1983).

Rank Xerox uses a measure of customer retention as part of a quarterly index of customer satisfaction used to determine bonuses and pay rises for management. Very simply the question they ask is 'How many of the customers that we had twelve months ago do we still have today?'

MANAGING INTERNAL MARKETS

A relationship approach to external markets will only succeed if the strategy is underpinned by an appropriate approach to the management of the organisation's 'internal markets'. By referring to the management of internal markets we mean both the management and coordination of profit centres within the organisation, and the management of the internal customer–supplier relationships (Gummesson, 1987; Collins and Payne, 1991).

Internal Marketing Planning

Whilst the fundamentals and techniques of external market planning are well developed and reasonably widespread in use, the application of the same logic to the internal market is less commonly encounted.

The principles of internal and external market planning are essentially the same. In planning for internal marketing effectiveness we are seeking to establish and quantify the requirements of internal customers, and to develop systems and procedures capable of meeting the goals of internal customers as cost-effectively as possible. The concept of internal supplier/customer 'linkages' is critical here. It is important that everyone in the organisation can see the linkage between what they do and its impact on the eventual customer. The internal marketing plan is a means of bringing these issues to the surface and focusing attention on the necessary actions to improve the performance of the internal customer chain. This appreciation of how each employee contributes ultimately to the delivery of customer satisfaction encourages and improves cross-functional working, and helps to promote, develop and sustain an ethos of heightened service quality for internal as well as external customers.

Culture, Climate and Employee Retention

The development and sustenance of a customer-orientated culture within the organisation is a critical determinant of long-term success in relationship marketing. It is an organisation's culture – its deep-seated, unwritten system of shared values and norms – which has the greatest impact on employees' behaviour and attitudes. The culture of an organisation in turn dictates its climate – the policies and practices which characterise the organisation and reflect its cultural beliefs (Webster, 1990).

A study of the retail banking industry in the US found that customers' perceptions of an organisation's climate were linked to customer retention (Schneider, 1973). A later study (also in retail banking) identified a direct relationship between well-designed service encounters, enhanced customer satisfaction and employee satisfaction (Schneider and Bowen, 1984). A satisfied employee is likely to be a retained employee. Employee retention becomes an important part of the equation when we consider that relationships are built and maintained by individuals, and customers are often more loyal to the employee who deals with them than to the wider organisation. Salesmen, hairdressers and professional service workers are notoriously good at taking favoured clients with them when they leave to work for rival businesses.

In most industries the connection between customer retention and employee retention is less obvious. The inadequacies of accounting systems mean that the costs of high employee turnover – such as the increased costs of recruitment and training, and the inefficiency of inexperienced workers – are rarely monitored. The impact of high staff turnover on customers' perceptions of service quality, customer satisfaction and retention are also unlikely to be realised (Schlesinger and Heskett, 1991; Schneider, 1980).

An integrated approach to marketing and human resource management is therefore needed, one that recognises employees as a valuable and finite resource, and a potential source of competitive advantage (Schlesinger and Heskett, 1991), because – despite the best technology and the most carefully planned procedures – in the final analysis relationship marketing stands or falls on the quality and willingness of the people who implement it.

The relationship chains focuses attention upon a number of critical processes and tasks, specifically: defining the value proposition; segmentation, targeting and positioning; operations and delivery systems; delivered satisfaction; and measurement and feedback. Each of these five elements of the chain are now discussed below. The central notion underpinning this discussion is that every element of the chain must be scrutinised to determine ways of adding value through relationship building.

DEFINING THE VALUE PROPOSITION

The notion of adding value has been highlighted by a number of actors. The value chain concept (Porter, 1985) points out the potential of primary and support activities to add value to products and services, and the value delivery sequence concept (Bower and Garda, 1986) reflects the need to create, deliver and communicate the value. Our concept of the value proposition reflects the importance of creating relationships that deliver value beyond that provided by the core product. This involves adding tangible and intangible elements to the core products thus creating or enhancing the 'product surround'. This results in the delivery of enhanced value through improved service quality (this is referred to later under the heading of delivered satisfaction). Three interrelated approaches help determine the key elements of the value proposition:

Identifying Key Service Issues

It is essential that research be undertaken to elicit the importance buyers attach to customer service *vis-à-vis* the other marketing mix elements and the specific importance they place on the individual components of customer service. Once these dimensions are defined, it is then possible to identify the relative importance of each one and the extent to which different types of customers are prepared to trade off one aspect of service for another.

Measuring Service Preferences

The 'trade-off' technique (Christopher, 1992) enables companies to evaluate very simply the implicit importance that a customer attaches to the separate elements of customer service. Using trade-off analysis it is of course also possible to identify groups of customers sharing common service preferences.

Competitive Benchmarking

Having identified the key components of service and the relative importance, the next step is to ask the customers to rate the company and its competitors on each of these elements in terms of their perceived performance.

SEGMENTATION, TARGETING AND POSITIONING

Having determined the importance attached by different customers to each of the service attributes identified in the first link of the relationship chain, the next step requires that we see if any patterns emerge among these customers. If one group of customers has, for example, a distinct set of priorities from another group then it would be reasonable to think of them both as different service segments. The company then has to decide which of these segments to target and how it should position the services offered to these segments in relation to the competition.

Service/Relationship Segmentation

One technique which we have used to identify these segments is *cluster analysis*. Thus if two respondents complete the trade-off matrix in a very similar way their importance scores on the various service dimensions would be similar and hence would be assigned to the same segment.

Customer Profitability Analysis

There are invariably significant differences in profitability between customers. Not only do different customers buy varying quantities of products but the costs to service these customers will vary dramatically. What will often emerge from these studies is that the largest customers in terms of volume, or even revenue, may not be the most profitable because of their high costs of service.

Database Marketing (Micro-Marketing)

Increasingly companies are coming to recognise the opportunities for using database marketing whereby the profiles of existing customers are analysed to correlate their demographic and other characteristics with their purchasing patterns. The purpose of this is to seek to maintain the closest contact with their customers, often through direct marketing, and hence to build long-lasting relationships.

Positioning

It has been suggested (Payne, 1993) that positioning is concerned with differentiation and using it to advantageously fit the organisation, and its products and services, to a market segment. It is possible to differentiate on the basis of subjective criteria such as image and communication, or objective criteria in terms of other elements of the marketing mix including product, processes, people and customer service. To this we would also add the possibility of positioning in terms of the nature, style and quality of relationships.

OPERATIONS AND DELIVERY SYSTEMS

It is now becoming more widely accepted that a powerful source of competitive advantage comes through 'capabilities' (Stalk, Evans and Sulman, 1992). What this implies is that the way we configure and manage our process becomes a critical element in achieving success in the market-place. The ability to meet the ever-increasing demands for variety, supported by ever-higher levels of service, calls for an unprecedented degree of flexibility in our operating and delivery systems. There are a number of critical aspects in the design, management and planning of operations and delivery systems and these are highlighted below.

Mass Customisation

The technological advances that made database marketing possible have also opened new opportunities in the next stage of the relationship chain. Following the path of Total Quality Management and just-in-time manufacturing, information technology has been harnessed to create manufacturing systems so flexible that one-off products can be produced at mass-market prices. With cost penalties removed, customers no longer have to compromise so that manufacturers can exploit the economics of scale. Each product can be produced to a customer's own specification.

Configuration by Segment

There is a lingering assumption in many organisations that, although customers' product requirements differ enormously, the delivery of these goods or services can best be executed through a uniform approach. This is simply not true in the vast majority of industries. These uniform delivery systems usually operate according to performance criteria derived from the most demanding customers. The result tends to be under performance for some, over performance for the rest, and unnecessarily expensive for everyone. Instead, it is possible to segment customers' delivery needs across a variety of criteria including response times, frequencies of orders, type and size of packaging, and value and complexity of the products usually purchased.

Partnering

Closer relationships with suppliers are also becoming more common as organisations re-examine the supply chain for opportunities to leverage and create greater value for their customers. The benefits can be considerable for those organisations which can replace a multitude of *ad hoc* and adversarial relationships with cooperative alliances or partnerships with a few high quality suppliers.

Process Benchmarking

To raise the standard of operations and delivery systems, emphasis must be placed upon the comparison of entire business processes. To do this an organisation must look beyond its usual customer and supplier relationships, and seek the cooperation of companies from other seemingly unrelated industries. The idea behind this is that much can be learned from how other companies manage service processes. Cross-industry comparisons are particularly useful because they allow organisations to see beyond their own established industry practices, and learn from the 'best in class' exponent of each process.

DELIVERED SATISFACTION

The way organisations can differentiate themselves from the competition is not just by the quality of the core product but by how it manages the 'product surround'. Customer satisfaction, and therefore the maintenance of the customer relationship, is in fact dependent on how well a product or service measures up to the customer's original expectations of quality. A review of cost/benefit for each segment and the delivery of appropriate service quality to enhance relationships are critical components of this element of the relationship chain.

Cost/Benefit By Segment (Value/Price)

Customers do not buy products, they seek benefits. In so doing they evaluate competing offers in terms of the totality of product and service as well as the 'relationship', or potential relationship, that could exist between themselves and the supplier and/or the brand. Delivered value can be thought of as the total value offered to a customer less the total cost to the customer. Total customer value can of course include service value, product value, people value and image value. Total customer cost on the other hand can include monetary price, time cost, energy cost and psychological cost.

Service Quality

In recent years a number of writers have attempted to define service quality, many of them stressing the subjective nature of the concept (Lewis, 1988; Parasuraman, Zeithaml and Berry, 1985). Nevertheless, when attempting to deliver customer satisfaction, it helps first to understand that a product or service must perform on more than one dimension.

Grönroos (1983) believed that service quality could be broken down into three dimensions. The first is the 'technical' quality of the service (ie whether the service fulfils its technical specifications); the second is functional quality (the manner in which the service is delivered). A third consideration, 'corporate image', may also influence customers' perceptions of quality.

MEASUREMENT AND FEEDBACK

To complete the relationship chain – and indeed to close the gaps so that the process of relationship management becomes a continuous cycle of improvement – systems of measurement and feedback must be installed. The aim should be for constant feedback, not *ad hoc* studies carried out from time to time. The challenge is to refine the processes on a continuing basis to create ever-better means of delivering customer satisfaction. Some of the more important approaches are now discussed.

Service Process Monitoring

An analogy between service processes and manufacturing processes is useful at this point. We have come to learn that it is not sufficient to *inspect* the final output of a production process as a way of controlling quality. Instead we have to *control* the process. If the process is under control then the quality of the output is guaranteed. The secret is to identify the critical points where failures or malfunctions can lead to a loss of quality. In a service process we should be equally concerned to monitor the critical fail points in our service delivery system. These are the 'moments of truth' which may occur at any point in the relationship chain, but which can have a considerable impact on delivered satisfaction as viewed by the customers.

Employee Satisfaction Studies

We are already aware of the relationship between employee satisfaction and customer satisfaction, so there is a case for monitoring employee satisfaction as a bellwether of performance. Back in 1969, researchers Smith, Kendall, and Hulin identified five factors which constitute the overall concept of job satisfaction: namely, satisfaction with the work itself, satisfaction with pay, satisfaction with promotion prospects, satisfaction with supervision, and satisfaction with co-workers. These determinants still form the backbone of employee satisfaction surveys today, although other factors (such as satisfaction with the working environment, corporate communications, senior management performance and company image) may also be included.

Customer Satisfaction Studies

Satisfaction must be measured on a regular basis because, while a product or service itself may not change over a lengthy period, customers' expectations rarely remain static. Customer satisfaction surveys whether in the form of questionnaires, interviews or focus groups, must be administered objectively. Whatever the method of data collection, the surveys must use criteria which reflect the needs and preferences of the customers, and the relative importance of each, as seen from the customers' perspectives (bearing in mind that different customer groups have differing priorities). Ideally, the results should then be compared with customer satisfaction data relating to competitors' product or service offerings.

CONCLUSIONS

In this chapter we have explored the limitations of traditional marketing, examined some key elements of the emerging paradigm of relationship marketing and proposed a new framework – the relationship management chain – for implementing an improved relationship focus.

The chain provides a structure to assist in the operationalisation of some key elements of relationship marketing strategy. More specifically, it provides a framework to explore means of adding value through the creation and delivery of relationship-enhancing activities and processes. The chain comprises five core components: defining the value proposition; segmentation, targeting and positioning; operations and delivery systems; delivered satisfaction; and measurement and feedback. Each of these components has critical activities, processes and linkages which need to be managed to implement relationship-focused strategies. The chain helps identify those value-adding activities that can be carried out in different elements of the chain. Once these activities have been identified, external and internal marketing plans need to be formulated to ensure communication and delivery of the value proposition.

The relationship chain provides a framework for identifying and delivering added value through relationship building. We contend that this focus on relationships represents a powerful way to create and deliver a value proposition. This view is supported by increasingly strong evidence that the linkages between the quality of relationships – such as those between customers and internal staff, and between employee retention and customer retention – can result in a significant improvement in long-term profitability and shareholder value. Using the chain as an analytical tool will also facilitate the improvement of flexibility and coordination as well as improve cross-functional communication within organisations. As a result it can simultaneously improve corporate performance and provide companies with a competitive advantage.

Our view of relationship marketing reflects an emerging paradigm of marketing that is cross-functional, relationship-driven and focuses upon processes as well as functions in achieving long-term customer satisfaction. The implementation of relationship marketing strategies will, however, require managers to go beyond their traditional roles focused upon functional performance. Instead they will need to take a much broader perspective and develop stronger cross-functional capabilities which will facilitate much closer relationships between suppliers, internal staff, customers and other relevant markets. This represents a significant challenge to senior management to reorient their thinking and actions towards building a more relationship-oriented and customer-focused organisation.

References

Bagozzi, R P (1975) 'Marketing as exchange', *Journal of Marketing,* October, pp 32–39.

Berry, L L (1983) 'Relationship marketing', in Berry, L L, Shostack, G L and Upah, G D (eds), *Emerging Perspectives on Services Marketing,* American Marketing Association, Chicago, pp 25–28.

Berry, L L and Gresham, L G (1986) 'Relationship retailing: transforming customers into clients', *Business Horizons,* November–December, pp 43–47.

Borden, N H (1965) 'The concept of the marketing mix', in Schwartz, G (ed.), *Science in Marketing,* John Wiley, New York, pp 386–397.

Bower, M and Garda, R A (1986) 'The role of marketing in management', in Buell, V P (ed.), *Handbook of Modern Marketing,* McGraw-Hill, New York.

Brownlie, B and Saren, M (1992) 'The four Ps of the marketing concept:

prescriptive, polemical, permanent and problematical', *European Journal of Marketing*, Vol 26, No 4, pp 34–47.

Business Week (1983) 4 April

Christopher, M (1992) *The Customer Service Planner*, Butterworth-Heinemann, Oxford.

Christopher, M, Payne, A F T and Ballantyne, D (1991) *Relationship Marketing: Bringing Quality, Customer Service and Marketing Together*, Butterworth-Heinemann, Oxford.

Collins, B and Payne, A F T (1991) 'Internal services marketing', *European Management Journal*, Vol 9, No 3, pp 216–270.

Crosby, L A and Stephens, N (1987) 'Effects of relationship marketing on satisfaction, retention and prices in the life insurance industry', *Journal of Marketing Research*, Vol 24, pp 404–411.

de Ferrer, R J (1986) 'A case for European management', *International Management Development Review*, Vol 2, pp 275–281.

Gluck, F W (1980) 'Strategic choice and resource allocation', *McKinsey Quarterly*, Winter, pp 22–23.

Grönroos, C (1978) 'A service-orientated approach to marketing of services', *European Journal of Marketing*, Vol 12, pp 588– 601.

Grönroos, C (1983) 'Innovative marketing strategies and organisational structures for service firms', in Berry, L L, Shostack, G L and Upah, G D (eds), *Emerging Perspectives on Services Marketing*, American Marketing association, Chicago, pp 9–21.

Grönroos, C (1990a) 'Marketing redefined', *Management Decision*, Vol 28, No 8, pp 5-9.

Grönroos, C (1990b) *The Marketing Strategy Continuum: Toward a Marketing Concept for the 1990s*, Working Paper No 201, Meddelanden Fran Svenska Handelshogskolan, Helsinki.

Grönroos, C (1990c) 'Relationship approach to marketing in service contexts: the marketing and organisational behaviour interface', *Journal of Business Research*, Vol 20, No 1, pp 3–11.

Gummesson, E (1981) 'Marketing costs concepts in service firms', *Industrial Marketing Management*, No 3.

Gummesson, E (1987) 'The new marketing – developing long-term interactive relationships', *Long Range Planning*, Vol 20, No 4, pp 10–20.

Hakansson, H (ed.) (1982) *International Marketing and Purchasing of Industrial Goods*, Wiley, New York.

Hart, C N L, Heskett, J L and Sasser, W E Jr (1990) 'The profitable art of service recovery', *Harvard Business Review*, July–August, pp 148–156.

Heskett, J L (1987) 'Lessons in the service sector', *Harvard Business Review*, March–April, pp 118–126.

Jackson, B (1985) 'Build customer relations that last', *Harvard Business Review*, November–December, pp 120–128.

Kotler, P (1984) *Marketing Management*, Prentice-Hall, Englewood Cliffs, NJ.

Levitt, T (1983) 'After the sale is over ...', *Harvard Business Review*, September–October, pp 87–93.

Lewis, B R (1988) *Customer Service Survey: A Major UK Bank*, Financial Services research Centre, Manchester School of Management, UMIST.

McDonald, M H B (1989) *Marketing Plans*, Heinemann Professional, Oxford.

McKenna, R (1991) *Relationship Marketing*, Century Business, London.

Ostroff, F and Smith, D (1992) 'The horizontal organisation', *McKinsey Quarterly*, Winter, pp 148–167.

Parasuraman, A Zeithmal, V A and Berry, L L (1985) 'A conceptual model of service quality and its implications for future research', *Journal of Marketing*, Vol 49, pp 44-50.

Payne, A F T (1993) *The Essence of Services Marketing*, Prentice-Hall, New Jersey.

Porter, M (1985) *Competitive Advantage: Creating and Sustaining Superior Performance*, Free Press, New York.

Reichheld, F and Sasser, W E Jr (1990) 'Zero defections: quality comes to services', *Harvard Business Review*, September–October, pp 105–216.

Rosenberg, L J and Czepiel, J A (1984) 'A marketing approach for customer retention', *Journal of Consumer Marketing*.

Schlesinger, L A and Heskett, J L (1991) 'Breaking the cycle of failure in service', *Sloan Management Review*, Spring, pp 17–28.

Schneider, B (1973) 'The perception of organisational culture: the customer's view', *Journal of Applied Psychology*, Vol 57, No 3, pp 248–256.

Schneider, B (1980) 'The service organisation, climate is critical', *Organizational Dynamics*, Autumn, pp 52–65.

Schneider, B and Bowen, D (1984) 'New services, design, development and implementation and the employee', in George, W E and Marshall, C E (eds) *Developing New Services*, American Marketing Association, Chicago, pp 82–101.

Smith, P C, Kendall, L M and Hulin, C L (1969) *The Measurement of Satisfaction in Work and Retirement*, Rand-McNally, Chicago.

Stalk, G, Evans, P and Sulman, L E (1992) 'Competing capabilities: the new rules of corporate strategy', *Harvard Business Review*, March–April, pp 57–69.

Webster, C (1990) 'Towards the measurement of the marketing culture of a service firm', *Journal of Business Research*, Vol 21, pp 345–362.

INDEX